The Dynamic of Secession

Seccessionist activity has been increasing in the developing wo....,
Western liberal democracies, and especially in the former communist
states of Eastern Europe. This timely book offers a general explanation for the occurrence of the phenomenon, arising from a comparative study of numerous historical examples of secession and
separatist conflict. The book develops a comprehensive framework,
specifying the elements necessary for a secession crisis, and discussing the moral issues underpinning such a decision. The author
examines the political, economic, and social costs and benefits of a
community's two alternatives – continued integration in the existing
state and secession – which enter into decision-making processes,
and argues that secessionist activity arises only when government
action or international developments change a community's view of
the balance among these costs and benefits. Her conclusion is that a
community's aspirations for independence change constantly with
circumstances, and that in some instances, sensitive government
policy can substantially mitigate secessionist sentiment, while, in
others, evolution in the prevailing international climate can outweigh
domestic factors in the dynamic of secession.

Viva Ona Bartkus is a consultant with McKinsey & Company. She
holds a doctorate from the University of Oxford.

CAMBRIDGE STUDIES IN INTERNATIONAL RELATIONS: 64

The dynamic of secession

Editorial Board

Cambridge Studies in International Relations is a joint initiative of Cambridge University Press and the British International Studies Association (BISA). The series will include a wide range of material, from undergraduate textbooks and surveys to research-based monographs and collaborative volumes. The aim of the series is to publish the best new scholarship in International Studies from Europe, North America, and the rest of the world.

CAMBRIDGE STUDIES IN INTERNATIONAL RELATIONS

The Dynamic of Secession

Viva Ona Bartkus

PUBLISHED BY THE PRESS SYNDICATE OF THE UNIVERSITY OF CAMBRIDGE
The Pitt Building, Trumpington Street, Cambridge CB2 1RP, United Kingdom

CAMBRIDGE UNIVERSITY PRESS
The Edinburgh Building, Cambridge CB2 2RU, UK   http://
www.cup.cam.ac.uk
40 West 20th Street, New York, NY 10011–4211, USA   http://www.cup.org
10 Stamford Road, Oakleigh, Melbourne 3166, Australia

© Viva Ona Bartkus 1999

First published 1999

Printed and bound in Great Britain by
Biddles Ltd, Guildford and King's Lynn

Printed in the United Kingdom at the University Press, Cambridge

Typeset in Palatino 10/12$\frac{1}{2}$ pt [CE]

A catalogue record for this book is available from the British Library

Library of Congress Cataloging in Publication data

Bartkus, Viva Ona.
  The dynamic of secession / Viva Ona Bartkus.
    p.   cm. – (Cambridge studies in international relations: 64.)
  Includes bibliographical references.
  ISBN 0 521 65032 1. – ISBN 0 521 65970 1 (pbk.)
  1. Secession. 2. Self-determination, National. 3. Sovereignty.
I. Title. II. Series.
JC327.B246   1999
320.1′5 – dc21   98–35138 CIP

ISBN 0 521 65032 1 hardback
ISBN 0 521 65970 1 paperback

Contents

Acknowledgments

A project considering the phenomenon of secession invariably involves the study of numerous historical instances of man's inhumanity to man. This was more than counterbalanced by the patience, encouragement, and support shown to me by faculty members of the Department of International Relations at the University of Oxford, fellow students, friends, and family. A simple reference on this page, unfortunately, will never be a sufficient tribute to the kindness that many people have shown me during the long hours of research and writing.

I am deeply indebted to Gowher Rizvi, who carefully oversaw this work, from its initial stages of the formulation of ideas to its completion and to Professor James Mayall, who consistently encouraged me. The book benefited greatly from the insightful criticisms and constructive comments provided by other faculty members of the Department of International Relations: Rosemary Foot, Andrew Walter, and Benedict Kingsbury. From initial research to final revisions, my brother Darius provided constant encouragement and support. Fellow graduate students and friends, Roger Hutchins, Byron Auguste, Holly Wyatt-Walter, Margaret Kean, Dhugal Bedford, Sharron Kraus and André Soldo provided engaging debate, humor, and friendship. Pat Oaklief suggested thoughtful editorial improvements. The assistance of numerous librarians at the Bodleian Library proved invaluable at each stage of research. The Rhodes Trust furnished the opportunity and the financial means to enable me to undertake such a study.

Most of all, I would like to dedicate this work to my father and mother. This book would not have been possible had they not constantly encouraged me to seek the very best in myself.

I   Introduction

1   Introduction

This book investigates secession. It seeks to answer a single question: why do groups decide to secede? Since secession is frequently a contested subject, it may be helpful at the outset to clarify both its meaning and my approach. Secession is the formal withdrawal from an established, internationally recognized state by a constituent unit to create a new sovereign state. The decision to secede represents an instance of political disintegration, when the citizens of a sub-system withdraw their political activities from the central government to focus them on a centre of their own. When the leaders of both a seceding community and the state express their positions in stark, absolute terms, the avenue of compromise is often precluded, thereby causing secessionist conflicts to be among the most bitter of struggles. To the observer, secession often appears irrational as it entails the ostensible sacrifice of economic opportunities and the endurance of social upheaval. Because of the coercive powers which the state can employ in these disputes, secessionist struggles frequently become violent and protracted, as both the seceding community and the state lose the willingness to accommodate each other's needs. Thus, secession is disintegrative in the most fundamental sense: it involves not the overthrow of existing government institutions, but rather the territorial dismemberment of a state. In this book, I refer to the groups attempting secession as "distinct communities."

The fact that secession seems to plague all types of societies – liberal democratic, former communist, and developing – implies the possible existence of many different routes to secession. The structured comparative study of numerous examples of secession and separatist agitation provides a broad perspective and enables the reformulation of the idiosyncratic motivations of each case into more general variables. I propose that the timing of the decision to secede can be understood within a framework structured around four primary variables: (1) the benefits of continued membership in the larger existing political entity;[1] (2) the costs of such membership; (3) the costs of secession; and (4) the benefits of secession. Some costs and benefits are clearly qualitative; others are extremely difficult or even impossible to quantify. To have impact, though, all must be perceived by the distinct community. A fluctuating phenomenon such as secession, however, cannot be explained by a constant, such as the four costs and benefits taken as static conditions. Secessions arise only when the distinct community determines that there has been a shift in the balance of these four variables. The types of changes the distinct community so identifies occur at both the level of the state and the international system. These changes include both rapidly moving events, such as a sequence of political or economic initiatives, and gradual transformations of attitudes, such as mounting discrimination or growing tolerance of diversity.

Secession, by its very nature, raises the basic question of justification. The perceived justice of the secessionist cause colors the opinions and potential support of members of the distinct community itself, the central government, foreign governments, and the broader international community. After a good deal of consideration, it seems to me that a community embarking upon secession has already assumed a moral right to secede. Therefore, since the book investigates secession crises, it will not delve deeply into the arguments regarding when secession would be morally justifiable or even desirable.[2] Rather, the book builds on the foundation of an existing body of arguments specifying and circumscribing the conditions under which there may be a "right" of secession in order to focus on exploring and explaining the timing of the secession decision. What is most important for the study of the dynamic of secession is not a resolution to this

---

[1] For the sake of brevity, the book will use "the benefits of membership" for those benefits associated with the distinct community's continued membership within the larger state. The same description applies to the "costs of membership."

[2] For a detailed discussion of the moral justifications for secession, see John Stuart Mill, *Collected Works* vol. XIX (London, 1963), p. 549; Harry Beran, "A Liberal Theory of Secession," *Political Studies* (1984), Vol. XXXII, pp. 21–31; Allen Buchanan, *Secession: The Morality of Political Divorce From Fort Sumter to Lithuania and Quebec* (Oxford: Westview Press, 1991); Lee Buchheit, *Secession: The Legitimacy of Self-Determination* (New Haven: Yale University Press, 1978); Michael Walzer, "The Reform of the International System" in Oyvind Osterud (ed.), *Studies of War and Peace* (Oslo: Norwegian University Press, 1986), p. 238.

ethical debate, but rather an understanding that the debate exists and will persist with each new secession crisis.

The book's focus is deliberately limited to the origins of secession, to explain why discontent leads to secession at certain times and to political demands short of separation under other circumstances. In other words, it focuses on a single "snapshot" in a set of rapidly changing events. Critical to understanding the snapshot, however, is an observation of the entire moving picture. The investigation of case studies spanning the period from the first stirrings of discontent to the outcomes of confrontation is crucial in order to place the moment of decision to secede in its proper context. Furthermore, in seeking to isolate the various constraints on the crucial decision, the book consistently comments on numerous intrinsic aspects of the state. The many differentiated routes to secession, to a certain extent, reflect changing conceptions of sovereignty and the state itself.

The argument rests on inferring the causes of secession decisions. A brief note on causality is necessary: discriminating analysis of historical documents such as the memoranda of secessionist organizations and autobiographies of their leaders paints only an incomplete picture of the dynamic of secession. Leaders cannot instigate a crisis without mass support. Due to the often diffuse nature of disaffection with the ruling regime among members of the community, their motivations for protest and even for secession cannot easily be determined. The argument is based upon the study of each case of secession within its own circumstances. The approach is to ascribe perceptions and apprehensions to the community through a process of scrutinizing and ultimately understanding the significant issues of the time. The approach does presuppose both the existence of basic human elements of motivation for such inspired acts as secession and the possibility that these common human elements of motivation can be discerned through comparative study.

The argument itself is organized into three main sections. Part I establishes the conceptual foundation for the subsequent analysis of secession. Potential territorial rearrangement and the creation of new states have not always been a possible outlet for discontent. Several elements are necessary for a secession crisis: an identifiable unit of people or "distinct community," territory, leaders, and discontent. The four chapters of Part II describe in detail the cost/benefit framework, its four variables, and the economic, political, and cultural factors which constitute each. Focusing on the dynamic of secession, Part III addresses directly the question of why groups decide to secede. Its four chapters explore the way in which changes in the balance among the four primary variables precipitate secession attempts.

Expressions of surprise have greeted the recent eruption of secessionary activity in Europe. None the less, a broader perspective of European history easily demonstrates that secession is not a novel phenomenon. As James Crawford notes, "... until this century, secession was certainly the most conspicuous, as well as probably the most usual method of the creation of new states".[3] Crawford lists numerous examples of secession between 1776 and 1900; if he had extended this time period to include the immediate post-World War I era, his list would have been substantially enlarged.[4]

Given the rising incidence of secessionist activity in developing countries, in the former communist countries of Eastern Europe, and in Western liberal democracies, this study of secession is a timely addition to this less-well-developed area of social science and international relations research. Potential extrapolations of such a study would involve reflections on sovereignty, since sovereign status is the key attribute of the state to which secessionists aspire. Moreover, the numerous case studies may reveal the extent to which a state's treatment of its distinct communities contributes to the decision to secede. A fuller explanation of the connection between changes in the four primary variables and the decision to secede would reveal the conditions under which states can influence such decisions. It would indicate the policies useful in the pursuit of particular outcomes in the secession dynamic and the limits of their effectiveness. Thus, from a better understanding of the "snapshot," we may be able to sketch in the rest of the moving picture. From a clearer understanding of the timing of the decision to secede, we may be able to draw conclusions on some of the means, which are theoretically possible, for the prevention and resolution of secession crises.

My intention is to gain a better understanding of the decision to secede; it is neither to condone nor to condemn specific secession attempts. The strength of the proposed framework lies in its cross-cultural applicability to secession and in its ability to help discern and organize the numerous causal patterns of secession. The book seeks to

---

[3] James Crawford, *The Creation of States in International Law* (Oxford: The Clarendon Press, 1979), p. 247.
[4] Finland, Poland, Lithuania, Latvia, and Estonia were but a few of the states created through the process of secession directly after World War I.

demonstrate that a comprehensive perspective on secession can provide a more useful approach than the currently prominent, segmented theories which concentrate on certain regional factors to explain secessionist difficulties. If it generates discussion and debate, I will consider it a success.

2   Theoretical foundation for analysis of the decision to secede

This chapter begins by discussing the process of disintegration, then introduces the four necessary elements for secession: a distinct community, territory, leaders, and discontent. Furthermore, while specifying these four elements, the chapter also discusses the use of "distinct community" in place of other terms such as "nation" or "ethnic group." The chapter then moves on to the debate concerning the "right" to secede in order to provide a solid foundation for the subsequent discussion of the analytical framework investigating the secession decision. The analytical framework is grounded in a set of costs and benefits, as perceived by the distinct community, of the political alternatives of continued membership in the existing state and secession. The cost/benefit approach elucidates many of the considerations and factors in a secession decision, but cannot and does not address the moral questions inherent in the secession dynamic. Critical to any specific secession is its own internal justification; of central importance to any study of secession crises are the moral issues concerning their justification. The analytical framework therefore rests on this normative bedrock underpinning secession. The book argues, however, that moral justifications, although integral to the understanding of a secession attempt, are not sufficient in and of themselves to explain the timing of the decision to secede. For a community to decide to secede, it must perceive a change in its circumstances and its political alternatives.

Disintegration and the "secession crisis"

Secession is a logical, although not inevitable, conclusion of the process of political disintegration. Borrowing Ernst Haas's definition, political integration is "the process whereby political actors in several distinct political systems are persuaded to shift their loyalties, expectations, and political activities toward a new center, the institutions of which possess or demand jurisdiction over the pre-existing subsystem."[1] By contrast, the decision to secede represents an instance of political disintegration, wherein political actors in one or more subsystems withdraw their loyalties from the jurisdictional center to focus them on a center of their own.

This process of disintegration, however, can ultimately result in numerous different outcomes due to the "the fickleness and elasticity" of separatists' demands.[2] The demands of a disgruntled community fluctuate. Although separatist movements vary widely in terms of intensity, degree of violence, and duration, their demands usually fall on a political spectrum somewhere between demanding greater regional autonomy and outright secession. At any particular time, a movement may include those who push for secession, and others who press for domestic change. Leaders may blur their demands due to their own uncertainty or due to strategic considerations. For instance, leaders may espouse secession as the primary goal to strengthen their negotiating position for greater devolution, or they may espouse separatist aims to consolidate their base of support and thus enable them to pursue secession in the future.

Nevertheless, a clear demarcation between separatism and secession is necessary because my aim is to investigate those factors which constrain a discontented community to settle for a position within the existing state in one instance, while provoking another similarly discontented community into declaring independence. For the purposes of this book, the crucial distinction between separatism and secession lies in the willingness or unwillingness of the discontented community to recognize the sovereignty of the existing political authority. The definition of secession used here emphasizes the formal withdrawal of a constituent unit from an established, internationally recognized state and the creation of a new sovereign state.

Employing this definition of secession, I have specifically excluded several different processes of disintegration. First, secessions from sub-state authorities are excluded. The protracted secession of the Jura districts from the canton of Bern from 1947 to 1977, the creation of the

---

[1] Ernst Haas, *The Uniting of Europe* (Stanford: Stanford University Press, 1968), p. 16.
[2] Donald Horowitz, "Patterns of Ethnic Separatism," *Comparative Studies of Society and History*, 23, 2 (April 1981), 169.

Hutt River Province in Western Australia in the 1970s, and the recent proposals for the withdrawal of Staten Island from New York City will not be investigated. Second, demands for a state to relinquish control of its overseas empire are excluded. The recognized process of decolonization during the post-World War II era will not be investigated.[3] In this argument, therefore, attention is restricted largely to the nineteenth and twentieth-century creation of the state.

Our working definition of the critical moment of secession, or "secession crisis," reinforces the centrality of the state:

> *A secession crisis occurs when the leaders representing a territorially concentrated and distinct community within a larger state translate discontent into demands for secession, and possess the power, either through sufficiently strong internal community mobilization or through the use of force, to compel the central government to react to those demands.*

The crucial distinction here lies in the requirement that the central government in fact reacts to the demands for secession.

The four necessary elements of a secession crisis

The proposed definition of a secession crisis implies four necessary elements: a "distinct community," territory, leaders, and discontent. First, the demands must be presented by an identifiable unit, or *distinct community*, which is smaller than the state and which threatens

---

[3] The arbitrariness of this division is apparent, as the numerous accusations of internal colonialism in the former Soviet Union reveal. Many Europeans, including the Russian monarchy, shared the imperial ambitions of the eighteenth and nineteenth centuries. Some achieved relatively more success in retaining control of the territory occupied during their period of imperial expansion. Writing in 1970, Robert Conquest in *The Nation Killers: The Soviet Deportation of Nationalities* (London: Macmillan, p. 10) has vividly pointed out this arbitrariness:

> the nations of the Crimea and the Caucusus [inhabited] territories which the Russians invaded only at the end of the 18th century, and did not finally subdue until the latter half of the 19th century. The Crimea was annexed only in 1783, at the time of the British annexation of Oudh, and by similar methods. The Caucasian annexations were only completed in the 1860s at the time of the British annexations in Africa. In fact, these territories are not old Russian lands, or even old dependencies, but were annexed as part of the great wave of European imperialist expansion.
>
> A comparison may indeed be made between the present situation of those parts of Asia similarly and simultaneously brought under the rule of Britain and Russia. The present map shows, instead of the vast stretch of dependent territory from the Persian Gulf to the China Sea, a few islands and strips of coast still coming under London's control. The area under Moscow's control remains the same as in Tsarist times.

to withdraw if not satisfied. Political protests would not normally lead to secession crises. The May 1989 mass demonstrations by Chinese students and workers in Tienanmen Square demanding increased political rights from a repressive totalitarian regime did not lead to a secession crisis, since the demonstrators' intentions were not to pull out of the People's Republic but rather to reform its government. The following section explains the reasons for using "distinct community" in place of other possible descriptions.[4]

Second, this identifiable unit of people must be associated with a geographical *territory*, on which it would presumably intend to establish its new independent state. Because they are dispersed across the United States, African Americans are unlikely to translate demands to end racial discrimination into calls for secession. Third, *leadership* of the movement is necessary both to translate the community's needs into demands for secession and to organize efforts to make its threats credible. Without effective leadership, threats to the community might merely generate social disorder and violence as pent-up frustrations are vented. Fourth, *discontent* with its current circumstances within the existing state is necessary to motivate this identifiable unit to demand change, although in any individual case the causes of discontent are not necessarily identical to the motivations for the secession decision. Often the distinct community is bound together by common claims or perceptions of discrimination, neglect, exploitation, or repression, in economic, political, cultural, linguistic, or religious terms. *The Declaration of Independence* points to the "unbearable tyranny of the state" as both the reason, in the sense of providing the motivating force, and the moral justification for secession.[5]

---

[4] The description of distinct community would logically include cross-border groups such as the Somalis. Although irredentism is not the book's primary focus, the pressures for and the process of irredentism change share some similarities with the dynamic of secession.

[5] The eloquence and precision with which *The Declaration of Independence* of the United States justifies secession from despotic rule deserves further quotation:

> When in the Course of Human Events, it becomes necessary for one People to dissolve the Political Bonds which have connected them with one another, and to assume among the Powers of the Earth, the separate and Equal Station to which the Laws of Nature and of Nature's God entitle them, a decent Respect to the Opinions of Mankind requires that they should declare the causes which impel them to the Separation.
>
> We hold these Truths to be self-evident, that all Men are created equal, that they are endowed by their Creator with certain unalienable Rights, that among these are Life, Liberty, and the Pursuit of Happiness – That to secure

This book is not the first to utilize the term "distinct community." The concept is grounded on observations made by contemporary scholars scrutinizing the origins, nature, and permanence of ethnic consciousness.[6] Disagreements surround the question as to whether an ethnic group could be defined by observers, or has to be "self-defined."[7] Disagreements also involve the role of integration, modernization, and industrialization as forces for assimilation, on the one hand, and as factors influencing the relative tenacity of community loyalties, on the other. Furthermore, different terms including "nation," "tribe," "ethnic group," or "minority group," abound for describing this grouping of people. Even though "nation" had been the most widely accepted term for such social groupings, it has since acquired a baggage of political connotations which has impaired its precision and consequently its usefulness in describing such phenomena. The meaning of "nation" has come to be used interchangeably with "state."

This rather remarkable conflation of state and nation – of a political organization with a subjective grouping of people – stems from the simultaneous rise of two trends in the nineteenth century: the creation and consolidation of the modern state, particularly in Europe, and the rise of "nationalism" as a theory of political legitimacy. The nationalist principle proposed that legitimacy rested on a state being coterminous with the nation. The logic of this principle seems to have been gradually turned backwards, almost upon itself, to the point where a

these Rights, Governments are instituted among Men, deriving their just Powers from the Consent of the Governed, that whenever any Form of Government becomes destructive of these Ends, it is the Right of the People to alter or to abolish it, and to institute new Government, laying its Foundation on such Principles, and organizing its Powers in such Form, as to them shall seem most likely to effect their Safety and Happiness. Prudence, indeed, will dictate that Governments long established should not be changed for light and transient Causes; and accordingly all Experience hath shown, that Mankind are more disposed to suffer, while Evils are sufferable, than to right themselves by abolishing the Forms to which they are accustomed. But when a long Train of Abuses and Usurpations, pursuing invariably the same Object, evinces a Design to reduce them under absolute Despotism, it is their Right, it is their Duty, to throw off such Government, and to provide new Guards for their future Security.

[6] Cynthia H. Enloe, *Ethnic Conflict and Political Development* (Boston: Little, Brown, 1973); Walker Connor, "Nation-Building or Nation-Destroying", *World Politics*, 24, 3 (April, 1972) 319–355; and Ernest Gellner, *Nations and Nationalism* (Oxford: Basil Blackwell, 1983).
[7] Walker Connor, "The Politics of Ethnonationalism" *Journal of International Affairs*, 27, 1 (1973) 1–21.

community would rarely be called a nation unless it possessed the attributes of the modern state.

Many discontented communities have specifically not been accorded national status in order to withhold a sense of recognized legitimacy for their aspirations. President Sékou Touré of Guinea was correct in more than one sense when he claimed in the early 1960s that "in Africa it is the state that creates the nation." To prevent the rearrangement of their continent's arbitrarily drawn colonial borders and to cultivate a sense of loyalty among their disparate citizens, many African leaders have pursued forceful policies of assimilation to create a sense of nationhood within the state. However, President Touré's statement possesses a second meaning. Using their access to international fora, many African leaders branded internal protests as "tribalisms," thereby seeking to dismiss them. These leaders feared that they would no longer be able to ignore a community if these demands were to garner international recognition as legitimate national claims. For there exists no principle of "tribal self-determination" comparable to the principle of national self-determination in international law. None the less, based on most objective definitions of the term, there exists no *a priori* reason that three million Welsh should be called a nation, while 12 million Ibos are not normally characterized by the same term. In fact, and more importantly, most communities seeking political autonomy have been denied the description of nation unless they successfully created their own state. In reference to Sir John Harington's famous dictum,[8]

> Treason doth never prosper, what's the reason?
> For if it prosper, none dare call it treason.

Ernest Gellner draws the implicit comparison:

> In a sense nationalisms are simply those tribalisms, for that matter any other kind of grouping, which through luck, effort, and circumstance succeed in becoming an effective force under modern circumstances. They are only identified *ex post factum*. Tribalism never prospers, for when it does, everyone will respect it as true nationalism, and no one will dare call it tribalism.[9]

Given this controversial quandary, one could adopt a number of different conventions. The chosen term would need to capture the

---

[8] Sir John Harington, *Of Treason*, book IV, no. 5 (London, 1618); reprinted in *The Oxford Dictionary of Quotations*, 3rd edn (London: Guild Publishing, 1988), p. 242.
[9] Ernest Gellner, *Nations and Nationalism* (Oxford: Basil Blackwell, 1983), p. 87.

subjective nature of this grouping of people whose existence depends
on its members' belief in its existence. Hugh Seton-Watson has outlined the difficulty of describing a phenomenon based on sentiment:

> What is the nation? Many people have tried to find a definition. But
> it seems to me, after a good deal of thought, that all we can say is
> that a nation exists when an active and fairly numerous section of its
> members are convinced that it exists. Not external objective charac-
> teristics, but subjective conviction is the decisive factor.[10]

Although clearly subjective, "nation" and "tribe" seem inappropriate
choices due to their other political associations discussed here.
"Nation" is further impaired by its close association with the possession of statehood. Other scholars have suggested "ethnic group."
Despite the fact that members of many communities are tied together
through bonds of ethnicity, this term is not quite appropriate either.
Walker Connor indicates its weakness: "[an] ethnic group may be
very apparent to an anthropologist or even an untrained observer, but
without a realization of this fact on the part of a sizable percentage of
its members, a nation does not exist."[11]

To set aside these disputed labels, I suggest an alternative. Any
territorially concentrated community of people seeking to change its
political situation, either through demands for increased autonomy or
for outright independence, either peacefully or through the use of
force, will be called not a nation, nor a tribe, nor an ethnic group, but
rather a "distinct community." This approach provides the analytical
framework with two benefits. First, the term does not invoke specific
political associations. Second, it is inclusive of all communities
seeking to alter their political circumstances, whether they are inside
the borders of an established state and willing to remain so or are
pressing for secession.

That the community is "distinct" acknowledges certain objective
characteristics, such as religion, language, culture, race, or ethnicity,
which can often be ascribed to it. More importantly, the people in this
group *perceive* characteristics which distinguish their members from
individuals not within the group. That this group is a "community"
emphasizes the subjective element and reinforces arguments made by
both Benedict Anderson, in his description of an "imagined commun-

[10] Hugh Seton-Watson, *Nationalism: Old and New* (Sydney: Sydney University Press, 1964), p. 5.
[11] Walker Connor, "Nation-Building or Nation-Destroying?" *World Politics*, 24, 3 (April, 1972), p. 337.

14

ity,"[12] and Ernest Gellner.[13] Both scholars argue that the mere category of persons, such as the speakers of a particular language or the inhabitants of a particular region, does not constitute a nation or a community, until those people recognize their mutual duties to each other by virtue of their shared membership in the group. As Anderson has indicated, most members of any such extended community will never meet, and yet they feel a commitment to each other. It is their commitment which transforms a mere category of people into a community.

A note on the moral justification underpinning secession

Embedded in any secession lies the perceived justice of its community's cause. Although the specific purpose of this book is to investigate the timing of the decision to secede, such an investigation must acknowledge the central importance of its justification. Moral questions lie at the very core of any secession, and thus provide the foundation from which a discussion of the secession decision must proceed.

Many scholars, philosophers, and secessionist leaders have attempted to reason from first principles such as freedom and liberty to the conditions under which secession would be justifiable and even desirable. The debate surrounding the "right" of secession revolves around, first, an argument that secession may be justifiable in circumstances where state rule over a community is particularly onerous or when the majority of a territorially concentrated community desires secession, and second, an argument that secession may be desirable due to the benefits it provides for communities to organize themselves by their own values and by possibly improving the chances for international peace if the desires of distinct communities are no longer denied. The following section discusses each of these arguments in turn.

Those seeking to justify secession extend the argument that if a society may overthrow a government when it has become unbearable, then a segment of the population may also remove itself from a government which is particularly objectionable to it. Although this

---

[12] Benedict Anderson, *Imagined Communities* (London: Verso, 1983), p. 6.
[13] Gellner, *Nations*, p. 7.

minority segment may not posses the right to overthrow and replace the government for the whole state, at minimum it must have the recourse to end that portion of the government's power directed at it. This recourse could include physically separating itself from the existing state. For revolution or secession, the underlying principle of protest is the same.

Several scholars have attempted to specify under what objectionable conditions this minority segment may be morally justified in withdrawing from the existing state. John Stuart Mill acknowledged that freedom and liberty may not be possible when the state is an artificial agglomeration of two or more distinct communities with one dominating the mechanisms of government, and thus, conceded that secession may be a necessary alternative to promote liberty. Mill prescribed a stern doctrine of self-help in these situations. He compared freedom for communities with virtue for the individual. Neither freedom nor virtue could be acquired with assistance from external actors. They must be cultivated independently, and in the case of freedom, through an "arduous struggle" on the part of the community.[14] The difficulty with Mill's prescription lies in situations where the discontented community may be fighting for secession with metaphorical bows and arrows against the superior fire-power of the state. The inequality of the struggle prejudices the outcome and may unjustly perpetrate alien rule over a community despite its valiant efforts in search of freedom.

In a recent investigation of numerous cases of secession, Alan Buchanan specifies further the circumstances under which a "right" to secede may exist, as long as the prerequisite – a valid claim to territory – has been satisfied by the seceding community. Buchanan's outline of such circumstances includes state violations of basic individual civil and political rights, state-perpetrated discriminatory redistribution, and defense of the distinct community's unique culture.[15]

Harry Beran reasons toward a justification for secession not from the direction of objectionable state rule, but rather by beginning with three liberal principles: freedom, sovereignty of the people, and legitimacy of majority rule. He proceeds to argue that "liberal political philosophy requires that secession be permitted if it is effectively

[14] Mill, *Collected Works*, p. 549.
[15] Allen Buchanan, *Secession: The Morality of Political Divorce From Fort Sumter to Lithuania and Quebec* (Oxford: Westview Press, 1991).

desired by a territorially concentrated group within a state."[16] Beran is quick to qualify his argument in two ways: first, with an outline of the conditions under which secession may not be permissible; and second, with the observation that even conditions which may permit secession do not necessarily imply that secession is desirable.

President Woodrow Wilson, and later Michael Walzer, address directly the question as to when secession may be not only justifiable, but also desirable. Wilson sought peace above all else. In his thinking, justice played a critical role in the preservation of peace: he believed that the subjugation of one distinct community by another was unjust, and thus, would inevitably lead to a threat to peace. Implicit in Wilson's approach lies a belief in the desirability of secession since it would create new states coterminous with national communities, despite their many problems.

Michael Walzer combines the previous arguments justifying secession with a further refinement of the Wilsonian perspective on the circumstances which make secession a desirable alternative. Like Mill and Buchanan, Walzer argues first that secession may be justifiable because some communities, such as the Armenians and Kurds, could best guarantee their safety and survival through the medium of sovereign power. Second, every historical nation should possess the same right to organize its communal life according to its own values. Third, secession may be a desirable outcome because international peace would continue to be disturbed if distinct communities were denied on the first two basic considerations. Walzer concludes:

> in many parts of the world, the completion of the state system is the first requirement – if only because its completion, and the festering discontent of stateless people, is one of the prime causes of violence, war, and Great Power confrontation ... The conflict of nationalism may be endless, but no particular conflict is necessarily endless, and each particular solution reforms even as it expands the state system and improves the chances of general peace.[17]

The difficulties surrounding a "right" to secession are certainly not in short supply. Secession, by its very nature, presents the international system with instability and chaos. The potential conclusion for the logic of secession would be the infinite division of existing political entities, given the lack of widely accepted objective criteria to

---

[16] Harry Beran, "A Liberal Theory of Secession", *Political Studies*, 22 (1984), 21–31.

[17] Michael Walzer, "The Reform of the International System" in Oyvind Osterud (ed.), *Studies of War and Peace* (Oslo: Norwegian University Press, 1986), p. 238.

delineate a distinct community. From a detailed study of several cases
of secession, Lee Buchheit proposes the establishment of internationally accepted standards concerning the legitimacy of a secession
attempt. He suggests that a United Nations resolution might explicitly
balance the "right" of a community to secession against the utilitarian
concern about the disruptive effects of the secession on both the state
directly affected and the international system in general.[18] Whether or
not one agrees with Buchheit's proposed approach, that some way to
bring secessionist struggles into the realms of international discourse
is urgently needed is not in debate.

The critical observation here, however, is that a discussion of its
justification does not explain the timing of that secession. Distinct
communities live with the factors reinforcing the perceived justice of
their cause for years, sometimes generations, without suffering a
secession crisis. Moral justifications for secession such as objectionable
state rule or simply the strong desire to organize communal life
according to its own values, although integral to an understanding of
the secession attempt, are not, in and of themselves, sufficient to
explain the timing of the decision to secede. The secession dynamic
rests on the community perceiving some change in its circumstances
and its political alternatives.

The framework

The framework to investigate the timing of the decision to secede
depends on four primary variables: the benefits of continued membership in the larger political entity, the costs of such membership, the
costs of secession, and the benefits of secession. As mentioned in the
Introduction, these costs and benefits must be apprehended by the
distinct community as it assesses its political options. The purpose of
the four chapters of Part II is to explain the four key costs and benefits.
In order to disclose the costs and benefits as conditions of a community's experience, the discussion rests on case studies in which the
particular primary variable has not been associated with an immediate secession attempt.

Exploration of what is the first variable in this situation, the benefits
of membership for a community, necessitates a brief examination of

[18] Lee Buchheit, *Secession: The Legitimacy of Self-Determination* (New Haven: Yale
University Press, 1978).

potential services provided by the state. Chapter 3 seeks to demon-strate that government services provide advantages that accrue to the distinct community as a whole, rather than simply to its members as individuals. The description of the security, economic, and social benefits of membership relies upon aspects of numerous case studies: the experiences of the Czechs and Slovaks, the constitution of Yugo-slavia, the special needs of the Karen in Burma, and the Romansch in Switzerland are but a few of the examples employed.

The costs of secession are contingent on state opposition and international hostility to secessionist activity. Following an overview of the considerations which frequently dominate a state's reaction to a secession attempt, Chapter 4 delves into state opposition. A survey of the secession crises involving the Nagas in India and the Kurds in Turkey, Iran, and Iraq discloses the various strategies available to states. None the less, the effect of state resistance in such situations is not constant. On the one hand, the state could suppress a secessionist insurrection without being able to force the distinct community to relinquish its aspirations for independence. On the other hand, efficient state repression could force the distinct community to recon-sider the feasibility of continuing its struggle. The credible threat of state opposition could even dissuade other discontented communities from seeking secession as a means to alleviate their grievances.

A discussion of the second category of the costs of secession – the international community's attitude toward secession – cannot avoid addressing the inherent conflict between the principle of self-determi-nation and that of territorial integrity. An investigation of a number of representative legal documents with particular reference to these two principles helps gauge the international community's attitude toward secession. Two specific secession crises – those of Katanga from the Congo, 1960–1961 – and of Biafra from Nigeria, 1966–1970 support the assertion of international hostility. These two costs of secession provide an effective barrier to the successful creation of an indepen-dent state through secession, while the benefits of membership act as an implicit restraint on the decision to secede.

In introducing the costs of membership, Chapter 5 investigates the manner in which state power has historically been utilized by ruling elites to threaten distinct communities residing within their jurisdic-tions. The costs of membership not only entail mortal threats, such as deportation, famine, and mass violence, but also political, economic, and cultural threats. These latter include official policies perpetuating political domination or economic exploitation of members of a certain ethnic group. The experiences of the Armenians and the Kurds in Turkey and several communities in the former Soviet Union serve to illustrate some of the human costs of membership. The actual degree of security from such threats is not as important as the distinct community's perception of its security.

Chapter 6 investigates the benefits of secession. The difficulty in defining this variable lies in its dual nature: these benefits can either stretch to encompass the entire distinct community or can be more narrowly limited to its elite. One of the primary benefits of secession lies in a distinct community's belief in its ability and right to be ruled by its own members through the medium of sovereign power. This conviction has its origins in the principle of national self-determination. While Chapter 4 assesses the relevance of this doctrine in international law, Chapter 6 indicates the power of its popular appeal. It also investigates the considerable opportunities for financial gain and social advancement for ethnic elites, historically associated with the domination of an independent state. Examination of separatist agitation in Nigeria, both under British colonial administration and during independence, reveals the way in which regional elites contemplated secession as a means of retaining their power base and privileges.

There are four essential elements of any secession crisis which, even though we have discussed them earlier, bear repetition before proceeding to an overview of the arguments presented in the four chapters of Part III. These include the distinct community itself, its claims to territory, its leadership, and discontent. These four elements must be present for a secession crisis to occur, although they need not be present in any specified or fixed amounts, levels, or proportions. Secession crises are possible when the distinct community's claims to a territory are more or less tenuous; or when the definitions of the distinct community's "distinctness" are more or less fluid; or when the sources of discontent cause more or less indignation; or when the leadership of the community is more or less inspired. On the one hand, relatively stronger community consciousness and sense of grievance require less inspirational leadership to provoke a secession crisis. On the other hand, skillful leaders can act as a catalyst to bring cultural or economic cleavages to prominence in political debates, although there exists no *a priori* reason for such divisions to be more politically salient than class or religious ones. In a secession crisis, leaders exert pressure on the state by mobilizing their community or commanding the resources of force. What is significant is their ability to force the state to react to demands for secession. Moreover, a secession crisis presupposes the community's belief in the inherent justice of its cause. Justifications for a community's "right" to secede could rest on accusations of state misrule or on the majority's desire for independence as disclosed through democratic processes, or on the simple wish to govern one's community according to its own values. The important point here is that the analysis of the decision to secede builds on an assumption of the four necessary elements of a secession crisis and on some moral justification for the attempt.

Secession is a consequence of a shift in, and thus an imbalance among, the four primary variables. The decision to secede can be thought of as the result of motion on a scale. On one side of the scale, high benefits of membership and costs of secession serve as the main restraints on secession. Reduction in these could precipitate a secession crisis. Similarly, an increase in either of the motivations for secession – the costs of membership or the benefits of secession – could also provoke secession crises. It is the balance among these costs and benefits that is critical.

A possible imbalance can arise from any number of shifts. These shifts can come in the form of rapidly moving events or as gradual transformations of attitudes. These changes can occur at the level of the current government, in terms of the various policies affecting its distinct communities, or at the level of the international system. Part III, therefore, seeks to explain the dynamic of secession. It chronicles examples of how such changes have provoked secessions as a consequence.

First, one of the most prevalent causes of secession is the sudden and objectionable rise in the costs of membership. Escalating threats to the physical safety or the cultural inheritance of a community generate fear and discontent, and can at times provoke a secession attempt. Faced by such desperate circumstances, the decision to secede becomes one of "last resort." Chapter 7 uses the secession crises of Biafra from Nigeria in 1966 and of the Bengalis from Pakistan in 1971 to elaborate the circumstances in which the distinct community chooses secession because it perceives its safety jeopardized by the ruling regime. The example of the Southern Sudanese insurrection shows that protection of a community's culture and religion may also be worthy of a secessionist war. In fact, the Southern Sudanese abandoned their struggle when the Khartoum government agreed to respect their cultural and religious rights in 1972, but took up arms again once Sudan began to enforce Islamic law in 1983.

Second, a sudden reduction in the potential costs of the endeavor has also motivated numerous historical cases of secession. The roots of discontent need not be the same as the motivations for secession. Discontented communities have attempted to secede when they perceived the likelihood of success to be greater – at "opportune moments." Chapter 8 investigates how the general weakening of a central government or external support for the separatist community have reduced the risks of effective state repression, and thus, have generated secession attempts as a result. The secessionist activity of multiple communities following the collapse of tsarist rule in Russia illustrates how secessions can occur at opportune moments. An investigation of India's intervention in Bangladesh's secessionist war and Turkey's invasion of Cyprus discloses the influence of foreign powers on the secession dynamic.

Third, Chapter 9 concentrates on how changes at the state or international system level which reduce the benefits of membership precipitate secessions or at least reinforce persistent separatism. As outlined in Chapter 4, once the government has failed in its duties to its citizens, it has forfeited the right to command their obedience. The distinct community may decide to seek secession because it perceives that the state is no longer providing the important services its members need. Norway's secession from Sweden in 1905 was at least partly provoked by Sweden's reluctance or inability to provide adequate consular services to Norwegian sailors, who by the turn of the century had built the third largest merchant marine in the world.

The persistence and even growth of some secession movements in the absence of circumstances understood as "last resorts" or "opportune moments" at first appears anomalous. Detailed scrutiny of the cases of Catalonia and Quebec indicates how Catalans and Quebecois may be more inclined to contemplate secession now that a gradual transformation of the international system has moderated the tradition security and economic benefits of integration into a larger state. In both cases, the usual costs of membership consisting of mortal or cultural threats are not in evidence. The 1978 Spanish constitution granted extensive autonomy to the Catalan regional government. The federal government in Ottawa has conceded considerable privileges to the Quebec provincial government. Both now possess the power to administer their own social, educational, and health programs, to raise taxes, and to pass legislation aimed at promoting their respective languages and cultures. Their prosperity and economic resources would normally be the envy of most other distinct communities. Furthermore, neither Spain nor Canada appears to suffer from recent structural weakening, so that the costs of secession have not been reduced. The persistence of these secessionist movements may be partly caused by evolution in the international security structure combined with the emergence of regional economic integration. Due to arrangements of collective security in Western Europe and North America, it is less crucial for each state to provide its own military defense. In terms of economic considerations, with the growth of a single market within the European Union and the North American Free Trade Association, the state may no longer be the appropriate level of political authority to provide certain economic advantages for its citizens. Together, these trends have reduced the benefits of membership for some communities. Consequently, members of some distinct communities may perceive independence as an increasingly viable political alternative.

Fourth, and so far, perhaps the least frequent occurrence, a rise in the benefits of secession may precipitate a secession crisis. Changes in such benefits, like changes in the benefits of membership, can also come from gradual shifts in the international system. With the guidance of recent scholarship on "quasi-states,"[19] Chapter 10 investigates the evolution in the normative context guiding relations between developed and developing states. The recent rise in the benefits of secession rests on the way in which the contemporary international system has undertaken the responsibility to promote the economic development, political stability, and survival of the many new weak states created through the process of decolonization. If a distinct community were successful in overcoming the numerous obstacles to gain independent statehood, it could reasonably expect political and especially economic assistance from the rest of the world.

Historical illustrations are critical to the argument. In every case study, a whole web of interconnecting factors influences the decisions, events, and outcomes. The book does not present any case study in its

[19] Robert Jackson, *Quasi-States: Sovereignty, International Relations, and the Third World* (Cambridge: Cambridge University Press, 1990).

entirety. A particular case has been chosen for its exemplary relevance to the particular point under discussion. Any one factor is unlikely to be influencing the situation in isolation from other factors, yet in the case chosen it is the key factor providing the essential impetus for an event.

There are certain limitations to such a theoretical framework. To its credit, the framework provides an instrument useful in the organization of analysis and in the discernment of causal patterns in the process of disintegration. The framework does not however, provide a hierarchy of the influential factors in theory. It does not indicate which of the primary variables could provide relatively stronger restraints on the decision to secede or which of the potential changes could provide stronger impetus for secession. This theoretical limitation can be overcome through the supplementary investigation of individual cases of secession crises. Judgments as to the relative motivational strength of a particular variable necessarily rest on scrutiny of the available historical evidence. Even though some of the primary variables may have greater effect on the secession dynamic, I present all four costs and benefits for the sake of thorough and comprehensive analysis. Such an exposition also lays the foundation for the subsequent greater development of the framework. It is intended that the framework be employed to analyze secession trends in the future.

A note on the cost/benefit approach

The terms "costs" and "benefits" are but labels chosen to describe the four primary variables. The terms of costs, benefits, and balance are controversial. It may be helpful to identify the sense in which I use them in this book. At its most fundamental level, "costs" are abstracted from their normal usage implying financial loss and revolve around the notion of a penalty, such as the loss of life or the loss of livelihood. The costs envisaged here can manifest themselves in terms of the sacrifice, seizure, or dispossession of economic opportunities, political rights, autonomy, or cultural heritage, and can escalate into political repression and systematic violence. For example, state opposition to and international hostility toward this type of endeavor determine the costs of secession. In other words, state policies which suppress separatist insurrections constitute the instrument of the costs of secession. They can lead, for the members of the distinct community, to human costs such as fear, suffering, and death. Meanwhile, the international community can cause hardship for the community seeking secession by withholding the economic and political privileges associated with sovereign statehood.

"Benefits" can be understood as the mirror image of costs. The definition of benefits also abstracts from potential economic profits and revolves around the right and opportunity to life and livelihood in the absence of external threat. "Costs" and "benefits" are strong words adopted to describe the four primary variables. Throughout the argument, this notion of costs and benefits must be understood implicitly, and not as part of a great decision-making balance sheet.

Separatist and secessionist movements, certainly in Western societies, have suffered from a negative, and perhaps at times justified, image of being the irrational endeavors of romantics. At first glance, even though the notion of costs and benefits has been carefully defined, it may still seem inappropriate to be using these particular labels to describe a phenomenon that both commentators and critics describe as emotive. Several responses exist to this problematic observation. First, it is possible to subject conflicting moralities and their associated emotions to rational and detached analysis. Furthermore, the cost/benefit framework proposed here concerning the decision to secede cannot and does not comment on the specific moral issues at stake with any secession, but rather assumes them as the prerequisite or bedrock underpinning the attempt. And, finally, the argument does assert that, at a fundamental level, human behavior is guided by rational criteria. In approaching a decision-making juncture, the members of a community complete an implicit weighing of the costs and benefits of the various alternatives. I do not claim that the proposed cost/benefit mechanism is a description of actual events in a secession crisis. The members of the distinct community do not congregate and evaluate together their various options and then choose the best alternative. From much observation and research, however, it appears that distinct communities act *as if* they have completed such an evaluation of potential costs and benefits. Consequently, it is a useful analytical instrument for interpreting historic occurrences of secession.

Furthermore, the book cannot claim to be the first to introduce the idea of costs and benefits to the study of secession, although it is the first to employ them in such a rigorous manner. Ralph Premdas, Anthony D. Smith, and John R. Wood propose various models to describe and interpret the frequent process of discourse, disagree-

Introduction

ment, and escalation into confrontation of secessionist struggles.[20] Peter Gourevitch and Donald Horowitz ascribe the motivations for separatist protests and demands for secession to variables related to the level of economic and social progress achieved by the community.[21] In describing his model of separatism resting on the relationship between relative group position and relative regional development, Horowitz declares: "In short, (separatist) precipitants may act either to raise the costs or to reduce the benefits of remaining in the state – provided, of course, that benefits and costs are understood to embrace non-material as well as material values."[22] Anthony Birch presents a utilitarian theory that links the likelihood of secession to changes in the overall "balance of advantages in any particular time"[23] which bears close resemblance to the cost/benefit framework introduced here.

Beyond the factors captured in the "costs" and "benefits," there are other complexities that deserve mention, which though they will introduce ambiguities into the analysis of the secession crisis, will also enrich such a study. A few of these less tangible factors in human motivation include behavior based on momentum, habit, tradition, or inertia. Surmounting these obstacles represents an additional implicit cost of secession. Also to be considered are the benefits associated with peaceful existence, even if under politically unappealing conditions.

A note on the units of analysis

Men and women identify themselves with others who share a similar culture and values, are of the same race, practice the same religion, or speak the same language. This tendency stands in radical opposition

[20] See Ralph Premdas, S. W. R. de A. Samarasinghe, and Alan B. Anderson (eds.), *Secessionist Movements in Comparative Perspective* (London: Pinter Press, 1990); Anthony D. Smith (ed.), *Nationalist Movements* (New York: Macmillan, 1976); and John R. Wood, "Secession: A Comparative Analytical Framework", *Canadian Journal of Political Science*, 14, 1 (March 1981), 107–134.
[21] See Peter A. Gourevitch, "The Reemergence of 'Peripheral Nationalisms': Some Comparative Speculation on the Spatial Distribution of Political Leadership and Economic Growth," *Comparative Studies of Society and History* (1979), 303–322; and Donald Horowitz, "Patterns of Ethnic Separatism," *Comparative Studies of Society and History*, 23, 2 (April 1981), 165–195; and "The Logic of Secession and Irredentism," in *Ethnic Groups in Conflict* (Berkeley: University of California Press, 1985), pp. 236–288.
[22] Horowitz, "Patterns of Ethnic Separatism," p. 193.
[23] Anthony H. Birch, "Minority Nationalist Movements and Theories of Political Integration," *World Politics*, 30, 3 (April 1978), 325–344.

26

to values propounded by eighteenth-century Enlightenment thinkers. It challenges both their fundamental principle of universalism and their preoccupation with individual rights. The Enlightenment may have been hostile to theories which devalue the individual in the name of the collective, but the fact of the matter remains that individual members of a community, when calculating their own self-interest, frequently take into account the needs and interests of the community as a whole as well. Thus, although individuals must still weigh on a daily basis the costs and benefits associated with different alternatives and act accordingly, the argument holds the distinct community in its entirety as its primary unit of analysis.

This choice is imperfect. The calculations made by individuals are susceptible to external encouragement, propaganda, and in particular, influence by their leaders. Leadership is necessary both for preventing discontent from degenerating into anarchical violence and for translating this discontent into effective demands for secession. However, leaders are not simply the mouthpiece of the community, organizing protests, mobilizing support, and negotiating with the central government. As with any sub-group or elite within a society, leaders pursue their own interests. In participatory democracy or in a revolutionary movement, the interests of the leaders parallel more closely those of the rest of the distinct community. Nevertheless, in many other cases elite interests diverge from those of the remainder of the community. Leaders of a secessionist community may stop weighing the costs and benefits for the entire group, and rather make decisions on the basis of the costs and benefits associated with their own personal ambitions. In numerous examples of violent separatist agitation, the desire to retain power and its trappings has become the goal of secessionist leaders. When policies seem to veer away from the perceived good of the entire community, the appropriate unit of analysis may become the individual who wields power. Chapter 6 discusses these issues in more detail when it turns to the benefits for elites associated with secession.

Despite these reservations, the use of the distinct community as the primary unit of analysis remains justified. When leaders make decisions consistently harmful to the community or which are not supported by its members, both the leaders and their policies become discredited over time. This process eventually leads to their loss of support, and even to their removal, as new leaders emerge who pursue policies closer to the perceived interests of the community as a whole. This transfer of power can, and often does, become an extended and painful struggle. In multiple examples, leaders have commanded sufficient resources to control their communities for extended periods of time. But if a set of leaders is pressing for secession without the continuing support of the distinct community, even if they do command significant resources, it is best not to underestimate the human desire for peace. The number of secession crises where community members have successfully pressed for just such a transfer of power to new leaders justifies the use of the distinct community as the primary unit of analysis for this framework.

The argument temporarily idealizes the distinct community, although this restriction is relaxed once the framework has been completely explained. This simplification abstracts from the internal diversity of the seceding community and imputes characteristics to it as a whole. This abstraction is necessary since the seceding community could be deeply divided before the secessionist struggle. For example, the Southern Sudanese secessionist movement lacks internal cultural unity. It includes the Western Nilote peoples (Dinka, Nuer, Shilluk, and Anuak), the Eastern Nilotes (Bari, Latuka, Taposa, and Turkana), the central Sudanic groups (Moru and Madi) and the West African related Azande.[24] The seceding community can also become deeply divided by differences in values, priorities, and interests once the struggle for secession has been completed. In the year following Lithuania's independence in 1991, its fragmentation into numerous political parties and factions nearly paralyzed the Lithuanian parliament.

Implicit in any study of ethnic conflict and secession lies a theory of the state. Conflictual and contractual theories pose different definitions of the state: either as an hegemony of one group ruling over a number of less powerful groups in the society or as a provider of services to meet basic social needs. This book employs both theories. On the one hand, the concept of the benefits of membership depends on contractarian principles of governance. On the other hand, the costs of membership utilize more of a conflictual theory perspective. In all cases, the term "state" is used to signify the regime or elites commanding the apparatus of power.

While it may be relatively easy to characterize distinct communities as united in their struggles, it is even easier to depict states as Goliaths

---

[24] Douglas H, Johnson, *The Southern Sudan* (London: Minority Rights Group, 1988), p. 4.

in their battles with dissenting portions of their populations. In both unitary and federal states, the central government normally possesses the established symbols of authority, commands the military, controls the central budget and other financial institutions, and has access to foreign support. Nevertheless, contrary to the distinct community's image of the state, it is often not a monolith. The central government is likely to be constituted by a coalition of several interests. The regime may also suffer from a lack of coordination in policy implementation due to its size. Although unquestionably very powerful, states are usually imperfect Goliaths.

Part of the success of any argument lies in circumscribing its field of inquiry. The explanatory power of the proposed framework ends if sustained violence has erupted in the secessionist conflict. The outbreak of violence almost certainly prolongs and complicates the dispute. Protracted violent struggle hardens the attitudes of leaders representing both sides, as compromise becomes an unpalatable alternative in principle. Frequently violence also detracts attention from the original causes of the conflict. None the less, a deeper scrutiny of the role of extended violence in the resolution of secessions lies beyond the limited scope of this book, which concentrates exclusively on the critical moment of decision to secede.

To ignore human emotions, however, would imply a gross misunderstanding of the frequently subjective nature of this phenomenon. Thus, even when all the rational explanations for secession crises are exhaustively explored and objectively weighed, there still remains the emotional appeal of an independent homeland. Conversely, those who possess the mechanism of established political power can also equally fervently desire the preservation of the territorial unity of the state and their privileges. The study of secession should therefore ignore neither the logic of group memory nor the history of a distinct community and the state in which it belongs. In the hands of a capable leader, ethnic differences and group memory could not only become salient to domestic political competition, but also provide the motivating force for political mobilization and the cornerstone of ideology. An effective ideology is no less powerful when it taps ethnic aspirations than when it outlines other emotive distinctions such as class. While it is clearly beyond the scope of this book to attempt to explain the origins, persistence, and power of nationalism, xenophobia, and other emotional drives which often lie at the root of passionate human conflict, these forces would play a part in a comprehensive analysis of secession. We can only seek empathy with the actors involved in the process.

Nevertheless, just as the inherent moral justification for secession is not sufficient to motivate the decision to secede, neither can such emotions in isolation motivate a community to secede. This is because they are primarily static conditions. Only change can motivate the secession dynamic. Although a community may desire its own country that is governed by its own members and embodying its values and culture, this desire would not, in and of itself, provoke a secession crisis. Decisions to secede only result from changes in the balance among the costs and benefits associated with its political alternatives as perceived by the distinct community.

II   The costs and benefits

3   The benefits of membership

Given the relative infrequency of this phenomenon, our metaphorical scales may be stacked against secession. The purpose of this chapter and Chapter 4 is to examine the main barriers to secession: first, the benefits of membership, and then, the costs of secession. The benefits of membership for a distinct community accrue from the services and advantages provided by the state. This chapter dissects these benefits into their constituent security, economic, and social factors. Critical to the argument, investigation of specific cases in which secession was a viable alternative and yet not chosen reveals that communities sometimes calculate that they can ill afford to forfeit the benefits associated with participation in a larger and more powerful state. In effect, this calculation provides a powerful restraint on secession attempts.

Security benefits

Security benefits of membership manifest themselves in the state's maintenance of internal order so as to protect citizens from violence at each other's hands and in its guarantee of defense from the aggression of foreign powers. With a few exceptions, before the middle of the twentieth century, force was deemed an acceptable means to settle political or economic disputes between states. One needs only to remember von Clausewitz's famous dictum in *Vom Kriege:* "War is a continuation of policy by other means."[1] As long as they could do so without suffering heavy repercussions, states regularly intervened in the affairs of neighboring countries in order to extend their own

---

[1] The main arguments on war as an instrument of policy are in Karl von Clausewitz, *On War*, 1832, vol. II, bk. 8.

power and influence. Security, as well as the protection and expansion of one's economic and political interests, depended on military strength. Military capacity in turn was a function of industrial, natural, and human resources. Small size in terms of population and territory, therefore, limited a state's defensive capabilities and consequently, its sovereignty and independence.[2] More powerful, expansionary states conquered smaller or weaker polities; two famous examples being the division of the weak Polish Commonwealth in 1797 among Prussia, Austria, and Russia and the unchallenged partition of Africa at the Berlin Conference of 1885.

Communities, and not just individual citizens, can and do readily recognize these security benefits. At the turn of the century, even though they suffered repression, weaker distinct communities in Europe did not normally contemplate independence as a remedy for their grievances. An investigation of Czech demands for reform and devolution within the framework of the Austro-Hungarian Empire reveals an acute awareness on the part of Czech leaders that they would surely face the prospect of even worse subjugation if they were to secede. Furthermore, a short examination of the events leading to the creation of Yugoslavia indicates the extent to which concerns for security preoccupied the Serb, Croat, and Slovene communities. Yugoslavia's hasty creation was to a great extent due to each community's similar judgment that its own particular interests would be better defended by integration into a larger and more powerful state of their creation.

Czech desires for a Bohemian Kingdom within the Austro-Hungarian Empire[3]

Until the imminent collapse of the Austro-Hungarian Empire during World War I, the Czech community consistently presented limited demands for political reforms, recoiling from a demand for outright

---

[2] One only has to think of China's semi-colonial status before 1949 to recognize that size alone could not guarantee security against foreign aggression. The lack of social cohesiveness, control over territory, and efficient organization of government functions could also impair a state's defense against foreign influence.

[3] Historical material for this section has been drawn mainly from Victor Mamatey and Radomir Luza (eds.), *A History of the Czechoslovak Republic, 1918–1948* (Princeton: Princeton University Press, 1973); and Joseph F. Zacek, "Nationalism in Czechoslovakia," in Peter F. Sugar and Ivo J. Lederer (eds.), *Nationalism in Eastern Europe* (Seattle: University of Washington Press, 1969), pp. 166–206.

independence. After the Austro-Hungarian *Ausgleich* (Compromise) of 1867, which created the Dual Monarchy, the primary ambition of Czech leaders was to convince Emperor Franz Josef I to restore the *Staatsrecht* of the Kingdom of Bohemia. This would enable the Czech lands to receive a level of autonomy analogous to that granted to the Kingdom of Hungary.[4] Despite the emperor's many promises to have himself crowned with the crown of St. Venceslas in Prague, Germans, fearful of Czech domination within the potentially autonomous Bohemia, successfully mobilized German opinion across the empire to pressure Franz Josef to abandon his promises.

The adoption of universal male suffrage in 1906 in the Austrian half of the empire assured the Czechs and other minorities there of representation in the *Reichsrat* in Vienna, and set the Czechs on a new strategy to pursue enhanced political rights and autonomy. Czech leaders sought alliances with other Slavs, who together constituted more than half of the imperial population, to exert greater pressure on the Austrian government for reform. But the Ukrainian and Polish *Reichsrat* members were reluctant to cooperate. This failure embittered and alienated many Czechs from the empire.[5]

Nevertheless, regardless of their differences, few of the main Czech political parties or organizations advocated secession as the solution for Czech discontent. In 1909, Tomas G. Masaryk, leader of the Czech Realist Party and future president of an independent Czechoslovak Republic, stated the compelling explanation for Czech moderation: "We want a federal Austria. We cannot be independent outside of Austria, next to a powerful Germany with Germans on our territory."[6] Victor Mamatey and Radomir Luza, two historians of Czechoslovakia, assert that the prevailing security conditions in Central Europe, and in particular the real threat posed by an expansionist Germany, prevented the Czechs from attempting to secede.[7] Greater autonomy and political freedoms within the decentralized Austro-Hungarian Empire served Czech interests better than independence. An independent Czech state was clearly perceived to lack the resources required to protect itself from intimidation and possible subjugation by the more powerful and potentially repressive German Empire.

[4] Mamatey and Luza, *Czechoslovak Republic*, p. 4.
[5] Ibid., p. 4.
[6] Quoted in Evzen Stern, *Opinions of T. G. Masaryk* (Prague, 1918), p. 60.
[7] Victor Mamatey and Radomir Luza, "The Establishment of the Republic," in *Czechoslovak Republic*, pp. 3–38.

The hasty creation of Yugoslavia[8]

Although Yugoslavia had its roots in romantic nineteenth century nationalist ideals, its creation was due to the common security threats faced by the Serb, Croat, and Slovene communities during World War I. These three communities judged that they could defend their integrity and interests better collectively than individually.

The "Illyrian movement" of the 1830s sought the political unification of the Southern Slavs. Although first debated within the Croat community after Napoleon's brief experiment of creating a single administrative unit called "Illyria" out of the Slovene and Croat provinces, it soon inspired many Slovenes, Croats, and Serbs.[9] Naturally each community was drawn to the prospect of unification because it offered the advancement of its own parochial interests. Despite the Illyrian movement's official suppression by the Hapsburgs in 1843, it was resurrected in the 1860s as another Croat initiative to counter the Austro-Hungarian policy of *divide et impera* over its Slav minorities. In the late nineteenth century, the Serbian government also adopted its main tenets as a means to liberate all South Slavs from Hapsburg rule. Croat and Slovene accusations that Serb pursuit of this ideal also served as "a cloak for Serbian territorial expansion" possessed some validity.[10]

This shared romantic inspiration of Southern Slav unity did not, however, lead to the creation of Yugoslavia. Immediate and daunting security threats against these three communities during World War I contributed to the creation of Yugoslavia. "Despite religious, cultural, and other differences, the Serbs, Croats, and Slovenes shared significant political and geostrategic interests … By the late 19th century, they also began to be drawn to each other by *a desire for collective security* against the great powers."[11] Specifically, in the 1915 secret treaty, the Entente promised Italy the Austro-Hungarian territories on the Dalmatian coast, namely Slovene and Croat lands. Serb leaders,

---

[8] Material for this section has been drawn mainly from Stephen Clissold (ed.), *A Short History of Yugoslavia: From Early Times to 1966* (Cambridge: Cambridge University Press, 1966); Steven L. Burg, *Conflict and Cohesion in Socialist Yugoslavia: Political Decision making since 1966* (Princeton: Princeton University Press, 1983); and Ivo J. Lederer, "Nationalism and the Yugoslavs" in Sugar and Ivo (eds.), *Nationalism in Eastern Europe*, pp. 396–438.
[9] Clissold (ed.), *Short History of Yugoslavia*, pp. 32–35.
[10] Lederer, "Nationalism and the Yugoslavs", p. 425.
[11] Ibid., p. 397. Emphasis added.

including Prime Minister Nikola Pašić had given some verbal support to the Yugoslav ideal, yet had no intention of sacrificing Serbian sovereignty for its realization. Two historians of Yugoslavia, Ivo Lederer and Steven Burg, argue that the Bulgarian invasion of Serbia in 1915 and the subsequent overthrow of the tsar in 1917, in which Serbia lost its most powerful supporter, forced the Serb leadership to compromise on its former intransigent stance.[12] In the summer of 1917, a meeting between Pašić and the Yugoslav Committee, an organization of Slovene and Croat *Reichsrat* members, produced the *Declaration of Corfu*. Both sides agreed in principle to the creation of a South Slav state as a constitutional monarchy under a Serb dynasty. Crucial for later developments, the Declaration also affirmed the formal equality of the three languages, different alphabets, and religions. The rapid Austrian surrender overtook negotiations and forced the establishment of the Kingdom of Serbs, Croats, and Slovenes on December 1, 1918. Their hasty union agreement left little time to settle the new country's future domestic political structures.

The institutions of the new Yugoslav state were certainly imperfect. The 1921 Vidovdan constitution created a unitary state. Its domination by Serb interests proved "a bitter disappointment" to Slovene and Croat expectations for a federal arrangement.[13] Failures by the central government to accommodate Slovene and Croat grievances caused domestic political instability during the inter-war years. The subsequent problems of the Yugoslav state do not, however, detract from the fact that, as Lederer points out, in a historic precedent Serbia and Montenegro voluntarily relinquished their sovereignty in the creation of this new state. The leaders of Serbia and Montenegro judged, as did the Croat and Slovene communities, that this larger Yugoslav state would more effectively protect their interests from external encroachment.[14] This pragmatism constrained each of their aspirations.

These cases illustrate the way in which foreign threats can serve to discourage distinct communities from attempting to establish their own independent state. Even under circumstances where current political authorities could not effectively oppose a secession attempt – a rare opportunity which the Slovenes and Croats faced with the

[12] Burg, *Conflict and Cohesion*; and Lederer, "Nationalism and the Yugoslavs," pp. 396–438.
[13] Paul Lendvai, "Yugoslavia without Yugoslavs: The Roots of the Crisis," *International Affairs*, 67, 2 (April 1991), pp. 253–254.
[14] Lederer, "Nationalism and the Yugoslavs,"p. 428.

Hapsburg collapse – distinct communities may still judge that the choice of secession would not serve their interests. In this case, the security benefits of membership in a larger state outweighed the more emotional appeal of an independent homeland.

Economic benefits

The economic benefits of membership also manifest themselves in two ways. First, by unifying many regional economies with a coherent set of regulations, the state provides its citizens with numerous advantages based on scale: access to a large market for their products, access to raw materials, integration into large transport and communications networks, to name but a few. Second, through the implementation of specific policies, the state can also provide the members of poorer communities with numerous economic benefits such as development assistance, technology transfers, and subsidies for health and educational programs.

Frequently those specific members within a distinct community who understand such economic advantages also oppose secession most strongly. For example, an investigation of the public pronouncements by the Quebec business community reveals a sharp awareness of the economic benefits for Quebec of remaining within the Canadian federation and market. Fearing the economic sacrifices clearly associated with independence, Quebec's prominent business leaders have consistently advised against the *Parti Quebecois* proposals for secession.

In addition, the beneficiaries of welfare programs or budget transfers from other more prosperous regions protest strongly against a country's disintegration. Such economic calculations can prove to be as compelling as the security assessments outlined in the previous section. Research into the Soviet Union's federal budgets reveals that the Soviet Central Asian republics were consistently the net recipients of an inter-republic system of resource redistribution. The constituent communities of these republics – the Tadjiks, Kazakhs, Uzbeks, Turkmen, and Kirghiz – were the beneficiaries of discriminatory social and educational policies. Not surprisingly, the Central Asian republics were also the ones which protested most vehemently against the demise of the former Soviet Union. They have continued to attempt to salvage some form of confederation, despite their ethnic differences. This is not to deny that the Central Asian republics also suffered disadvantages such as Russian immigration, pollution, and environmental disasters. None the less, their struggle becomes understandable once one realises the extent of the economic advantages they lost with the Soviet Union's collapse.

The severely underdeveloped nature of the Central Asian economies contrasts with the self-assuredness of Quebec. Quebec's prosperity is based on the province's possession of enviable economic resources including raw materials, industry, services, an admirable educational system, and the enterprise of its skilled workforce. Yet these republics and Quebec shared a common privilege within their respective federations. Membership in a larger state often provides cumulative economic benefits not only to communities with developing economies, but also to those possessing more advanced systems.

Quebec: economic ties that bind[15]

By reversing Ottawa's centralizing tendencies and using its own resources to direct economic initiatives, Quebec currently possesses "more powers than almost any subnational government in the world."[16] Through increases in its powers of taxation and the introduction of conditionality into federal funding in the 1930s, the Canadian federal government consolidated numerous fiscal powers. More specifically, federal grants were made conditional on the provincial governments' agreement to participate in federal social programs such as health care, pensions, unemployment, and the education system. In 1965, the Liberal government of Quebec won a major concession when the federal government allowed it to opt out of federal cost-sharing programs without financial penalty.[17] These special fiscal privileges enabled the provincial government to proceed with its ambitious restructuring of Quebec society, a process now known as the "Quiet Revolution."[18] The provincial government

[15] Contemporary material for this section was drawn mainly from articles in *The Nation of Toronto*, *The Globe and Mail of Toronto*, *The New York Times*, and *The Economist*. Historical material was drawn mainly from Kenneth McRoberts and Dale Postgate, *Quebec: Social Change and Political Crisis* (Toronto: McClelland & Stewart, 1988); and Hubert Guidon, *Quebec Society: Tradition, Modernity, and Nationhood* (Toronto: University of Toronto Press, 1988).
[16] "For Want of Glue: A Survey of Canada," *The Economist*, 29 January, 1991, p. 16.
[17] Camille Legendre, *French Canada in Crisis: A New Society in the Making?* (London: Minority Rights Group, 1979), p. 10.
[18] See Postgate and McRoberts, *Quebec*, for detailed description.

became more directly involved in business, education, labor, and other social matters. Reinforcing its interventionist economic policies, Quebec then negotiated additional privileges in the North American Free Trade Agreement of the late 1980s; its provincial government was exempt from the restrictions placed on state subsidies for business.

In the recent debates on secession, it has been respected leaders of the Quebec business community who have warned the public of the economic sacrifices associated with independence. The Quebec public was stunned and alienated when other provincial governments rejected the Meech Lake constitutional arrangements in 1990. The popularity of the Parti Quebecois and its secessionist agenda immediately surged. None the less, business leaders made a forceful public stance against secession. These businessmen include Ghislian Dufour, head of the Conseil du Patronat du Quebec – a business group whose membership includes most of Quebec's largest corporations; Claude Castonguay, the founder of the Laurentian Group, one of Canada's largest financial services conglomerates; Purdy Crawford, chairman of Imasco – the giant retailing, banking, and tobacco corporation; and M. Menard, chairman of the Montreal Expos baseball club. Menard summarised their public stand: "The crucial change is that Quebeckers must better understand that the province's inherent economic strength might not outweigh the importance of economic linkages and economic association with the rest of Canada."[19] A 1992 survey conducted by the *Nation of Toronto* found that 92 per cent of Quebec's top business executives believed that Quebec independence would have either a "negative" or a "very negative" effect on their companies.[20] Castonguay explained this conscious abandonment of secessionist fervor as "a change in corporate thinking ... [which] flows in part from a fresh appreciation of the benefits of economic union and a cooler analysis of the high costs of independence."[21] The list of possible economic difficulties is extensive. Higher interest rates, a reduced pool of capital for investment, higher unemployment, a renegotiation of the North American Free Trade Agreement with the probable loss of interventionist privileges, and the unavoidable onus of debt due to the redistribu-

---

[19] Quoted in Clyde Farnsworth, "Separatist Fervour Fades in Quebec: The Cost of Seceding Is Seen As Too High," *The New York Times*, September 10, 1991, p. C1.
[20] Bertrand Marotte, "Unity Debate Biting into Business, CEOs Say: Independence would be Worse," *The Nation of Toronto*, March 6, 1992, p. B1.
[21] Farnsworth, "Separatist Fervour Fades," p. C1.

tion of Canada's public debt whilst floating new replacement government bonds, have been cited as some of the daunting economic problems associated with separation.

The abandoned Soviet Central Asian republics[22]

Soviet efforts to modernize and industrialize their economy before World War II and in the 1950s and 1960s led to a great effort to equalize development and education levels across the Soviet Union. As the least developed region, the Central Asian republics became the main beneficiaries. Within the Unified State Budget, only the five Central Asian republics consistently retained 100% of the income tax collected within their borders, while the Baltic republics, by contrast, retained between two-thirds and three-quarters of their taxes.[23] These republics also received additional subsidies to sustain high per capita rates of infrastructure investment, and of public health and education expenditure.[24] Besides such significant budgetary concessions, the economic well-being of these republics also depended on inter-republic trade in industrial products and on the large, protected Russian market for their raw materials, such as cotton and wheat.

Once economic stagnation had limited the growth of new opportunities for social mobility, the redistributive development strategy imposed upon a geographically segmented, multinational federation provoked protest from the more advanced communities. For example, the USSR State Planning Committee's officials consistently encountered great difficulties in finalizing capital investment plans with the Ukrainian Council of Ministers. Ukrainian government officials "always stubbornly try to increase capital investment funds, basing their demands on the production quotas which the Ukraine contributes to the all-Union fund. *They openly speak of being*

[22] Historical material for this section was drawn primarily from Bohdan Nahaylo and Victor Swoboda, *Soviet Disunion: A History of the Nationalities Problem in the USSR* (New York: Macmillan, 1989); Philip G. Roeder, "Soviet Federalism and Ethnic Mobilization," *World Politics*, 43 (January 1991), pp. 196–232; and Richard E. Ericson, "The Classical Soviet-Type Economy: Nature of the System and Implications for Reform," *Journal of Economic Perspectives* (5:4 1991), 11–27. Contemporary material was drawn mainly from articles in *The New York Times, The Independent (London)*, and *The Economist*.
[23] In 1988, Latvia retained the lowest proportion of its taxes: 56.8%, while Estonia retained 79.4%. *Prava*, October 29, 1988 quoted in Philip G. Roeder, "Soviet Federalism and Ethnic Mobilization," *World Politics*, (January 1991), 216.
[24] Ibid. For example, in 1988 these additional subsidies ranged from 321 million rubles for Tadjikistan and 2.7 billion rubles for Kazakhstan.

robbed."[25] Ukrainian or Baltic proposals for increased decentralization of economic decision-making and fiscal autonomy for the
republics triggered harsh criticism by the Central Asian republics.
To illustrate, in the 1988 meeting of the all-union Supreme Soviet,
President Khabiballaev of Uzbekistan and President Pallaev of
Tadjikistan voiced the strongest opposition to Estonia's "self-finan-
cing" schemes, which the Supreme Soviet subsequently vetoed.[26]

As a result, the leaders of the Central Asian republics spearheaded
efforts to prevent the dissolution of Soviet authority. For instance, in
the fall and winter of 1990, President Nursultan Nazarbaev of Kazakhstan worked tirelessly to salvage some form of confederation by
bringing together other republican leaders with President Gorbachev.
The so-called "nine plus one" process led to the creation of the short-
lived State Council.[27] "Loyalty has remained the motto of Kazakh
President Nazarbaev, who has been the least enthusiastic [of the
former republican] leaders to see the old Soviet Union disintegrate."[28]
During the coup against Gorbachev in August, 1991, when most other
republics including Ukraine, Azerbaijan, Georgia, Moldova,
Lithuania, Latvia, and Estonia declared their independence, the
governments of the Central Asian republics remained silent, except
for Tadjik President Kaklar Makhkamov, who openly supported the
coup attempt.[29] Turkmenistan, Kazakhstan, Tadjikistan, Kirghizia,
and Uzbekistan were the most eager to participate in Gorbachev's
proposal for an economic union treaty.[30] Faced with massive budgetary shortfalls since local taxes could only cover about one quarter
of proposed spending, and without the resources to clean up the
ecological disasters of the Aral Sea and the Semipalatinsk nuclear
testing area, the Central Asian republics still relied heavily on the
center.[31] When Uzbekistan and Kirghizia finally did declare independence on August 30, 1991, they simultaneously issued statements
declaring their willingness to sign the proposed economic union

[25] Teresa Rakowska-Harmstone, "The Dialectics of Nationalism in the USSR," *The Problems of Communism*, 23 (May–June 1974), 14. Emphasis added.
[26] Roeder, "Soviet Federalism," p. 218.
[27] Serge Schmemann, "Kazakh Chief, Seeking What Works, Backs Both Order and Free Economy," *The New York Times*, September 8, 1991, p. 11.
[28] "Vegas of the East," *The Economist*, March 7, 1992, p. 60.
[29] Bill Keller, "Soviets Prepare to Design New System," *The New York Times*, September 1, 1991, pp. 1–6.
[30] Francis X. Clives, "Proposals for Economic Union Offered," *The New York Times*, September 12, 1991, p. A7.
[31] "The Silk Revolution," *The Economist*, October 19, 1991, p. 17.

treaty. Their declarations of independence reflected a need to position themselves as formal equals before negotiating the terms of the new treaty.

Harsh economic realities forced these former Soviet republics to reconsider their independent status. The agenda of the summit meeting of the leaders of the Commonwealth of Independent States, of October 9–10, 1992, in Bishkek, Kirghizia, was little less than a refederation. Supported by the leaders of Kirghizia, Tadjikistan, and Uzbekistan, President Nazarbaev tabled a proposal for closer coordination of economic legislation with the Russian parliament, full monetary union, and combined fiscal policy which would be designed to re-establish the pattern of budgetary transfers under the former Soviet Union.[32] The leaders of Turkmenistan, although not formal sponsors of the motion, were amenable to its content. Debate over this proposal dominated the summit. Within only two years, due to the economic hardships endured by their populations, the prospect of a union between Russia and the Central Asian republics was no longer considered "unimaginable."[33]

This section has attempted to show that both underdeveloped and economically advanced distinct communities are often unwilling to secede due to the economic sacrifices such a decision would entail. Even when the community is presented with the opportunity to secede without major costs in terms of state opposition – an option that the Soviet Central Asian republics faced after the August 1991 bungled coup attempt and the subsequent virtual collapse of the central government in Moscow – it may still decide not to secede because it judges that it can ill afford to forfeit the economic benefits of membership. Independence would bring its members greater economic hardship.

Social benefits

Most liberal political philosophy has maintained that a state's legitimacy rests on the proper relationship between the individual citizen and the state. More recently, the notion that the state bears a responsibility to its distinct communities as groups rather than as collections of individuals has entered political discourse. International law now

[32] Anne McElvoy, "Republics Seek Reunion with Moscow," *The Times of London*, October 10, 1992.
[33] Ibid.

recognizes the beneficial aspects of cultural diversity and the need for states to help protect and promote that diversity. The United Nations has played a significant role in effecting this normative change. The Resolution of the UN Subcommission on the Prevention of Discrimination and Protection of Minorities of June 1949 codified these new responsibilities. The document acknowledges that distinct communities "wish for a measure of differential treatment in order to preserve basic characteristics which they possess and which distinguish them from the majority of the population." It proceeds to declare that "differential treatment of such groups or of individuals belonging to such groups is justified."[34] The United Nations Convention on the Elimination of All Forms of Racial Discrimination stipulates that states "shall, when circumstances so warrant, take special measures to ensure the adequate development and protection of certain racial groups or individuals belonging to them for the purpose of guaranteeing them the full and equal enjoyment of human rights."[35]

In this way, the third benefit constitutes the greater social opportunities which the larger established state can offer the distinct community. Though not entirely distinct from the previously discussed economic interests, the social benefits of membership merit separate investigation. Historically, their small size has precluded numerous distinct communities from achieving economic and social progress. Without sufficient resources, they have been unable to provide their members with the social programs, most significantly educational opportunities, to which they may aspire. Such distinct communities have often benefited from government subsidies for social initiatives. For example, the Swiss federal government has heavily subsidized the preservation of the Romansch language and community. Karen leaders have come to realise that they can not provide sufficient educational opportunities for their children. Expectations of future assistance from the Burmese government contributed to the Karen National Union's 1984 abandonment of secession as the explicit goal of its long struggle against the military regime. A promise of Czech assistance in establishing governmental and educational institutions in Slovakia contributed to the Slovak agreement for a united Czecho-Slovak Republic in 1917.

[34] E/CN.4/Sub.2/40/Rev.I, cited in Vernon Van Dyke, "The Individual, the State, and Ethnic Communities in Political Theory," *World Politics*, 29:3 (April 1977), pp. 356–7.
[35] E/CN.4/641, cited in Van Dyke, "The Individual, the State," p. 357.

The Romansch[36]

There is no doubt that genuine advantages exist for Switzerland's four linguistic communities to remain within its borders. Regional security threats prompted the Uri, Schwyz, and Unterwalden cantons into a defensive alliance in 1291. Subsequent external threats motivated other cantons to join the emerging Swiss confederation. Further, since the federal government has consistently responded flexibly to its citizens' needs, economic and social benefits of membership have also grown in importance. For instance, the Romansch community of the Graubunden canton formally requested a constitutional amendment to declare its language as the fourth national language of Switzerland in 1935. In a referendum three years later, 92 per cent of Swiss voters approved the request despite the huge costs incurred by society to make government services quadrilingual. The prevalent feeling was that although Romansch-speakers constituted only 0.5% of the population, if they felt their culture threatened, the Swiss federation should help them.[37] A referendum in March 1996 raised the status of Romansch to a "semi-official" language, just one step below the full "official" rating accorded to German, French, and Italian. As a result, the Romansch people are now able to deal with the federal government in their native tongue and receive larger federal subsidies for social programs.[38] Through a system of inter-cantonal taxation and resource redistribution, the federal government has historically provided eleven times greater financial subsidies per Romansch pupil than for its German counterpart.[39] The state has been instrumental in protecting the Romansch language and culture from erosion due to powerful social trends of urbanization, industrialization, and communication sophistication.

[36] Material for this section was drawn mainly from Kenneth McRae, *Conflict and Compromise in Multilingual Societies: The Case of Switzerland* (Waterloo: Wilfred Laurier University Press, 1983); and William Keech, "Linguistic Diversity and Political Conflict: Some Observations Based on Four Swiss Cantons," *Comparative Politics*, 4:3 (1972), 384–404.

[37] Kenneth McRae, *Conflict and Compromise in Multilingual Societies: The Case of Switzerland* (Waterloo: Wilfred Laurier University Press, 1983).

[38] "The Swiss fortify Romansch," *The Economist*, March 30, 1996, p. 51.

[39] Part of the additional expense arises from the fact that Romansch has several dialects which are sufficiently different to require that school books be printed in each. William Keech, "Linguistic Diversity and Political Conflict: Some Observations Based on Four Swiss Cantons," *Comparative Politics*, 4:3 (April, 1972), 393.

The Karen[40]

A hill people inhabiting the eastern mountains and jungles of Burma, the Karen distinguish themselves from the majority Burmans[41] by their own language and culture. The Karen form a very small, predominantly Christian enclave surrounded by a sea of Buddhism. A history of antagonism and the lack of an agreement on the post-colonial government contributed to Karen fears of domination in a Burman-ruled state. This fear influenced Karen soldiers in the Burmese army to mutiny directly before the declaration of independence on January 4, 1948. They quickly formed the core of the insurgency. In the first few years, the Karen achieved startling success on the battlefields in the Burmese plains, nearly over-running Rangoon. As the chief-of-staff, General Ne Win, slowly built up the discipline of Burmese troops in the 1950s, the army was able to force the Karen to retreat into the rugged Tenasserim district on the Thai border. The war settled into a cyclical stalemate following the changing of the seasons. During the dry season from November to June, the Burmese army would launch attacks on Karen strongholds such as Mannerplaw. The lack of all-weather roads through the jungle and the already dangerous stretching of its supply lines would force the Burmese army to retreat during the rainy season. Despite this fierce Burmese opposition, the leadership of the Karen community, the Karen National Union (KNU), succeeded in controlling a long, narrow territory along the Thai-Burmese border, at its height about 30 miles wide and 700 miles long. Within this area, the KNU provided rudimentary government services which it financed by taxing the blackmarket cross-border trade in consumer goods between Thailand and Burma.

In 1979 the Karen, along with eight other secessionist groups including the Wa, Kachin, Chin, Shan, and Mon formed the National Democratic Front (NDF) initially to prevent internecine fighting and

[40] Historical material for this section is largely drawn from *Burma in Brief* (Washington, DC: The International Centre for Development Policy, 1989), Amnesty International, *Burma: Extrajudicial Execution and Torture of Members of Ethnic Minorities* (London: Amnesty International, 1988), and articles in the *Far East Economic Review*. The texts of legal documents such as the Panglong Agreement, the Draft Constitution of the Federal Union of the Democratic National States of Burma, and declarations and statements made by the Karen National Union or the National Democratic Front have been provided to the author by the Karen National Union foreign secretary, Dr. Em Marta.
[41] "Burman" signifies membership in the dominant linguistic, cultural, and ethnic group in Burma. "Burmese" connotes any member of the entire population of Burma.

later to expedite coordination of joint operations against the Burmese army. Five years later, the leaders of the nine rebel organizations, in a momentous and unanimous decision, used the NDF forum to renounce secession as their ultimate goal.[42] A. Ganemy Kunoo, secretary to KNU leader General Bo Mya, has candidly encapsulated the reasons for such a policy reversal: "We are too small to make progress. We need to help one another. We need help from Rangoon, from the wealthier provinces in terms of technical assistance and redistribution of taxes."[43] Public pronouncements by Karen leaders like General Bo Mya and Dr. Em Marta, foreign secretary of the KNU, the specific articles of the KNU proposed constitution for Burma, and the Karen proposals on educational reform reinforce Kunoo's assessment.

Kunoo further indicated that of primary concern was the fact that, without supplemental resources, the KNU could provide only primary and some secondary education. These circumstances created the unfortunate situation in which he and most older Karen leaders had benefited more from educational opportunities than they could provide for subsequent generations. Karen educational proposals reveal their expectations that once the civil war is over, Karen students would benefit from the greater opportunities that the Burmese society has to offer. Fearing that Karen students would be handicapped by their primitive schools in the jungle, the KNU suggests that, at least initially, faculties such as engineering and medicine in prominent universities in Rangoon and Mandalay admit Karen and other disadvantaged ethnic minority students on a quota system.[44]

The KNU Draft Constitution for a Democratic Federal Burma addresses both the necessity for regional autonomy to protect cultural distinctiveness, and the fact that fiscal autonomy would be insufficient to promote each community's aspirations for social progress. The constitution outlines a federal arrangement in which each of the twelve distinct communities residing within the borders of Burma would receive its own state.[45] Article 109 of the constitution stipulates

[42] National Democratic Front, "Statement Issued by the Third Plenary Central Presidium Meeting" (unpublished), October 30, 1984. Text provided to the author by the Karen National Union Foreign Secretary, Dr. Em Marta.
[43] The statement was made during a series of interviews with the author in Mannerplaw, July 9–11, 1991.
[44] A. Ganemy Kunoo, secretary to General Bo Mya, outlined these Karen proposals in a series of interviews conducted by the author in Mannerplaw, July 9–11, 1991.
[45] The Preamble of the constitution lists the twelve distinct communities as the Arakanese, Burmans, Chin, Kachin, Karen, Karennis, Mon, Shan, Lahu, Palaung, Pao, and Wa.

that these future states have the right to legislate and collect taxes to pay for local government and its programs.[46] Each distinct community would possess the right to administer its own cultural, educational, and social affairs. Given the recognition that their own community's resources would be insufficient to finance such activities, the Karen have been careful to add a proviso that the federal government would be required to vote funds to meet the expected budgetary shortfalls. To this end, Article 75 guarantees the states a share of federal revenues generated from national taxes on incomes, excise, and corporations. Furthermore, Article 108 stipulates that the states are entitled to grants from the federal government not only to meet the additional expenses of implementing federal legislation, but also as assistance to cover state budget deficits. Thus, part of the reason that the Karen have relinquished their secessionist aspirations is their judgment that they might become the net beneficiaries of an eventually redistributive system of government within Burma. Their long-term political demands are now shaped by this prospect for future generations.

The Slovaks and the creation of Czechoslovakia[47]

In the Austro-Hungarian *Ausgleich* in 1867, Emperor Franz Josef traded the rights of all national minorities in the Hungarian half of his empire for the sworn allegiance of Hungarian aristocrats. As a result, the Slovaks endured over fifty years of cultural and social repression. Hungarian noblemen consistently rejected Slovak petitions for the recognition of Slovak nationhood, the official use of the Slovak language for administration and primary school education in the Slovak lands, or the establishment of a Slovak university. They closed the Slovenska Matica, an influencial center for Slovak scholarship and education, in 1875.[48] Hungarian speakers even dominated the Slovak Catholic Church. The systematic attempts to force Magyar assimilation and the high level of poverty precipitated a mass emigration of Slovaks to North America. This exodus further weakened the Slovak community by depriving it of its most enterprising, industrious, and

[46] The Draft Constitution of the Federal Union of the Democratic National States of Burma has been provided to the author by the Karen National Union foreign secretary, Dr. Em Marta.
[47] Material for this section has been drawn mainly from Mamatey and Luza (eds.), *Czechoslovak Republic*; and Zacek, "Nationalism," pp. 166–206.
[48] Hugh Seton-Watson, *Nations and States: An Enquiry into the Origins of Nations and the Politics of Nationalism* (Boulder, CO: Westview Press, 1977), p. 172.

intelligent members. Strict restrictions on parliamentary representation and ethnic organizations prevented Slovaks from mobilizing support for their aspirations. Therefore, whilst a full range of well-organized political parties proliferated in the more progressive and relatively wealthy Czech lands, Slovakia could boast only of the impotent Slovak National Party and the liberal Hlasisti movement, named after its review, *Hlas* (Voice).[49] Under Hungarian rule, Slovak social and cultural progress had been effectively thwarted: "Isolated from the major currents of European affairs, the feeble Slovak culture and Slovak national consciousness were dying in 1914. In another generation, assimilation by the Magyars would have been complete."[50]

With the announcement by the new emperor, Charles, in April 1917 of the convocation of the *Reichsrat* in May, Vovro Srobar, leader of the Hlasisti, traveled to Prague. He requested that Czech leaders speak on behalf of the Slovak community which was disenfranchised by living in the Hungarian half of the empire.[51] Proposals for a joint Czecho-Slovak future were presented in the *Reichsrat* by Czech representatives of all ideological backgrounds. Despite vehement protests by the Hungarian government against interference in its domestic affairs, Czech leaders in Vienna and the West, like Professor Masaryk and Eduard Beneš, lobbied the Austrian and Allied governments on behalf of both communities.[52] It is a testimony to the virtually complete repression of Slovak political and cultural activity in Slovakia that Masaryk traveled not to Bratislava, but rather to Pittsburg, to discuss the future unification of Czech and Slovak communities into a single state. In the Pittsburg Agreement of 1917, Czech leaders promised that they would assist the Slovaks in establishing their own administration, parliament, courts, and schools. All government business in Slovakia would be conducted in the Slovak language.[53] Czechoslovak historians such as Joseph Zacek, Victor Mamatey, and Radomir Luza assert that part of the reason that the Slovak community was willing to participate in the new state was not only its hope of escaping Hungarian repression, but also its expectation of new

[49] Mamatey and Luza (eds.), *Czechoslovak Republic*, p. 8.
[50] Zacek, "Nationalism," p. 190.
[51] Mamatey and Luza, *Czechoslovak Republic*, pp. 16–18.
[52] For the eleven memoranda on Czecho-Slovak claims which Beneš presented to the Allied powers at the Versailles Conference, see Eduard Beneš, *Memoirs* (Paris, 1919).
[53] Zacek, "Nationalism," p. 194.

opportunities for educational and social advancement through employing the greater resources and experience of the Czech community.

To summarize the propositions put forward thus far, communities gain security, economic, and social advantages by maintaining their position within the larger, existing state. The relative importance of each of the three constitutive benefits is difficult to determine as it varies from case to case. In general experience, however, a community would face a mixture of all three types of benefits. The calculation of such benefits has dissuaded some communities from the secessionist path, since they judged that they could ill afford to sacrifice these advantages. It therefore acts as an implicit restraint on secession attempts.

The secession dynamic depends on the balance among the four costs and benefits of membership and secession. A reduction in the implicit restraints can precipitate secession attempts. Specifically, reductions in the benefits of membership – either through a series of government actions or due to gradual changes in the international system – can motivate a secession crisis. Chapter 9 examines how the Swedish government's neglect of duties deemed vital to the Norwegians motivated Norway's secession from Sweden. It also investigates the way evolution in the international system has moderated for some communities the security and economic benefits described here. This investigation establishes the context necessary to explore the persistence of modern Catalan and Quebecois separatism.

4 The costs of secession

Due to perceived benefits of membership, most distinct communities do not consider secession as a viable option. But, if they were to consider secession, they would immediately run into a second barrier: the costs of secession. State opposition and international hostility can force a distinct community to give up its independence struggle or not to embark on one in the first place. Furthermore, these costs of secession are the most effective obstacle to success even if the distinct community continues its struggle. More often than not, states have effectively opposed secession attempts. And even if the secessionist community were to win on the battlefield, it still stands to lose the diplomatic contest. The principle of territorial integrity as one of the fundamental norms of post-1945 international relations limits secession as a means of altering existing borders. As a consequence, the international community has consistently withheld diplomatic recognition and the associated privileges from secessionist entities.

Secession involves an "arduous struggle." State resistance to and international hostility toward secession contribute to its arduousness. John Stuart Mill described the Hungarian attempted secession from the Austrian Empire in 1848 as such an ardrous struggle. The combined forces of the Austrian and Russian armies defeated and then violently suppressed Hungarian aspirations for independence. Historically, the struggle for secession has often entailed dreadful costs in terms of lives and human suffering. In a remarkable example, the Eritrean community has made an enormous sacrifice, in the form of approximately 500,000 dead out of a total population of about 4 million, in its nearly three-decade long struggle to secede from Ethiopia.[1]

---

[1] "An Unborn Nation," *The Economist*, October 20, 1990, p. 104.

Because the primary focus here is on the decisions of the distinct community, this chapter comments only peripherally on states' resistance to secession. Detailed analysis of the many reasons for such state opposition is beyond the scope of this investigation. But some considerations which have historically led most states to oppose their own territorial dismemberment will be discussed.

If the prospect of state resistance is well-nigh a constant, the reaction of the distinct community to state opposition is far from uniform. In numerous cases state opposition has not deterred secession movements. Indeed, the Tamil and Southern Sudanese struggles have become nearly a perpetual feature in Sri Lankan and Sudanese politics. For four decades, every year during the dry season the Karen National Union and the Burmese army took up arms in their struggle. This chapter investigates two cases of state opposition to secession: the first in which effective government opposition has compelled a distinct community to give up secession as a goal, and the second in which multiple states' resistance has effectively prevented secession although it has not forced a relinquishment of separatist agitation. In the case of the Nagas, Indian army pressure forced them to negotiate a compromise to resolve the secession crisis. In the case of the Kurds, each secession attempt has been met by fierce opposition on the part of Iran, Iraq, and Turkey, and their predecessors in the Ottoman and Persian Empires. This has forced the Kurds to cease their struggle for a few years.[2] Evidence exists to support the cautious conclusion that the Nagas have begun a process of accommodation into India. By contrast, the Kurds have not abandoned their secessionist goals. Although it would be difficult to prove, one can imagine that the credible threat of state opposition has dissuaded other distinct communities from embarking on the secessionist path in the first place. The variability of the distinct community's reaction lies in the fact that other factors are always involved. One observation is certain: state opposition is one of the most effective barriers in the creation of new sovereign states through secession. Only a few communities have been able to overcome this obstacle.

Those few communities which have won on the battlefield have frequently lost the diplomatic struggle. The chapter also explores the inherent conflict between the principle of self-determination and that

[2] Additional small minorities of Kurds reside in Lebanon, Syria, and in the territory of the former Soviet Union.

of territorial integrity. A discriminating scrutiny of international documents, including the United Nations Charter and resolutions, the Final Act of the Helsinki Conference on Security and Cooperation in Europe, and the Organization of African Unity Charter and resolutions, gauges the attitude of the international community toward secession. By restricting the application of the principle of self-determination, and by raising territorial integrity to the level of a nearly absolute principle, the international system has implicitly condemned secession. Indeed, on several occasions the international community has made this implicit condemnation explicit.

This chapter mentions but does not investigate in detail the numerous economic challenges that are also associated with secession. For example, the government of a newly independent state must concern itself with the creation of a currency, commerce, and banking system. It must adopt credible fiscal and monetary policies in order to regulate its economy. It must also create legislative, judicial, and executive institutions, administer the education system, and establish external embassies to administer foreign policy. To a newly emerging country possessing only limited resources, these economic challenges can prove daunting. Conversely, independent statehood can also provide both new opportunities for previously disadvantaged ethnic elites and the possibility of receiving international financial assistance. Chapter 6 explores these propositions in greater detail as they constitute some of the main benefits of secession. For our purposes, however, it is sufficient to note that economic constraints posed by independence constitute a low priority in secession calculations. This point is emphasized by Odemjegwu Ojukwu, the former military governor of the Eastern Region of Nigeria and head of state of the seceding Republic of Biafra from 1967 to 1970. In 1968, during the throes of the Biafran secession, Ojukwu declared: "In the question of independence and self-determination, *viability is usually given a very, very low priority.*"[3] Secessionist leaders appear to be relatively more preoccupied with the reactions of the state and the international system than with the economic challenges associated with independence.

---

[3] Odemjegwu Ojukwu quoted in A. H. M. Kirk-Green (ed.) *Crisis and Conflict in Nigeria – A Documentary Source Book, 1966–1969*, vol. I (London: Oxford University Press, 1971), p. 395. Emphasis added.

State opposition

The leaders of a distinct community force the central government to react to their demands for political change through the organization of protests which threaten economic loss or destruction of the social order. No longer able to ignore these protests, the state must decide whether to allow or to resist the demands. Many government decisions have been based upon the perception, widely held before the twentieth century and currently still prominent in many parts of the world, that the deprivation of territory would necessarily damage three separate state interests – security, wealth, and prestige. This perception of interests has propelled states facing demands for secession almost uniformly to oppose them.

Historically, security depended directly on military strength, which in turn depended on domestic resources. Defense of foreign policy objectives often became the means by which rulers generated political cohesion in the domestic sphere. Furthermore, the domestic economy appeared pre-eminent before the remarkable growth of international capital and trade flows in the post-war era. Economic and strategic interests often converged on protection of the domestic market and an overseas empire. For example, economic and security concerns weighed heavily in the minds of British leaders as they tried to suppress rebellion in the thirteen American colonies. If these colonies were to secede from the empire, it was argued, British industrialists would lose their guaranteed source of inexpensive raw materials and a captive market for their products. The Royal Navy would lose both important naval supplies, in particular timber, and strategic harbors from which it had been extending its command of the world's oceans. Britain also feared that the loss of its American colonies would upset the balance of power in Europe, as continental rivals, perceiving a momentary weakness of Britain, would use the opportunity to extend their own influence in other regions. In another example, in 1848 the Hapsburgs requested the assistance of the Russian army in crushing the Hungarian insurrection. The ruling aristocracy feared that the loss of Hungarian land and population would cause imperial Austria nearly irreparable loss of power and prestige. Further, one of the fears of Abraham Lincoln and other Northern leaders was that if the Southern states were allowed to secede and form the Confederacy, then America would suffer a territorial rivalry and arms race of two security-conscious powers, rapidly expanding across the continent.

On several rare occasions before 1991, however, governments have not opposed a secession. The costs of trying to prevent the withdrawal outweighed the benefits of retaining the territory. Although Sweden did not look favorably upon Norway's bid for independence in 1905, it could tolerate it. Norway's secession would not threaten Sweden's security, partly because Norway was so much smaller, and partly because Sweden had enjoyed non-threatening relations with all of its neighbors for at least half a century. Swedish leaders judged that neither Britain, Russia, Denmark, nor Germany would use the opportunity to overturn the balance of power in the North. When the Russian and German emperors discussed the Scandinavian situation in a meeting on the Russian imperial yacht off Bjorko, in July 1905, both were preoccupied with their own foreign concerns and decided to press for a diplomatic settlement of the disagreement.[4] Moreover, the Swedish king and his government judged that a civil war fought to retain Norwegian territory would be extremely costly in terms of the potential loss of life, domestic economic growth, and foreign trade. None the less, Norway's peaceful secession from Sweden and Iceland's from Denmark in 1944 are exceptional cases. Rarely before 1991 have net security, economic, and prestige interests weighed in favor of the state allowing a secession without mitigating circumstances.

Yet resolve must be complemented by ability. The governing regime commands potentially coercive powers that enable it to crush dissent. Though they may suffer from underdeveloped political institutions, even small and weak countries can still mobilize the police, army, and bureaucracy. This monopoly of force, when used efficiently, can defeat most incipient secessionist movements.

The experience of the Nagas in India serves to illustrate three points about state opposition. First, a chronicle of the specific strategies which one state – India – has employed in repressing a secessionist community indicates some of the various methods available to all states. Second, effective government coercion forced the Nagas to begin negotiating a resolution to the civil war, and thus, to forfeit secession as their goal. Third, during the decade-long struggle

[4] The kaiser was preoccupied with the diplomatic conflict with the British and French governments over German claims in Morocco, while the tsar's throne was unstable due to the defeat of the Russian army in the war against Japan. For details, see T. K. Derry, *History of Scandinavia: Norway, Sweden, Denmark, Finland, and Iceland* (London: George Allen & Unwin, 1979), pp. 272–276.

between Naga guerrillas and the Indian army, the central government earned credibility for its oft-repeated threat to defeat any secession attempt. The Naga experience would serve as a strong precedent in subsequent confrontations between the Indian government and the discontented Mizo, Ghurka, Tamil, Assamese, Kashmiri, Punjabi, and Sikh communities.

Because the Kurdish community makes its home in the mountains stretching across the borders of three Middle Eastern states, its aspirations for autonomy or secession have been opposed either collectively or individually by Turkey, Iran, and Iraq. Repressive government policies motivated Kurdish rebellion. Chapter 5 investigates the specific reasons for Kurdish discontent with their plight in Turkey as an illustration of the costs of membership. The experience of the Kurds is used here to elucidate two different points concerning state opposition. First, although Kurdish efforts have been impaired by other factors, such as their chronic disunity, state opposition has proved the primary factor in preventing the creation of an independent Kurdistan. Second, all types of regimes resist secessionist activity. While neither Iran, nor Iraq, nor Turkey is beyond providing logistical assistance to neighboring Kurds to destabilise regional rivals, none wishes to see a truly autonomous Kurdish entity established. All three states share the same fear: that one Kurdish success will prove an irresistible beacon for the irridentist hopes of the Kurds within their own borders. Motivated by this fear, each has effectively prevented a Kurdish secession.

The Nagas: the precedent for Indian policy[5]

The Indian sub-continent's fragmentation along numerous different religious, linguistic, cultural, and ethnic lines caused enormous problems for India after independence. The experience of partition and the vast human suffering caused by the migration of millions of Muslims and Hindus across the border left a deep impression on both Pakistani and Indian leaders. The Naga secessionist movement began even

---

[5] Historical material for this section is largely drawn from Luingam Luithui and Nandita Haksar, *Nagaland File: A Question of Human Rights* (New Delhi, 1984); Paul Pimomo (ed.), *Nagaland Yearbook* (Shillong: Neelam Press, 1984); and Neville Maxwell, *India, the Nagas, and the Northeast* (London: The Minority Rights Group, 1987). Legal documents such as the Hydari Agreement, the Sixteen Point Agreement, and the Indian constitution are taken from *The Naga Nation and Its Struggle Against Genocide*, International Working Group for Indigenous Affairs Document No. 56 (Copenhagen, 1986).

before India gained its independence, thereby presenting one of the earliest challenges to its territorial integrity. Although later demands by the much more populous Tamils for the reconstitution of the former Madras province had the potential to prove a much more daunting threat to the unity of the Indian state, the leadership of the Congress Party established its policy toward separatism in response to Naga demands. It was in a meeting with Naga leaders that Jawaharlal Nehru first articulated what would become India's firm policy of opposition to all secessionist tendencies.

Numbering between 500,000 and 1 million,[6] and inhabiting about 15,000 sparsely populated square miles in the rugged north-eastern corner of India, on the border with Burma, the Nagas constitute a very small component of the Indian Union.[7] The widespread adoption of Christianity in the Naga community reflects the influence of nine-teenth-century Baptist missionaries.[8] Possessing distinctive traditions and no caste system, and thus fearful of assimilation into the dominant Hindu culture, Naga leaders had articulated demands for separation consistently and unfalteringly from 1929 onwards. When the Naga delegation presented its proposals before the Simon Commission on constitutional reforms, it urged that when the British left India, the Nagas should return to the independence they enjoyed before their informal incorporation into the British Empire.[9] With British with-drawal imminent, the Naga National Council (NNC) was formed in 1946 to provide the necessary political leadership as the Naga com-munity intensified its efforts to negotiate a peaceful settlement of differences with both the retreating British and the Congress Party.[10] Negotiations between the NNC and the British-appointed governor of Assam, Sir Akbar Hydari, produced a nine point agreement in June 1947. The Hydari Agreement recognized the NNC as the legitimate future government of the Nagas and granted it extensive legislative and judicial autonomy within its own administrative unit. Perhaps more importantly to the Nagas, Article 9 stated that the agreement would remain in effect for ten years, after which time the NNC could

[6] The wide variance in the estimates of the Naga population results from the lack of a census in the hill tracts since the British left India.
[7] *The Naga Nation*, p. 6.
[8] V. K. Nuh, *The Nagaland Church and Politics* (Kohima, Nagaland: Vision Press, 1986).
[9] Ela Dutt-Luithui, "Violence in India: The Case of the Naga National Movement," *South Asia Bulletin*, 5,2 (Fall, 1985), 39. The Naga memorandum to the Simon Commis-sion is also reprinted in Nuh, *Nagaland Church*, pp. 81–84.
[10] *The Naga Nation*, p. 21.

reassess the situation. The NNC could then decide either to extend the existing arrangements or to negotiate a new agreement.[11] This rather vague concluding statement was interpreted differently by both parties; Naga leaders such as A. Z. Pizho understood it as permitting them the right to secede after ten years in the Indian Union.[12]

Nehru and other Congress Party leaders judged that they could not approve the Hydari Agreement without courting the complete dissolution of the new Indian state. The leaders of other potentially separatist communities including the Mizos, the Assamese, the Tamils, and the rulers of many princely states, especially the nizam of Hyderabad, were observing the central government's treatment of Naga demands. These leaders were considering whether to press for full independence or autonomy within the Indian Union.[13] Explicitly with an eye on this uncertainty, Nehru enunciated the Congress policy toward separatism in a meeting with NNC leader A. Z. Pizho in July 1947. "We can give you complete autonomy, but never independence. You can never hope to be independent. No state, big or small, in India will be allowed to remain independent. We will use all our influence and power to suppress such tendencies."[14] During the following decade, the Indian army earned the credibility for this official policy through its campaigns in the Naga hill tracts.

The intransigence of the Congress Party and the confrontational actions of the Nagas led to a degeneration of the formerly peaceful dispute into violence. In August, only one day before India's independence, the NNC sent the following telegram to the Indian government and to the secretary general of the United Nations: "Southern Nagas including Manipur Hill Nagas and Cachar Nagas with Konyak Nagas declare independence, today, the 14th of August 1947."[15] A plebiscite conducted in the Naga lands in May 1951, recorded a nearly unanimous vote for independence. Organised under the auspices of the influential Nagaland Baptist Church, the vote demonstrated that NNC demands represented the desires of the Naga community.[16] As the

[11]   The Hydari Agreement is reprinted in *The Naga Nation*, pp. 198–201.
[12]   Asoso Yonuo, *The Rising Nagas: A Historical and Political Study* (New Delhi: Vivek Publishing House, 1974), pp. 167–170.
[13]   Neville Maxwell, *India, the Nagas, and the Northeast* (London: The Minority Rights Group, 1987), p. 9.
[14]   Ibid., p. 4.
[15]   Ibid.; *The Naga Nation*, p. 27.
[16]   The results of the 1951 referendum showed that over 90% of the Naga community supported independence. Nuh, *Nagaland Church*, pp. 118–123. Also see Maxwell, *India*, p. 4.

Indian government continued to ignore their demands, the Naga campaign of civil disobedience escalated into violence.

Though its objective remained constant – to oppose the Naga secession – the Indian government's policy progressed through several stages, employing different powers along the way. Initially, it attempted to neutralise Naga leadership. The traditional focus of local self-government, the Naga Tribal Councils, Regional Courts, and Village Assemblies were abolished by the Standing Order of October 1953, while individual Naga leaders were imprisoned or forced into exile.[17] Yet this strategy backfired in that the new generation of leaders was much more strident in its demands. By 1956, the NNC proclaimed the establishment of the Federal Government of Nagaland (NFG), complete with its own standing army, the Nagaland Home Guard (NHG).[18] Guerrilla warfare escalated.

The central government made a brief attempt to quell the violence utilizing regional police forces but quickly had to deploy the army. The provincial government of Assam gained direct control of the Naga lands and deployed the Assam Rifles, a paramilitary force. But the police could not restore order in the hill tracts. The federal government then declared the Naga hills a "disturbed" area and deployed the army to surpress the revolt.[19] In September 1953, the central government proclaimed the much hated Regulation of Forced Labour, which allowed Indian military forces to impress Naga civilians to work as porters.[20] The former director of India's Intelligence Bureau, B. N. Mullik, calculated that by the end of 1956 nearly two divisions of the army and thirty-five battalions of the Assam Rifles participated in operations in the Naga Hills "exerting maximum pressure."[21] The Indian parliament and the provincial Assamese legislature granted the army wide latitude for action through the 1958 Armed Forces Special Powers Regulation, which in effect placed the entire hill tracts under its complete authority.[22] The army forcibly relocated the entire rural population into new walled villages, often

---

[17] Luingam Luithui and Nandita Haksar, *Nagaland File: A Question of Human Rights* (New Delhi, 1984), p. 91.
[18] Yonuo, *Rising Nagas*, p. 215; *The Naga Nation*, p. 28.
[19] Yonuo, *Rising Nagas*, p. 213; *The Naga Nation*, p. 27.
[20] For a survey of the various "acts" and their effect on the Naga population, see *Endless War: Disturbed Areas in the North-East* (New Delhi: Peoples Union for Democratic Rights, 1983).
[21] Luithui and Haksar, *Nagaland File*, p. 27.
[22] Dutt-Luithui, "Violence in India," p. 41.

setting fire to homes, granaries, and crops in the process. Reports of army massacres of civilians accumulated.[23]

During the bloody war of attrition, the army inflicted enormous suffering upon Naga guerrillas and non-combatants. This suffering prompted some Nagas to search for alternative ways to resolve the crisis. Thus, the army did play an instrumental role in intimidating the Nagas into submission. There can be no doubt that, when the Nagas voted in the 1951 referendum, an overwhelming majority favored secession. However, by the late 1950s members of the Naga community and Indian leaders began to debate the merits and the practicability of granting the Naga lands statehood within India. The Indian army had already cowed the Nagas, yet the Indian government was unwilling to accept a situation of continued repression in the hill tracts. Such a policy would subvert its attempts to build consensus throughout the sub-continent and negate its experiment in parliamentary democracy. Detailed and difficult negotiations between the statehood movement, the Naga People's Convention (NPC), and the Federal Government were finalised in June 1960, with the Sixteen Point Agreement.[24] The state of Nagaland, with extensive fiscal, legislative, and judicial autonomy, was inaugurated on December 1, 1963. The Peace Council of the Nagaland Baptist Church assisted in negotiating a cease-fire in the following year and reintegrating the Nagaland Federal Government and many former guerrillas into Naga society.[25]

Although direct influence is difficult to prove, knowledge of the government's substantial efforts to suppress the Naga insurrection could not but impress other distinct communities like the Tamils and Assamese who were also dissatisfied with their current political situation. With the Indian government's deployment of thousands of troops into the hill tracts, the "disturbances" in the north-east began to receive more coverage in the Indian press.[26] Once the central government had committed itself to making significant concessions to those willing to relinquish their secessionist aspirations, the focus of domestic pressure turned to the complete reorganization of states along linguistic lines. The major movement in the Andhra region of

---

[23] The series of Reports by Naga People's Movement for Human Rights are reprinted in Luithui and Haksar, *Nagaland File*, pp. 209–240.

[24] The Sixteen Point Agreement is reprinted in *The Naga Nation*, pp. 205–210.

[25] The 1964 cease-fire agreement between the NFG and the Indian Union government is reprinted in *The Naga Nation*, pp. 202–204.

[26] Yonuo, *Rising Nagas*, p. vii; Luithui and Haksar, *Nagaland File*, p. 25.

the old Madras province led to the formation of the State Reorganization Commission in 1954. Its 1955 Report outlined the subsequent
States Reorganization Act of 1956, which redrew the state boundaries
so that administrative units would be coterminous with the main
distinct communities. The Indian government even granted "statehood" status[27] to the previously secessionist Tamil group, the DMK,
after it had foresworn its separatist demands.[28]

By way of a summary, the Naga example reveals two additional
considerations influencing a state's hostility to secession beyond the
security, economic, and prestige interests outlined earlier and also
illustrates some of the ways a state can force a distinct community to
abandon its secession attempt. The Naga territory possessed neither
strategic significance, nor sources of wealth for India. In fact, the Naga
case demonstrates how perceptions of internal security threats can be
an equally strong motivation. Fear of a "domino effect" created by
one successful secession compelled Indian leaders to resist Naga
demands for independence. Nehru encapsulated the Indian position
thus: "India has been prepared to share her independence, but not to
divide it."[29]

Further, the Naga example discloses that the political or moral
ideals of government leaders could motivate them to oppose secession. Governing elites may perceive their country as embodying an
ideal based on the promotion of cultural diversity and a plural society.
Other citizens may share their conviction. The ruling elites may incur
great costs in maintaining their country's integrity since they could
not allow secession without witnessing the corresponding dissolution of this ideal. In the Naga case, the opposition of Indian leaders
was at least partly motivated by the desire to preserve their vision of
India as a secular state constituted by numerous distinct communities,
yet building consensus in diversity through the democratic process. In
another similar example, such considerations contributed to President
Abraham Lincoln's resolve in resisting the secession of the Southern
states. As Garry Wills has persuasively argued, Lincoln fervently
believed that the United States possessed a special mission to prove to

[27] "Statehood" in the Indian domestic political context signifies for a distinct community the circumscribed right to a certain level of autonomous government, while still
recognising the ultimate sovereignty of the Indian Union.
[28] Paul R. Brass, *The New Cambridge History of India* (Cambridge: Cambridge University
Press, 1990), pp. 160–166.
[29] Maxwell, *India*, p. 10.

the dynastic realms of Europe that the American experiment in liberal democracy based on the principle that all men were created equal could succeed.[30]

Finally, through its handling of the Naga crisis, the Indian government gradually developed the model for responding to the demands of other separatist groups. In subsequent cases, the army was deployed to suppress the secessionist movements led by the Mizo National Front in the late 1960s and the Gurkha National Liberation Front in the late 1980s. This policy has also defined the Indian approach to the "disturbed" provinces of Kashmir, Punjab, and Assam to the present day. "The Government of India has demonstrated its resoluteness and its ability to suppress both secessionist and revolutionary movements among minorities and its willingness to apply whatever force is necessary to do so."[31] None the less, the role of military coercion should not be overemphasized as it was consistently coupled with political concessions. The official treatment of the Nagas set a credible precedent for the Indian government's policy as a combination of ruthless repression of separatist aspirations and concessions of maximum autonomy for distinct communities short of secession.

The Kurds: repression on three fronts[32]

"The Kurds have no friends."
Old Kurdish proverb[33]

Kurdish aspirations for independence can be traced to the early nineteenth century.[34] Even though the struggle of the Kurds has been impaired by two factors, namely their territorial division among a number of states and their internal discord, the primary impediment

[30] Garry Wills, *Lincoln at Gettysburg: The Words That Remade America* (New York: Simon & Schuster, 1992).
[31] Brass, *History of India*, p. 188.
[32] Historical material for this section is largely drawn from Gerard Chaliand (ed.), *People Without a Country: The Kurds and Kurdistan* (London: Zed Press 1980); David McDowall, *The Kurds*, 2nd edn (London: Minority Rights Group, 1985); legal documents are cited in Hurst Hannum, "The Kurds," in *Autonomy, Sovereignty, and Self-Determination: The Accommodation of Conflicting Rights* (Philadelphia: University of Pennsylvania Press, 1990), ch. 9, pp. 178–201.
[33] Quoted in Alexis Heraclides, *The Self-Determination of Minorities in International Politics* (London: Frank Cass, 1991), p. 107.
[34] The earliest Kurdish rebellion against the Ottoman empire was recorded in 1806. See Hurst Hannum, *Autonomy, Sovereignty, and Self-Determination: The Accommodation of Conflicting Rights* (Philadelphia: University of Pennsylvania Press, 1990), p. 184.

to the establishment of an autonomous Kurdistan has been opposition by ruling authorities. The experience of the Kurds, then, has differed from that of the Nagas in the following significant respect. The Indian army succeeded both in suppressing the insurrection and in forcing the Nagas to reconsider their pursuit of secessionist goals. Once the Nagas had perceived that the likely costs of the continuing failure of their secession attempt were too high, they gradually abandoned their ambitions for independence. The Indian government's political concession provided a further incentive to coax them in their transition toward accommodation within the Indian Union. In contrast, state opposition to Kurdish insurrections has been less effective. It has prevented the fulfillment of independence aspirations nurtured by the Kurdish community for at least a century, but has not forced their relinquishment.

A brief chronological account of a few representative examples of official opposition to Kurdish rebellions reveals that Turkey, Iran, and Iraq and their imperial predecessors have consistently adopted similar stances on secession. This similarity is despite their espousal of extremely different ideologies and possession of vastly different political institutions. The threat of territorial dismemberment appears to unite most states in opposition.

The earliest specific call for an autonomous Kurdistan came in the 1870s and 1880s from the Kurdish religious leader, Sheikh Ubaydallah. In 1878 Ubaydallah outlined the Kurdish manifesto for autonomy in a letter to the British vice-consul:

> The Kurdish nation is a people apart. Their religion is different and their laws and customs are distinct ... The chiefs and rulers of Kurdistan, whether Turkish or Persian subjects, and the inhabitants of Kurdistan one and all are agreed that matters cannot be carried on in this way with the two governments.[35]

Enjoying widespread support among Kurds in both the Persian and Ottoman Empires, Ubaydallah led a major rebellion. The strength of the combined armies of the sultan and the shah defeated the Kurds within a few months.

The closest that the Kurds came to possessing their own state came with the defeat of the Ottoman Empire. The Treaty of Sèvres of 1920 between the Allied and Turkish governments explicitly recognized the

---

[35] Quoted in Derk Kinnane, *The Kurds and Kurdistan* (London: Oxford University Press, 1964), p. 24.

Kurdish claim to independence. Article 62 entrusted the League of
Nations with the responsibility to assist in the creation of the new
state, as long as a majority of the inhabitants voted for independence
in a referendum. In Article 64, Turkey renounced all rights and titles
to the Kurdish areas.[36] Yet with Ataturk's rise to power, Turkey
repudiated the provisions of the Treaty. Rebellion followed. Led by
the liberation organization, *Khoyboun*, and aided by Iran, the Kurds
had gained control over a sizeable area by 1925.[37] This rebellion,
however, initiated a pattern which would repeat itself. Neighboring
regimes were not beyond interfering in the domestic affairs of regional
rivals, and, in particular, in aiding Kurdish rebels, as long as such aid
did not sufficiently strengthen the Kurds to make them a threat to
their own stability or territorial integrity. However, the new shah of
Iran, Reza Khan, who came to power in 1925, doubted the advisability
of such an approach. The protection of his own empire's unity was his
priority. Already facing his own Kurdish uprising, the shah feared
that a strong Kurdish community in Turkey could lend support to this
rebellion. In a sudden decision – one which would have an eerie echo
in a decision by his successor fifty years later – the shah ended
assistance to the Kurds and even permitted the Turkish army to move
through Iranian territory to encircle and defeat the Kurdish forces. He
concentrated his own attention on the most serious uprising within
his own territory – that lead by the Kurdish chief, Isma'il Shakkah
Simko. This insurrection in Iran lasted nine years until its defeat in
1930 by the shah's military expedition.[38]

Kurdish aspirations for independence next manifested themselves
in the creation, with the assistance of the Red army, of the Republic of
Mahabad in northern Iran in 1946.[39] Yet when the Soviet government
withdrew its support, Iranian troops crushed this brief expression of
Kurdish autonomy and executed its president, Qazi Muhammad, and
other prominent members of this government. Iran continued to
suffer resistance coordinated by the Kurdish Democratic Party (KDPI)
in the late 1960s and 1970s. The KDPI used the opportunity created by
the Iranian revolution in 1979 to extend its *de facto* control over large

[36] McDowall, *The Kurds*, p. 11.
[37] Chaliand Gerard (ed.), *People Without a Country: The Kurds and Kurdistan* (London: Zed Press, 1980), pp. 64–66.
[38] Hannum, *Autonomy*, pp. 184–185.
[39] Archie Roosevelt, "The Kurdish Republic of Mahabad," in Chaliand, *People without a Country*, pp. 135–152.

areas of Iranian Kurdistan. An Iranian offensive sent by the Ayatolla Khomeini defeated and massacred the KDPI in 1983.[40]

Kurdish politics in Iraq were dominated for decades by Mustafa Barzani, who, as agha and mullah,[41] held both secular and religious leadership roles. In 1970 the Iraqi government agreed to provide Kurds extensive devolution, although it never implemented the detailed provisions.[42] With the collapse of this agreement, Barzani and his followers took up arms against the Ba'athist regime.[43] The shah of Iran, Mossad, and the CIA provided arms and advisers.[44] In a matter of weeks after the March 1975 Algiers Agreement between Iran and Iraq, in which the shah promised to cut off all logistical support to the Kurds, the Iraqi army succeeded in crushing the revolt. The Kurds attempted to use the opportunity created by the Iran–Iraq war in the 1980s to again gain control over their own territory. In response, Saddam Hussein launched a "scorched earth" campaign, razing some 5,000 Kurdish villages. He also ordered the 1988 chemical weapons attack on the Kurdish town of Halabja. The attack killed over 5,000 people and forced several hundred thousand to seek refuge in Turkey or Iran.[45]

In a recent reincarnation of the Kurdish struggle, the Iraqi Kurdish *pashmergas* attempted to liberate Kurdish towns in March 1991, directly after Iraq's defeat in the Gulf War. The *pashmergas* succeeded in over-running local military bases but could not contend with the superior firepower of the Republican Guards armed with helicopter gunships, tanks, and heavy artillery. The Republican Guards recaptured most of Iraqi Kurdistan in less than four days,[46] forcing 1 million Kurds to seek refuge in Iran and an additional 700,000 to flee to Turkey through dangerous and freezing mountain passes.[47] It is ironic that after the creation of "safe havens" in northern Iraq, they

[40] Hannum, *Autonomy*, p. 196.
[41] In the hierarchy of the Ottoman Empire, an "agha" was a chief military or civil officer, although in many contemporary Middle Eastern societies it has become a title of distinction. "Mullah" is the Islamic title for one learned in theology and sacred law.
[42] The Peace Agreement of March 11, 1970 between representatives of the Iraqi government and the Kurds is reprinted in Martin Short and Anthony McDermott, *The Kurds* (London: The Minority Rights Group, 1975), pp. 25–26.
[43] Ismet Sheriff Vanly, "Kurdistan in Iraq," in Chaliand, *People Without a Country.*
[44] Lee Buchheit, *Secession: The Legitimacy of Self-Determination* (New Haven: Yale University Press, 1978), p. 119; and James Mayall, *Nationalism and the International System* (Cambridge: Cambridge University Press 1990), p. 66.
[45] Ron Moreau, "Saddam's Slaughter," *Newsweek*, April 15, 1991, p. 12.
[46] "An Iraqi Prison Diary," *The Economist*, May 4, 1991, p. 70.
[47] "Cavalry to the rescue," *The Economist*, April 20, 1991, p. 69.

were first invaded not by Iraqi Republican Guards, but rather by thousands of Turkish troops in search of guerrillas from the Kurdish Worker's Party (PKK). The PKK had been fighting for Kurdish independence from Turkey since 1984. The Turkish government justified its attack with accusations that PKK guerrillas had taken advantage of the power vacuum in northern Iraq to establish their own bases. By penetrating Iraqi territory about 16 kilometers, Turkish security forces created a buffer zone inside Iraq, which they patrolled frequently.[48]

What Nader Entessar has called the "Kurdish mosaic of discord"[49] has certainly hampered Kurdish resistance. Fragmentation within the community has been caused by different Kurdish dialects being mutually unintelligible, physical separation by the mountains, cultural differences between mountain and plains Kurds, and disputes arising from contemporary ideologies and ancient family rivalries. No fewer than seven separate political organizations in Turkey, Iran, and Iraq compete for the support of the Kurdish community in their commitment to win greater autonomy.[50] These traditional rivalries fatally impeded the defense of the Republic of Mahabad. Furthermore, by accepting assistance from one neighboring state, Kurdish leaders have had to renounce the provision of support for their kinsmen across the border. In order to gain Iranian support, Barzani was forced to cease assisting the KDPI, which lead directly to the KDPI's temporary demise in the 1960s.[51] Kurds in northern Iraq have pleaded with PKK guerrillas to remain quiet or to leave, since they fear the wrath of the Turkish security forces.[52]

To sum up, whatever the level of internal unity or division within the Kurdish community, even such a brief outline of their history demonstrates that the primary constraint on their search for greater autonomy has been the resolve of Turkey, Iran, and Iraq to use the most extreme forms of repression. Significantly, Barzani acknowledged this constraint directly when he described Iraqi Kurdish demands as a function of the military strength of his men relative to the military strength of his adversaries in the Iraqi government.

[48] "Wages of defeat," *The Economist*, August 17, 1991, p. 36.
[49] Nader Entessar, "Kurdish mosaic of discord," *Third World Quarterly*, 11, 4 (October, 1989), 83.
[50] For a description of the various Kurdish parties, see McDowall, *The Kurds*, pp. 29–30.
[51] Hannum, *Autonomy*, p. 195.
[52] "Wages of defeat," *The Economist*, August 17, 1991, p. 36.

Perhaps more intriguing is the fact these three very different regimes have not qualitatively differed in their treatment of the Kurds. After the revolution in 1979, Iran attempted to create an Islamic Republic. Iraq possesses an authoritarian Ba'athist regime loosely embracing a socialist creed. Turkey has attempted to remold itself into a secular and Western state. These ideological differences have not precluded them from employing equally ruthless approaches to their Kurds, ranging from outright denial of their existence to chemical weapons attacks on their towns.[53] Natural resources in Kurdistan, strategic security considerations, and superpower pressures may have contributed to the decision of each state to support Kurdish separatism in its neighbors. But Turkey, Iraq, and Iran have all strenuously and successfully opposed Kurdish demands for separate statehood or meaningful autonomy.

Before discussing the second cost of secession – hostility on the part of the international community – let us summarize the thrust of the argument thus far. Like India, Turkey, Iran, and Iraq, most states facing secessionist turmoil have historically possessed the resolve and commanded the resources to oppose a secession. They have inflicted heavy losses in terms of lives and livelihoods on the members of the seceding community. Although he was investigating separatist movements in the West, Milton Esman's description applies to almost all states facing secessionist activity:

> At present the balance [of advantages in secessionist conflicts] favors the central elites ... In the absense of overwhelming support for secession, [they] command impressive capabilities to accommodate moderate ethnoregional claims and to repress their extreme or violent manifestations within the existing frameworks and state boundaries.[54]

As in the case of the Kurds, state strategies can often dampen, if perhaps not completely eradicate, such dissent. In other cases, such as that of the Nagas, the central government can force the reconsideration and perhaps relinquishment of the secessionist struggle through concurrent policies of repression and concession. The credible threat of state opposition has probably dissuaded other distinct communities from choosing the secessionist path. State capabilities provide one of the more effective obstacles to successful secessions.

[53] Moreau, "Saddam's Slaughter," p. 12.
[54] Milton Esman (ed.), *Ethnic Conflict in the Western World* (Ithaca: Cornell University Press, 1977), p. 389.

International hostility

State opposition clearly causes mental and physical anguish to those attempting secession. International hostility can cause similar human costs of secession by relegating secessionist entities to diplomatic isolation. Exploring the causes of the international community's general opposition to secession quickly reveals the limitations of using a cost/benefit approach to address the fundamental normative questions inherent in the subject of secession. The purpose of this section is not to answer these value-laden questions, but rather to trace out from which moral principles of post-1945 international relations this hostility to secession arises.

Seceding communities and states can both find support for their respective causes in international law. Distinct communities have attempted to gain the moral high ground by couching their aspirations in terms of the principle of self-determination. States justify their opposition by arguing for the primacy of territorial integrity. With particular reference to these two contending principles, a careful investigation of international documents serves to determine the international system's position on secession in general. By severely limiting the justifiable application of self-determination and by raising territorial integrity to the level of nearly an absolute principle, the international system has implicitly condemned secession. Further, the Katangan crisis in the Congo in 1960–1961 and the Biafran crisis in Nigeria from 1966 to 1970 show the international community's reaction to specific secession crises. These two examples were chosen from a number of other post-war secession crises because the United Nations and other regional organizations issued a large number of public proclamations concerning them. In most secession cases, international organizations have in fact remained silent. In trying to protect their interests, states have successfully kept these other crises off the agenda of the United Nations and other international organizations. In the proclamations concerning Katanga and Biafra, however, the international community has made its implicit condemnation of secession explicit.

Self-determination

There is no doubt that self-determination as a "right" has captured the popular imagination of many distinct communities around the world. Chapter 6 explores its historical and contemporary appeal in greater detail when it considers the benefits of secession. The following overview of the term's use in more recent international resolutions demonstrates its prominence in international law as well. Having established its relevance, this section attempts to unravel its ambiguities.

Numerous international documents have espoused this principle, including President Woodrow Wilson's Fourteen Points, the Versailles Peace Treaty and the Atlantic Charter. An investigation of the resolutions of the UN, the Organization of African Unity, and the Conference on Security and Cooperation in Europe confirms its current relevance. To begin with, through the enumeration of the UN's purposes, Article 1(2) of the UN Charter recognizes the right of self-determination, albeit in a restricted fashion:[55] "To develop friendly relations among nations based on respect for the principle of equal rights and the self-determination of peoples." Article 55 also emphasizes its importance in conjunction with the promotion of international economic and social cooperation. However, by also emphasizing other principles of international law, like mutual recognition and non-intervention, post-war statesmen carefully circumscribed self-determination as a potential guiding principle for the UN.

The UN General Assembly Resolution 1514, Declaration on the Granting of Independence to Colonial Countries and Peoples, unanimously adopted on December 14, 1960, elevated the principle of self-determination to greater prominence.[56] Written as an authoritative interpretation of the UN Charter rather than as a recommendation, the resolution specifically related the widely accepted concept of human rights to that of the rights of national groups, and in particular, to self-determination:

> Conscious of the need for the creation of conditions of stability and well-being and peaceful and friendly relations based on respect for the principle of equal rights and self-determination of all peoples, and of universal respect for and observance of, human rights and fundamental freedoms without distinction as to race, sex, language or religion;

---

[55] Relevant provisions of the United Nations Charter are reprinted in Ian Brownlie (ed.), *Basic Documents on Human Rights*, 2nd edn (Oxford: The Clarendon Press, 1981), pp. 3–14.
[56] The Declaration on the Granting of Independence to Colonial Countries and Peoples reprinted in Brownlie, *Basic Documents on Human Rights*, pp. 28–30.

The General Assembly Declares that:

> (1) the subjection of peoples to alien subjugation, domination, and exploitation constitutes a denial of fundamental human rights, is contrary to the Charter of the United Nations, and is an impediment to the promotion of world peace and cooperation;
> (2) all peoples have the right to self-determination; by virtue of that right they freely determine their political status, freely pursue their economic, social, and cultural development.

The ramifications of the overwhelming passage of Resolution 1514 constituted a profound change in international relations. By specifically stating that "inadequacy of political, economic, social, or educational preparedness should never serve as a pretext for delaying independence," Resolution 1514 undercut the arguments presented by colonial offices in the metropolitan capitals of Europe to make the granting of independence contingent on sufficient political preparation and economic viability.[57] These arguments were considered morally inferior to the claims of peoples colonised by Western powers for self-determination. This revision of international norms accelerated the process of decolonization. Ian Brownlie argues that with the UN Charter, Resolution 1514, and the 1966 Covenant on Civil and Political Rights, self-determination has become part of the *jus cogens* of international law.[58]

The meaning of self-determination, nevertheless, continues to be ambiguous. With its roots in the notions of popular sovereignty in the late eighteenth century, the idea of self-determination proposed that the basis of international legitimacy must depend on the desires of the people and not their ruling elites. Its ambiguity arises from the question of which groups should receive self-determination as a right. Moreover, as the doctrine has been applied to novel situations, it has metamorphosed.[59] Her far-ranging scholarship enables Rosalyn

---

[57] In a representative example of such arguments, in December, 1948 the British colonial secretary, Arthur Creech-Jones, told the Commonwealth Affairs Committee that complete independence for a colony would only be achieved when the territory was "economically viable and capable of defending its own interests". Creech-Jones is quoted by Robert Jackson, *Quasi-States: Sovereignty, International Relations, and The Third World* (Cambridge: Cambridge University Press, 1990), p. 93; and by D. J. Morgan, *Guidance Towards Self-Government in British Colonies, 1941–1971, The Official History of Colonial Development*, vol. V (London, 1980), p. 21.

[58] Ian Brownlie, *Principles of Public International Law* (Oxford: Oxford University Press, 1979) p. 515.

[59] A detailed account of the metamorphosis of the principle of self-determination is presented in chapter 6 of this book.

Higgins to identify the units to which self-determination applies as a right in contemporary international law.[60] She argues that it has become restricted to the right of the majority to exercise power within an internationally recognized political unit. The key aspect of self-determination is to effect change within boundaries, not to change the boundaries themselves. Higgins utilizes the case of the Nagas to emphasize that small communities cannot claim self-determination as a right. Since the Nagas reside within the internationally recognized political unit of India and constitute only a very small minority therein, "there can be no such thing as self-determination for the Nagas".[61] Although the international community may embrace the conventions on self-determination as Higgins details them, this acceptance clearly does not extend to small distinct communities such as the Nagas who have been fighting for secession.

Territorial integrity

The reverence for self-determination is at least equalled, if not superseded, by the emphasis on territorial integrity. Article 2(4) of the UN Charter reflects this attitude:

> The Organization and its Members, in pursuit of the Purposes stated in Article 1, shall act in accordance with the following Principles:
> ... (4) all members shall refrain in their international relations from the threat or use of force against the territorial integrity or political independence of any State.

Resolution 1514, which elevated the status of self-determination, also emphasized territorial integrity.

The United Nations General Assembly Declares that:

> (6) any attempt aimed at the partial or total disruption of national unity and territorial integrity of a country is incompatible with the Purposes and Principles of the Charter of the United Nations;
> (7) all States shall observe faithfully and strictly the provisions of the Charter of the United Nations, the Universal Declaration of Human Rights and the present Declaration on the basis of equality and non-interference in the internal affairs of all States, and respect the sovereign rights of all peoples and their territorial integrity.

That these two contradictory principles were often conflated not

---

[60] Rosalyn Higgins, *The Development of International Law Through the Political Organs of the United Nations* (Oxford: Oxford University Press, 1963).
[61] Ibid., p. 105.

only in the same international document, but even in the same clause reveals the international community's ambivalent attitude toward this dilemma. Part VIII of the Final Act of the 1975 Helsinki Conference on Security and Cooperation in Europe, while setting out a policy statement on "The Equal Rights and Self-Determination of Peoples," actually emphasizes the primacy of territorial integrity:[62]

> The participating States will respect the equal rights of peoples and their right to self-determination, acting at all times in conformity with the purposes and principles of the Charter of the United Nations and with relevant norms of international law, including those relating to territorial integrity of states.

The African states as a group have not shared the international community's ambivalence toward the debate between self-determination and territorial integrity. They have systematically used the mechanism of international law to raise territorial integrity to nearly an absolute principle. Recognizing their mutual vulnerability due to arbitrary borders and societies divided by deep cultural cleavages, they have developed what Onyeonoro Kamanu has described as "the current doctrinaire emphasis of the Organization of African Unity (OAU) on the absolute preservation of the territorial integrity of member states and on the sanctity of existing frontiers."[63] Not only does the OAU deny the right of self-determination to historic African communities who do not currently possess a state, the organization itself denies a forum for those communities seeking to publicise their grievances. As one of the leaders of the Southern Sudanese secessionist struggle, Major-General Joseph Lagu laments: "We have endured more deaths ... than all the other African freedom movements combined. And yet the OAU will not even allow our story to be told."[64]

Numerous OAU resolutions have entrenched this position. Adopted by the Conference of Heads of State and Government in Addis Ababa on May 25, 1963, the Charter of the Organization of African Unity states:[65]

---

[62] The text of the Final Act of The Helsinki Conference is reprinted in Brownlie, *Basic Documents*, pp. 320–332.
[63] Onyeonoro S. Kamanu, "Secession and the Right of Self-Determination: an OAU Dilemma," *Journal of Modern African Studies*, 12, 3 (1974), 363.
[64] Lagu was head of the Anya-Nya and the Southern Sudanese Liberation Movement. He is quoted by Alexis Heraclides, *The Self-Determination of Minorities in International Politics* (London: Frank Cass, 1991), p. 107.
[65] Charter of the OAU is reprinted in Ian Brownlie (ed.), *Basic Documents on African Affairs* (Oxford: The Clarendon Press, 1971), pp. 2–8.

Determined to safeguard and consolidate the hard-won independence as well as the sovereignty and territorial integrity of our States,
and to resist neo-colonialism in all its forms;

The purposes of the Organization of African Unity are:

(2) to defend [its member states'] sovereignty, their territorial integrity, and their independence.

The OAU Resolution on Border Disputes, adopted in Cairo on July 21,
1964, further clarified the duties of member states:[66]

Considering further that the borders of African states, on the day of
their independence constitute a tangible reality...
[The Assembly] solemnly declares that all Member States pledge
themselves to respect frontiers existing on their achievement of
national independence.

Thus, Article 2 of the OAU Charter and Article 3(3) of the OAU
Resolution on Border Disputes impose an obligation on members far
beyond similar provisions in the UN Charter. Article 2(4) of the UN
Charter concentrates on the negative or passive obligation of member
states. It merely requires that they abstain from violating the territorial
integrity or political independence of any other state. Meanwhile, the
OAU Charter requires the organization "to defend" the sovereignty
and territorial integrity of its members – a positive or active obligation. Moreover, the OAU Charter presumably commits the organization to defend the territorial integrity of its member states from both
external aggression and internal threats.

Explicit condemnation of secession

The restricted application of self-determination and the elevation of
territorial integrity to nearly an absolute principle unite to form the
basis of the international system's implicit opposition to secession.
With the Katangan crisis in 1960–1961, this implicit opposition
became explicit condemnation.

Even though the rapid Belgian withdrawal from the Congo and the
vast mineral wealth of the Katangan province made its declaration of
independence on July 17, 1960 extremely controversial, the United
Nations at first did not address the question of Katanga's status. The
Security Council in its Resolution S/4405 of July 22 "recommended

---

[66] The OAU Resolution on Border Disputes reprinted in Brownlie, *Basic Documents on
African Affairs*, pp. 360–361.

the admission of the Republic of Congo to membership in the United Nations as a unit."[67] This implied an objection to the secession attempt. Subsequent resolutions in September and November, 1960[68] further reinforced the UN's support for the Congo's continued territorial integrity. Despite widespread disapproval of the Katangan position, the UN Secretary General Dag Hammarskjold meticulously refrained from altering the domestic balance of power between Leopoldville and Elisabethville. The Security Council, through adoption of Resolution 4741 on February 20–21, 1961, instructed Hammarskjold to negotiate the replacement of foreign military personnel in Katanga, both Belgian and mercenary, with UN troops. The underlying assumption was that the Katangan secession, dependent on external aid, would collapse once foreign advisers and troops had been removed.

Katangan inflexibility combined with Hammarskjold's tragic death led the UN to adopt a more intransigent position toward the secession. In an unprecedented act, the Security Council passed Resolution 5002 on November 24, 1961, which deserves to be quoted at length:[69]

> Reaffirming the policies and purposes of the United Nations with respect to the Congo as set out in the aforesaid resolutions, namely (a) to maintain the territorial integrity and political independence of the Republic of the Congo; (b) to assist the central government of the Congo in the restoration and maintenance of law and order; (c) to prevent the occurrence of civil war in the Congo; (d) to secure immediate withdrawal and evacuation from the Congo of all foreign military, para-military, and advisory personnel not under UN command, and all mercenaries; and (e) to render technical assistance; Deploring all armed action in opposition to the Government of the Republic of Congo *specifically secessionist activities,* and armed action now being carried on by the provincial administration of Katanga with the aid of external resources and foreign mercenaries, and *completely rejecting the claim that Katanga is a 'sovereign independent nation.'*

The United Nations Security Council:

(1) *Strongly deprecates the secessionist activities illegally carried out by the*

---

[67] The series of UN resolutions concerning the situation in the Congo, 1960–1964, is reprinted in Brownlie, *Basic Documents on African Affairs*, pp. 510–525.
[68] These were UNGA Resolutions 1474 and 1498.
[69] Resolution 5002 is reprinted in Brownlie, *Basic Documents on African Affairs*, pp. 516–517. Emphasis added.

provisional administration of Katanga with the aid of external resources and manned by foreign mercenaries ...

(2) Declares that all secessionist activities against the Government of Congo are contrary to the *Loi fundamentale* and Security Council decisions and *specifically demands that such activities which are now taking place in Katanga shall cease forthwith.*

In her history of the Congo, Catherine Hoskyns places this resolution in its proper perspective: "From a legal point of view, the most striking aspect of this resolution was its condemnation not just of external aid to secession, but of secession itself, and the fact that a mandatory call was made not only to outside states but also to the Congolese to desist from secessionist activities."[70]

Perhaps even more surprising than the UN's outright condemnation was the fact that its troops were directly responsible for the suppression of the secession.[71] Under the legal cover provided by Security Council Resolution 4741, which authorised "the use of force, if necessary" to take measures "for the immediate withdrawal and evacuation from the Congo of all Belgian and other foreign military personnel ...," UN troops organized operation RUMPUNCH against foreign troops on August 28, 1961. This operation escalated on September 13 into a full-scale assault on mercenaries. When foreign and Katangan forces attacked UN positions in December, UN commanders used a wide definition of self-defense to justify their occupation of centers of military importance in Elisabethville, such as the radio station, barracks, and government buildings.[72] Having captured Katangan leader Moise Tshombe, UN commanders forced him to negotiate directly with the Congolese federal president, Adoula. Under such UN pressure, Tshombe signed the Kitona Agreement on December 21, thereby renouncing all secessionist aspirations for Katanga.[73] The UN troops defeated a secession movement which its 1960 Declaration on the Granting of Independence to Colonial Countries and Peoples would seemingly have validated.

Having suffered much criticism of its handling of the Katangan

[70] Catherine Hoskyns, *The Congo Since Independence: January, 1960–December, 1961* (Oxford: Oxford University Press, 1965), p. 445.
[71] For a detailed study of the way in which UN troops were instrumental in ending the secession, see Conor Cruise O'Brien, *To Katanga and Back: A UN Case History* (London: 1962).
[72] For details of operations RUMPUNCH and MORTHOR, see Hoskyns, *The Congo*, pp. 402–435.
[73] Ibid., p. 454–455.

crisis, the UN formally remained silent on the Biafran secession from
Nigeria six years later. The Organization of African Unity, by contrast,
condemned the Biafran secession. The Resolution on the Situation in
Nigeria in September 1967 declared:[74]

> Solemnly reaffirming their adherence to the principle of respect for
> the sovereignty and territorial integrity of Member States;
> Reiterating their condemnation of secession in any Member State.

The OAU Conference of Heads of State and Government also resolved
to "send a consultative mission of six heads of state to the head of the
Federal Government of Nigeria to assure him of the Assembly's desire
for the territorial integrity, unity, and peace of Nigeria".[75] By effectively using international law and forums like the UN and the OAU,
African states created the pressure to precipitate this remarkable shift
in international norms.

Therefore, in the rare instance where the distinct community has
defeated the government's military forces, it still faces the nearly
insurmountable obstacle of gaining international recognition. Before
1991, the domestic and international constraints on secession have
been, by any measure, nearly prohibitive of the creation of new states
through secession. The accelerated European withdrawal from their
African and Asian colonies in the 1950s and 1960s forced the international community to recognize many new states. Once the process
of decolonization ended, however, the international system reverted
to its former reluctance to recognize newly seceded entities, as if a
certain class of states – those created through decolonization – had
been acceptable, while others were not.

Meanwhile, the pursuit by the United States and the Soviet Union
of their own ideological agendas and national interests did not contra-
vene these subtle changes in the normative framework underlying
inter-state relations. Both superpowers judged separatist agitation in
the Third World primarily as opportunities to extend their own
influence. As a result, many purely domestic disputes became the
grounds for open competition between the superpowers. Both governments provided arms and other support to one side or the other in
these conflicts. The secession crisis in the Congo serves as a good
example of the superpower scramble for influence. In general terms,

[74] The OAU Resolution on the Situation in Nigeria is reprinted in Brownlie, *Basic
Documents on African Affairs*, p. 364.
[75] Brownlie, Basic Documents on African Affairs, p. 364.

superpower intervention did not usually provoke secessionist struggles in developing countries. However, their involvement arguably played a role in making such conflicts more difficult to resolve, as both the central government and the discontented community were assured of sufficient arms, material, and financial support to avoid an outright military defeat.

In conclusion, let us re-examine the main propositions discussed in the last two chapters. Although the relative importance of the two types of barriers is difficult to determine, their combined absolute importance is great. Their influence can be inferred from the fact that in Ernest Gellner's calculation, about 8,000 separate languages exist in the world today, yet the number of states, secessions, and separatist movements are far fewer.[76] There are many reasons for this dichotomy. To begin with, distinct communities can be organized around other shared characteristics besides language, such as religion, race, territorial home, and culture. Further, a distinct community may only desire to be left alone. The aspirations of the Inuit and other Native Americans do not extend to sovereign statehood. Other communities may not contemplate secession due to factors such as inertia, tradition, or an appreciation of the benefits of cultural diversity. Finally, powerful restraints on secession lie in the benefits of membership and costs of secession. The calculation of such benefits dissuades communities from secession, since they could not afford to sacrifice the security, economic, and social advantages associated with participation in a larger state. Moreover, the credible threat of state opposition combined with likely international hostility has also restrained distinct communities from embarking on the secessionist path. While assessment of the benefits of membership acts as an implicit restraint on secession attempts, the costs of secession act as an explicit obstacle. Indeed, the scales appear to be weighed against secession.

Yet the decision to secede rests on the community's perception of a change in the balance of costs and benefits associated with membership and secession. The discontented community is more likely to attempt secession when the perceived likelihood of success has been enhanced. Reductions in the barriers to secession can create such "opportune moments" for secession. Chapter 8 demonstrates the way in which the weakening of the central government or foreign inter-

[76] Ernest Gellner, *Nations and Nationalism* (Oxford: Basil Blackwell, 1983), p. 47.

vention on behalf of the distinct community – by reducing the potential costs of secession – creates just such "opportune moments." It describes how numerous peripheral communities took advantage of tsarist Russia's collapse in 1917 to gain their independence. It also explores how the Indian army's intervention in the Bengali war for secession and the Turkish military involvement in Cyprus proved instrumental in creating Bangladesh and the quasi-state of Northern Cyprus. Chapter 9 examines how reduction in the implicit restraints on secession – the benefits of membership – can also motivate secession crises.

5　The costs of membership

This chapter begins to explore that side of our allegorical scales which provides the motivations and frequently the justification for secession: the costs of membership and the benefits of secession. The potential costs of integration into a larger heterogeneous state constitute the logical counterweight to the benefits of membership examined in Chapter 3. This chapter utilizes multiple cases to investigate the two broad categories of such potential disadvantages: first, physical hardships such as hunger, dispossession, and even mortal threats, and second, cultural threats. One can but recoil from instances where the government mobilizes its resources to force deportation or cultural assimilation onto one group of its citizens. Although still possible, such gross abuses are less likely when governments are in some way directly accountable to those they govern. None the less, it is the persecuted community that bears the costs when governments sacrifice the preservation of human life and unique culture to pursue other priorities.

It is perhaps useful to restate the sense in which I used the terms "costs" and "benefits" in this analytical framework. At a fundamental level, "costs" are abstracted from their normal usage implying financial loss and revolve around the notion of a penalty, such as the loss of life or livelihood or opportunity. The investigation of instances of injustice or dispossession or even murder is by its very nature a value-laden exercise, and thus, fits only awkwardly into a cost/benefit approach to the subject of secession. This effort is required and justified, however, because developing a perspective on how a distinctive community perceives the state and its own position within it is critical to understanding how changes in those circumstances could provoke a secession.

In the first section, Soviet deportations in 1943–1945 of eight Transcaucasus and Crimean communities, the Ukrainian famine of 1931–1933, and Turkish repression of its Armenian community during World War I indicate the level of human suffering which is possible when regimes use their coercive powers against distinct communities within their territories. In the second section, the chapter examines possible threats to a community's culture. Historically states have pursued vigorous policies of forcible cultural assimilation to eliminate potential treasonous elements. A poet's portrayal of the nightmare of ultimate extinction expresses the emotional anguish associated with such cultural threats. Official Turkish denigration of the Kurdish cultural heritage illustrates the fears which haunt many powerless distinct communities.

Mortal threats to the distinct community

Throughout history, many states have treated the communities within their borders in abhorrent ways. States have often justified their actions by accusing these communities of harboring treacherous elements. The cases of the Soviet minorities and the Armenians do not analyze the precise motivations for the deportations or murders. Rather, they illustrate that, notwithstanding the repugnance to human conscience, such extreme discrimination is possible. In the end, such systematic abuses frequently become essential moral justifications for secession attempts.

Deportation and famine: Soviet mistreatment of its minorities, 1930–1945[1]

After painstaking research into the experiences of the disparate populations of the Soviet Union during World War II, historians Bohdan Nahaylo, Victor Swoboda, and Robert Conquest independently arrived at the same conclusion: Soviet authorities dispossessed eight nationalities of their historic lands and deported them *en masse*

---

[1] Historical material for this section was drawn primarily from Bohdan Nahaylo and Victor Swoboda, *Soviet Disunion: A History of the Nationalities Problem in the U.S.S.R.* (New York: Macmillan, 1989); Robert Conquest, *Soviet Nationalities Policy and Practice* (London: Bodley Head, 1967); Robert Conquest, *The Nation Killers: The Soviet Deportation of Nationalities* (London: Macmillan, 1970); and Bohdan Nahaylo and C. J. Peters, *The Ukrainians and the Georgians* (London: Minority Rights Group, 1980).

to Siberia and Central Asia.[2] Those communities deported in 1943–1945 were native inhabitants of the Ukraine – Crimean Tatars and Volga Germans – and the Transcaucasus – Chechens, Ingushi, Karachai, Balkans, Kalmyks, and Meskhetians. In 1939, the population of these distinct communities stood at the following levels:[3]

407,690	Chechen
92,074	Ingushi
75,737	Karachai
42,666	Balkans
134,271	Kalmyks
380,000	Volga German
200,000	Crimean Tatars
200,000	Meskhetians

Soviet censuses indicate that over 1 million people were deported. Such an operation required the transfer of extensive resources from the war effort. Soviet authorities justified the deportations with accusations that these groups collaborated with advancing German forces. Records indicate that the German army had limited success in recruiting some Tatars and Volga Germans into its ranks, but there is little proof to sustain the accusation against the remaining six communities. The German advance did not come within hundreds of miles of their territory.[4]

Although the actual deportations took place in 1944, a Supreme Soviet decree in 1946 justified the treatment of Crimean Tatars, Chechens, and Ingushi in terms of their supposed duplicity during the war.[5] The treatment of the other communities received neither

---

[2] Nahaylo and Swoboda, *Soviet Disunion*, pp. 96–97; and Conquest, *Soviet Nationalities Policy*, p. 102.
[3] Conquest, *Soviet Nationalities Policy*, p. 104
[4] Conquest, *The Nation Killers*, pp. 48–49.
[5] The 1946 Law concerning the Abolition of the Chechen-Ingushi Autonomous Soviet Socialist Republic and the Changing of the Crimean Autonomous Soviet Socialist Republic into the Crimean Province reads as follows:

> During the Great Patriotic War, when USSR fought against the German Fascist invaders, many Chechens and Crimean Tatars joined volunteer units organized by the Germans and engaged in armed battles against Red Army. The main mass of the population of the Chechen-Ingushi and Crimean ASSRs took no counter-action against these betrayers of the fatherland.
> In connection with this, the Chechens and the Crimean Tatars were resettled in other regions of the USSR, where they were given land, together with the necessary governmental assistance for their economic establishment. On the proposal of the Presidium of the Supreme Soviet of the RSFSR the Chechen-

official justification nor recognition. Their deportation had to be deduced from omissions in cartographic publications. For ten years after the war, Soviet legal documents ignored not only their experiences, but their very existence. For example, the 1947 edition of the *Soviet Encyclopedia* completely neglected to mention them in its list of Soviet nationalities, although previous editions had included them.[6] Their autonomous regions, created by the 1924 Soviet federal constitution, were erased. None of these groups participated in the post-war sessions of the Council of Nationalities. Only after a decade of official silence were these distinct communities, with the exception of the Meskhetians, rehabilitated into national politics. They were granted some limited self-government in their new residences in Siberia and Central Asia. At the time, however, they were not granted the right to return to their ancestral homelands. The experience of the Meskhetians remained officially unacknowledged for a full twenty-five years until 1968.

What is remarkable about these cases is that the state employed its resources to deport an entire distinct community. Soviet authorities had employed similar measures earlier to impair resistance to Soviet rule. Having occupied the Baltic republics in 1940, the Soviet regime singled out and deported potential resistance leaders as a means to defeat the armed partisans. It is estimated that by July, 1941, 170,000 educated persons including doctors, lawyers, government officials, clergy, professors, and those with contacts abroad, including former Red Cross officials, had been forcibly expelled from the Baltic States.[7] In the post-war years, having reoccupied the Baltic states after the German retreat, the Soviet regime resumed its deportations. From

Ingushi ASSR was abolished and the Crimean ASSR was changed into the Crimean Province by decrees of the Presidium of the Supreme Soviet.
The Supreme Soviet of the RSFSR resolves:
1. To confirm the abolition of Chechen-Ingushi ASSR and the changing of the Crimean ASSR into the Crimean Province.
2. To make the necessary alterations and additions to Article 14 of the Constitution of the RSFSR.
Chairman, Presidium of the Supreme Soviet of the RSFSR, I. Vlasov.
Secretary, Presidium of the Supreme Soviet of the RSFSR, P. Bakhmurov.
Moscow, Kremlin, 23 June 1946. (Conquest, *The Nation Killers*, pp. 46–47)
[6] Conquest, *Soviet Nationalities Policy*, p. 105.
[7] Kestutis K. Girnius, *Partizanų Kovos Lietuvoje* (Chicago, 1987), p. 138; Thomas Remeikis, *Opposition to Soviet Rule in Lithuania*, 1945–1980 (Chicago: Institute of Lithuanian Studies Press, 1980), pp. 19–20.

refugee evidence it appears that some 400,000 Lithuanians were deported toward the end of 1948, about 150,000 Latvians between then and the beginning of 1949, and in May, 1949 alone, 35,000 Estonians.[8]

Besides deportation, those resisting Stalinist initiatives also faced famine. During the 1930s collectivization campaign, local authorities requisitioned all grain from farmers. Effective execution of this procurement policy resulted in a massive, artificially induced famine in Ukraine – one of the Soviet Union's most fertile regions.[9] Between 1932 and 1933, while the Soviet Union exported grain to Western Europe to earn hard currency, at least 10% of the Ukrainian population died from starvation.[10] Soviet historians in the West, such as James Mace, have researched and presented in a chilling light the calculations of Soviet leaders. Their priorities included agricultural collectivization and suppression of Ukrainian dissent.[11] Medvedev has estimated, rather conservatively, that the famine resulted in the deaths of approximately 6 million people.[12]

The artificial famine in Ukraine and the deportation of Lithuanians, Latvians, and Estonians resisting Soviet rule, although devastating to the families involved, differs from the experiences of the eight wartime deportations cited earlier in two crucial respects. First, although perhaps affecting greater absolute numbers, the famine and deportations did not deprive an entire community of its ancestral lands. Since the 1960s, the eight communities, with the Crimean Tatars in the lead, vociferously demanded the right to return to the Crimea or the Transcaucasus.[13] Second, Soviet authorities did not deny the events during the collectivization period and Baltic occupation. By contrast, for between a decade and a quarter century, the Soviet

---

[8] V. Stanley Vardys, "The Partisan Movement in Postwar Lithuania," in *Lithuania Under the Soviets: Portrait of a Nation, 1940–1965* (New York: Frederick Praeger, 1965) pp. 108–110; Conquest, *Soviet Nationalities Policy,* pp. 108–112.

[9] For both a series of eyewitness accounts of the famine and analysis of Soviet policies, see James E. Mace, "Famine and Nationalism in Soviet Ukraine," *Problems of Communism,* 33, 3 (May–June, 1984), 37–50.

[10] Bohdan Nahaylo and C. J. Peters, *The Ukrainians and the Georgians* (London: Minority Rights Group, 1980), p. 7.

[11] Mace, "Famine," pp. 49–51.

[12] Medvedev's estimates are quoted in Nahaylo and Swoboda, *Soviet Disunion,* p. 67.

[13] "The Crimean Question," *The Economist,* January 12, 1992, pp. 47–48; Bill Keller, "Tatars Seek Split with the Russians," *The New York Times,* September 8, 1991, pp. 1, 11; and "Tatar Sauce," *The Economist,* September 11, 1991, p. 46.

government wiped its history books clean of the experiences and very existence of the Kalmyks, Balkars, Karachai, and Meskhetians.

Turkish mistreatment of its Armenian community, 1915–1917[14]

The costs of membership can be even more dire: mass murder. Numerous conventions in international law now outlaw mass murder and genocide as repugnant to international morality and the human conscience.[15] With sufficient resources and will, however, a regime could rid itself of an entire distinct community considered troublesome. An investigation of Turkish mistreatment of its Armenian population during World War I indicates the way in which a community without the medium of sovereign power can be caught defenseless against such deliberate and systematic mortal threats. Michael Walzer, Harry Beran, and other political philosophers have used this specific Armenian experience as one of multiple examples to argue that this threat posed by the state to the safety of a community provides one of the most compelling justifications for secession and the creation of an independent country dedicated to its preservation.

Expatriate Armenian organizations have long accused the Turkish government of seeking "to liquidate the Armenian problem through extermination of the Armenian people" between 1915 and 1917.[16] In their defense, Turkish officials and historians have argued that accusations of genocide are ungrounded. Strong government measures were required due to the civil war between the Armenians and Turks. They claim that the entire Armenian community constituted a dangerous security threat due to its sympathies with the Entente powers and

[14] Historical material for this section is drawn largely from Vahakn N. Dadrian, "The Naim–Andonian Documents on the World War I Destruction of the Ottoman Armenians: The Anatomy of Genocide," *International Journal of Middle East Studies*, 17, 3 (August, 1986), 311–360; W. E. D. Allen and Paul Muratoff, *Caucasian Battlefields* (Cambridge: Cambridge University Press, 1953); and David Marshall Lang and Christopher J. Walker, *The Armenians* (London: Minority Rights Group, 1980).
[15] For a brief introduction of the main issues regarding genocide, see Leo Kuper's *International Action Against Genocide* (London: Minority Rights Group, 1982). For a more detailed discussion of genocides arising on the basis of internal division within a society, an assessment of the United Nations' performance in providing protection from genocide and other gross violations of human rights under the Genocide Convention of 1948, and an outline of strategies for the future prevention of genocide, see Leo Kuper, *Genocide* (New Haven: Yale University Press, 1981), and *The Prevention of Genocide* (New Haven, 1985).
[16] Lang and Walker, *The Armenians*, p. 3.

Russia. No conflict is ever unambiguous. There is some truth in Turkish accusations: the Armenians rebelled several times against their Ottoman rulers.[17] Toward the end of the nineteenth century, some Armenians began to form armed revolutionary societies to protect their community from the growing arbitrary violence of Ottoman officials. In their first significant act of defiance, the revolutionary societies organized a rebellion in Susan in 1894. Following its suppression, Ottoman reprisals included a series of massacres in 1894 and 1895. Contemporary observers, including British consuls, estimated that as many as 300,000 Armenians may have perished.[18] Violent clashes between Armenians and Turkish armed forces continued sporadically until World War I.

Despite Turkish denials, it would appear that Turkish authorities attempted to deport and then destroy the entire Armenian population of Asia Minor. Records from 1915 reveal that the Istanbul government first executed without trial thousands of Armenian intellectuals and professionals.[19] The loss of most of its young male population fighting in World War I compounded by the loss of its intellectual leadership impaired the Armenian community's ability to mount effective resistance to subsequent deportations. Those who did not perish during the enforced march to the deserts of northern Syria were executed upon arrival in the Dier ez-Zor prisoner-of-war camp.[20] After careful study of the conflict, military historians W. E. D. Allen and Paul Muratoff have refuted Turkish allegations of a civil war.[21] From the meticulous collection of Turkish documents, historian Vahakn Dadrian provides a compelling argument for official complicity in the Armenian deaths.[22] He bases his argument on the discovery that most Turkish officers in Ottoman Syria received two sets of orders, one

[17] The three largest of these revolutionary societies were formed by the Armenakans of Van in 1885, the Hunchaks in 1887, and the Dashnaks in 1890. For their history, see Louis Nalbandian, *The Armenian Revolutionary Movement* (Los Angeles: University of California Press, 1963).
[18] See generally, Sir Robert Graves, *Storm Centers of the Near East: Personal Memories, 1879–1919* (London, 1933); Viscount James Bryce, *Transcaucasus and the Ararat* (London: 1896); and A. J. B. Toynbee, "The Extermination of the Armenians," *The Times History of the War*, vol. VIII (London: 1916).
[19] Lang and Walker, *Armenians*, p. 6.
[20] Ibid., p. 7.
[21] W. E. D. Allen and Paul Muratoff, *Caucasian Battlefields* (Cambridge: Cambridge University Press, 1953).
[22] Vahakn N. Dadrian, "The Naim–Andonian Documents on the World War I Destruction of the Ottoman Armenians: The Anatomy of Genocide," *International Journal of Middle East Studies*, 17, 3 (August, 1986), 311–360.

open and one secret. The secret orders authorized the murder of Armenians in the camps. The mobilization of massive resources and the systematic implementation of orders implies that these actions resulted from policy decisions taken at the highest level of government and were not just a matter of "isolated incidents." This episode was neither civil war nor a cumulation of incidents, but rather the use of wartime conditions for the state's massive assault on a minority community.

Estimates of Armenian deaths vary. In a speech to the House of Lords on October 6, 1915, Viscount James Bryce, a historian of the region, placed the figure then "around 800,000."[23] Since the massacres continued in 1916 and 1917, Bryce has surely underestimated the number of deaths. Before 1914, Ottoman authorities had estimated their Armenian population at around 2 million out of a total world Armenian population of 4.5 million. Since World War I this figure has not exceeded 100,000. Given that approximately half a million Armenians sought refuge outside Turkey, historians estimate that about 1.5 million perished as a consequence of the Turkish actions.[24]

In summary, it may be worthwhile to tie together the main propositions thus far concerning the costs of membership. One can but react in horror to the capacity of governing elites to mobilize state resources to threaten their fellow citizens. Such ill-treatment is less likely, although still possible, when governments are in some way directly accountable to their citizens. None the less, it is the individuals and their communities who bear the enormous costs when the protection of human life is subordinated to other priorities. In the Soviet and Turkish examples, the superior force and organization of the state overcame each community's initial resistance to repression. Having lost their battle with the state, the members of the Transcaucasus, Ukrainian, Baltic, and Armenian communities suffered untold mental anguish and physical hardships.

Cultural threats to the distinct community

The state may threaten not only lives, but also cultures. Those states attempting cultural homogenization of their populations rarely rely

---

[23] Bryce's speech to the House of Lords is quoted in Lang and Walker, *The Armenians*, p. 8.
[24] Lang and Walker, *Armenians*, p. 12.

on the voluntary transfer of allegiances. Such initiatives invariably emphasize forcible assimilation. Those discriminated against face an unenviable choice of retaining their cultural, linguistic, or religious background and forfeiting any opportunity for economic or social progress or obtaining a chance for upward mobility while sacrificing their cultural heritage. This stark choice has frequently represented the beginning of the obliteration of a unique culture.

By contrast, John Stuart Mill and Henry Sidgwick are but two adherents of the idea that it was both advisable and desirable for smaller and less progressive distinct communities to assimilate into a dominant culture. Mill argued that members of smaller communities might voluntarily choose this route:

> Experience proves that it is possible for one nationality to merge and be absorbed in another: and when it was originally an inferior or more backward portion of the human race, the absorption is greatly to its advantage. Nobody can suppose that it is not more beneficial to a Breton, or a Basque of the French Navarre, to be brought into the current of ideas and feelings of a highly civilized and cultivated people – to be a member of the French nationality, admitted on equal terms to all the privileges of French citizenship, sharing the advantages of French protection, and the dignity and prestige of French power – than to sulk on his own rocks, the half savage relic of past times, revolving in his own little mental orbit, without participation or interest in the general movement of the world. The same remark applies to the Welshman or the Scottish highlander, as members of the British nation.[25]

No doubt many individuals have transferred their loyalties to a culture not of their birth. But Mill overlooks the possibility that even the educated may continue to identify with their "half savage past." If the assimilation of individuals frequently occurs, it is rarely the case that an entire distinct community chooses to forgo its unique cultural inheritance. Despite centuries of integration, continuing Basque, Breton, and Scottish rumblings for greater autonomy show that such "backward" people sometimes reject the privileges associated with assimilation within "a more highly civilized and cultivated people."

---

[25] John Stuart Mill, *Collected Works*, vol. XIX (London, 1963), p. 549. Also see Henry Sidgwick's justification of the German annexation of Alsace-Lorraine after the Franco-Prussian War of 1870, *The Elements of Politics* (London, 1891), pp. 268–287.

"The Last Huron syndrome"

To express the fear of losing one's culture requires a poet's sensitivity. After British forces crushed the 1838 French Canadian rebellion, Francois Xavier Garneau captured the concerns of a people defeated, dispersed, and facing the pressure of assimilation in *Le Dernier Huron*:

> Their names, their eyes, their festivals, their history
> Buried with them forever
> And I remain alone to speak their memorial
> To the people of our day.[26]

The Hurons were a Native American tribe who lived in the Great Lakes region. Their pacifism resulting from their conversion to Christianity by Jesuit priests rendered them defenseless against assaults by other tribes. In a series of attacks, their traditional enemies, the Iroquois, succeeded in massacring nearly every Huron. "The Last Huron Syndrome" came to encapsulate French Canadian fears of cultural extinction.[27] After the suppression of the 1838 rebellion, the British government sent the Earl of Durham to investigate the grievances which provoked the uprising. Durham expected to find "a contest between a government and a people." Instead, he found "two nations warring in the bosom of a single state." In his report he recommended that the only long-term solution would be to anglicise the French community. To this end, Upper and Lower Canada (Ontario and Quebec) were joined into a single province in the 1840 Act of Union. The British colonial administration began implementing a series of assimilationist policies.[28]

The fear of cultural obliteration pervades the consciousness of numerous weak communities, in particular those residing in states which do not value diversity. This type of membership cost therefore includes feelings of loss when one cannot participate fully in one's heritage. The prohibition of folk songs, folklore, and religious worship deprives the community of the very means to build its social bonds.

---

[26] Francois Xavier Garneau's poem is quoted in Ramsey Cook, *Canada, Quebec, and the Uses of Nationalism* (Toronto: McClelland and Stewart, 1986), p. 50.
[27] Ibid., for more detailed discussion of the cultural fears of the French Canadians.
[28] For a description of the political institutions of the United Province of Canada, see William Ormsby, "The Providence of Canada: The Emergence of Consociational Politics," in Kenneth D. McRae (ed.), *Consociational Democracy: Political Accommodation in Segmented Societies* (Toronto: McClelland & Stewart, 1974), pp. 271–279.

Such restrictions prevent communities from teaching future generations about their unique cultural identity.

Many leaders have judged, as Lord Durham did, that their country's strength depends on eliminating competing sources of loyalty. Policies of forced assimilation have naturally varied in tenacity, duration, and repressiveness. During the process of state-building in Europe, rulers employed numerous devices such as the denigration of a subjugated people's culture or religion, linguistic repression, and dilution of their presence in their historic lands. Hugh Seton-Watson chronicles the way in which the tsars and the Hungarian aristocrats used nineteenth-century policies of Russification and Magyarization to eradicate cultural differences within their territories. They outlawed local languages and customs, closed schools, and prohibited traditional worship in the Baltic and Transcaucasus regions and in Slovakia.[29]

What is surprising is that the relics of such policies have lingered in more liberal and democratic Western societies. For example, in a study of regional ethnicity in France, Morvan Lebesque argues that French society consistently stigmatized Breton cultural distinctiveness. Signs on public transportation, in government offices, and on street posters bore the inscription: "No spitting and no Breton."[30]

In other cases, particularly in developing countries, assimilation pressure may also be the consequence of other rivalries. Competition for scarce resources in underdeveloped countries is fierce, thereby provoking commensurate competition for control of the political institutions which allocate those resources. The arbitrary borders of post-colonial states which include many disparate peoples worsen the ethnic nature of such competition. Once one particular group gains a dominant position, its efforts to protect and promote its own interests often cause hardship for other communities. In many cases, opportunities for higher education, employment, and social advancement depend on institutionalized discrimination on the basis of language, religion, or race. Those discriminated against face the unenviable choice of either retaining their cultural identity and suffering subordi-

---

[29] Hugh Seton-Watson, *Nations and States: An Inquiry into the Origins of Nations and the Politics of Nationalism* (Boulder, CO: Westview Press, 1977), pp. 77–87, 163–169.
[30] Morvan Lebesque, *Comment peut-on etre Breton: Essai sur la democratie française* (Paris: Seuil, 1970), quoted in Suzanne Berger, "Bretons, Basques, Scots, and other European Nations," *Journal of Interdisciplinary History,* 3 (1972–1973), p. 170.

nate status or obtaining a chance for social mobility through the loss of their heritage.

Forcible cultural assimilation: the Kurds as "mountain Turks"[31]

Chapter 4 explored the various Turkish, Iraqi, and Iranian initiatives to suppress Kurdish rebellions, demonstrating one set of potential costs of secession. The plight of Kurds in modern Turkey illustrates the cultural costs of membership.

Since its founding until the 1990s, Turkey has systematically attempted to eradicate Kurdish culture. The justice minister in Ataturk's government clearly stated in 1930 the status Kurds could expect in Turkey: "[we] live in a country called Turkey, the freest country in the world ... I believe that the Turk must be the only lord, the only master of this country. Those who are not of pure Turkish stock can have only one right in this country, the right to be servants and slaves."[32] Under the cover of maintaining martial law in Kurdish areas until 1946, the Turkish government implemented legislation, approved in 1924, which outlawed the Kurdish language, names, and all manifestations of Kurdish culture such as folk dress, folk songs, and folklore. The government also closed Kurdish schools, associations, and publications.[33] Significantly, the new constitution adopted in 1982 entrenched the policies seeking to eliminate the Kurdish identity. Under Article 14, Kurdish demands for regional autonomy were made illegal, since they would violate "the indivisible integrity of the State with its territory and nation." In regulating political parties, Article 89 stipulated: "No political party may concern itself with the defense, development, or diffusion of any non-Turkish language or culture; nor may they seek to create minorities within our frontiers or to destroy our national unity."[34]

[31] Historical material for this section is largely drawn from Gerard Chaliand (ed.), *People Without a Country: The Kurds and Kurdistan* (London: Zed Press 1980); David McDowall, *The Kurds* (London: Minority Rights Group, 1985). Legal documents concerning the Kurds are cited in Hurst Hannum, "The Kurds," in *Autonomy, Sovereignty, and Self-Determination: The Accommodation of Conflicting Rights* (Philadelphia: University of Pennsylvania Press, 1990), ch. 9, pp. 178–201.
[32] Quoted by Kendal, "The Kurds under the Ottoman Empire," in Gerard Chaliand (ed.), *People Without a Country* (London: Zed Press, 1980), p. 65.
[33] Relevant articles of the Constitution of Turkey reprinted in Hannum, "The Kurds," pp. 188–190.
[34] Ibid., p 189.

Perhaps most critically, until 1991, Turkey even denied all existence of the Kurdish population by referring to them as "mountain Turks." Yet names, language, and traditions are perceived to retain power as weapons. To deprive a community of its unique names and culture and to refer to its protests as "tribalism" is a subtle attempt to deny legitimacy to its demands.

Before the 1990s, neither the gradual democraticization of domestic Turkish politics, nor the protests of international organizations and foreign governments achieved much success in moderating Turkish discrimination against its Kurdish population. Human rights organizations such as Amnesty International and Helsinki Watch have called attention to Turkey's mistreatment of the Kurds. In its report, the Helsinki Watch Committee forcefully argued that "the consistent policy of the state of Turkey from its inception has been the destruction of the Kurdish culture and the forced assimilation of Kurds into a purely Turkish society."[35] Furthermore, in 1982, the governments of France, Denmark, the Netherlands, Norway, and Sweden filed a complaint with the European Commission of Human Rights in protest against the alleged widespread human rights violations in Turkey. Even the US government, a close military ally of Turkey, in its annual Country Reports acknowledges that:

> the [Turkish] Government remains adamantly opposed to any assertion of a Kurdish ethnic identity and has taken a number of steps to suppress it. Publication of books, newspapers, and any other materials in Kurdish is forbidden, as are books or any other materials in Turkish dealing with Kurdish history, culture, or ethnic identity. Use of the Kurdish language is not permitted for any official purposes, e.g., in the courts, nor is it allowed in certain private situations such as receiving visitors in prison.[36]

The Kurds have therefore faced the unenviable choice of either assimilation into the culture of their oppressors or continuing to live as Kurds in poverty. Unless they relinquish their cultural heritage, Kurds are effectively prohibited from pursuit of educational opportunities, and thus social mobility. Even denial of their ancestry would make them merely tolerated at the fringe of Turkish society. Naturally, such a choice under duress of assimilation for social progress pos-

---

[35] *Destroying Ethnic Identity: the Kurds of Turkey* (New York: US Helsinki Watch Committee, 1988), p. 10.
[36] *Country Reports on Human Rights Practices for 1986*, quoted in Hannum, "The Kurds," p. 189.

sesses its own mental anguish. Consequently, the Kurds living in south-east Turkey have been caught in the vicious and demoralizing cycle of escalating poverty leading to escalating discontent, while protests or appeals to change their situation provoke greater official repression.

In summary, any notion of the progressive adoption of basic human rights to protect life and culture has been limited by the far stronger moral privileging of existing borders as the foundation of international relations. As a consequence, numerous states, developed or underdeveloped, have been able to threaten the physical and cultural well-being of communities within their boundaries, based on ethnic differences. The Soviet Union deserves special recognition for the brutality and efficiency with which it mobilized state resources in the execution of such policies. As Zbigniew Brzezinski once commented, "if under the tsars Russia had been a prison of nations, then under Stalin the Soviet Union came to resemble a graveyard of nations."[37] The experiences of Soviet minorities were at least eventually recorded. The Turkish abuses were also well known. One is left only to imagine the suffering of those peoples fully vanquished, deported, or assimilated, whom the victorious did not even bother to mention in their history books; those who did not possess a poet like Francois Xavier Garneau to transcribe their story.

In both the Soviet Union and Turkey, the ruling elites commanded significant resources to implement their discriminatory policies. The resources of the subjugated communities, by contrast, were limited. Hence, they were unable to mount an effective defense. In the absence of external allies supporting the minority group, the state almost invariably has the advantage in such unequal contests.

A state with unintegrated institutions and lacking in efficient communication and transportation networks, however, cannot pose such mortal or cultural threats to its distinct communities. It is unable to extend its authority over all the territories it claims. Historically, isolation has preserved some cultures. For instance, the Kurds lived for centuries in relative peace under the formal rule of the Ottoman Empire partly due to their privileged position as the warrior class, and partly because their villages were in mountainous regions relatively inaccessible to imperial authorities. The growing integration and modernization of the Turkish state empowered it to threaten the

---

[37] Brzezinski is quoted in Nahaylo and Swoboda, *Soviet Disunion*, p. 353.

lives, livelihoods, and cultural autonomy of Kurds even in the mountains.

Furthermore, within a more integrated heterogeneous state, even in the absence of forcible assimilation or official discrimination, members of smaller communities face significant cultural costs of membership on a daily basis. Walker Connor points out that greater accessibility of different forms of media can erode the essence of a distinct community.[38] The impact of radio, cinema, and especially television, should not be underestimated. Television programs bring the dominant language and culture into every village and home. Continual participation in such entertainment distances children from their parent's traditions and values as effectively, if not more so, as the linguistic requirements for educational or employment opportunities. Significantly, television differs from publishing in its enormous production costs. Many distinct communities can establish newspapers and publishing houses, but could not support a television station. It is revealing that among the primary concerns of both Welsh and Basque nationalists have been demands for central government assistance to broadcast television programs in their own languages.[39]

States have traditionally justified their assimilationist initiatives as the necessary solution for potential internal security threats or for economic progress. They attempt to eliminate the smaller community or gradually decrease its members' feelings of distinctness, thereby prompting a transfer of loyalties to state institutions. The resilience of many threatened minority groups attests to the failure of such policies. Despite the assumptions about the desirability or the inevitability of assimilation, as Antony Alcock declares, "it is the exact opposite which is true. The point about culturally divided societies ... is that *they wish to remain divided* ... Those who see division as a source of conflict overlook that conflict arises because of threats to the factors which make for that division."[40]

Associated with general economic and political progress, there has

[38] Walker Connor, "Nation-Building or Nation-Destroying," *World Politics*, 24, 3 (April 1972), 329.
[39] "Welsh spoken here," *The Economist*, May 16, 1992, p. 30; and "Spain: A Survey," *The Economist*, April 25, 1992, p. 22.
[40] Antony E. Alcock, "The Development of Governmental Attitudes to Cultural Minorities in Western Industrial States," in Antony E. Alcock, Brian K. Taylor, and John M. Welton (eds.), *The Future of Cultural Minorities* (London: Macmillan, 1979), p. 108. Emphasis in original.

been a trend toward greater tolerance in Western societies. As a consequence, some states have begun to emphasize the benefits of diversity. Some governments, like Canada and Switzerland, have even allocated significant official resources to maintain cultural diversity. These trends would reduce the probability that central governments would inflict upon their citizens the costs described in this chapter. Nevertheless, they would not alter the structural dominance of the state with respect to portions of its population. It is the state's dominance which perpetuates the possibility of the costs of membership, and therefore, of continuing conflict.

It is surely understandable that protests occur when groups determine that the government has placed certain objectives above the protection of their lives. Yet participation in a cultural community is also integral to the human experience. The community that one chooses necessarily varies; its manifestations are diffuse, fluid, associated with land or experience. These feelings of shared values and culture – the bonds which maintain the coherence of a community – coalesce when its members perceive themselves embattled. Herein lies the reason why cultural threats are so objectionable. It is still rarely the case that the dominant community abstains from giving primacy to its own interests within the society. The frequent result is that the weaker communities perceive either their safety or their cultural heritage to be in jeopardy. It is therefore not surprising that their members reject the state's priorities or legitimacy. For them, integration represents painful compromise and submission. Conflict and strife often arise because the threatened community can only choose among limited and unpalatable options: assimilation, acceptance of an inferior second-class status, or an active challenge of the state's authority to perpetrate perceived injustices. Demands for redistribution of resources and reform of governing institutions, in particular for greater devolution and autonomy, are one potential remedy of such grievances. Rebellion or social revolution has proved to be a frequent response when reform is denied. Under certain circumstances, secession is another recourse to end long-standing mistreatment.

Secession is a consequence of a shift in, and thus imbalance among, the four costs and benefits of membership and secession. One of the most prevalent causes of secession is the sudden and objectionable rise in the costs of membership. In these instances, because the community regards the state as a direct threat, the decision to secede is one of "last resort." Chapter 7 traces the outbreaks of three secession crises – the Ibos from Nigeria, the Bengalis from Pakistan, and the Southern Sudanese – to the rapid increase in the mortal and cultural costs of membership.

6   The benefits of secession

The benefits of secession are a constant force for the endeavor. They can be understood as benefits either for the elites or for the community in general. For the narrow class of political elites, the material and prestige advantages associated with an independent state are extensive. Secession sometimes represents an acceptable means toward achievement of these advantages. The case of Nigerian politics during the last decade before formal British withdrawal illustrates the point. Furthermore, for the community as a whole, secession can represent the fulfillment of dreams inspired by the principle of national self-determination. Grounded in nineteenth-century notions of popular sovereignty, the doctrine established an intimate connection between the nation and the political organization of a state. It originally proposed that the basis of legitimacy must depend on the people's desires, rather than the ruling monarchs. Although this political ideal remains elusive, it has captured the imagination of numerous subjected communities. As a result, it has made foreign rule not only objectionable, but at times untenable as well. The principle of national self-determination has therefore provided both the catalyst and the justification for demands for territorial adjustments and political change, usually in the form of unification, irredentism, or secession. Returning to our metaphorical scales, in the balance of the costs and benefits associated with the decision to secede, both factors – elite self-interest and popular self-determination – weigh heavily in favor of the attempt.

Elite interests

The questions addressed here are twofold: what are the advantages for elites in controlling their own state institutions? and how does pursuit of those advantages lead to separatist agitation? The main focus is on the challenges facing many post-colonial states, because under conditions of economic dependence, the patterns of elite political competition are more clearly discernible. The long-running domestic confrontations in Nigeria lend credence to John Stuart Mill's pessimistic assertion: "Free institutions are next to impossible in a country made up of different nationalities."[1]

The Nigerian case possesses several important features typical of many post-colonial African and Asian countries, and, therefore, provides a suitable vehicle to investigate the consequences of those common conditions. These features include ethnic division, a dependent colonial economy, a hierarchy with a segregated ethnic dominant class, and nominally democratic institutions. During the experiment of self-government, ferocious political confrontations nearly threatened the country with civil war; hence, the Nigerian experience provides a crystalization of the potentially destabilizing interaction of these four factors. Furthermore, this discussion also serves as preparation for the subsequent analysis of the dynamic of secession in Part III. Chapter 7 returns to the Nigerian example, this time to examine the Biafran secession from 1967 to 1970 – an attempt by the Ibo-dominated Eastern Region to withdraw from Nigeria.[2]

The unit of analysis is no longer the distinct community, but rather its governing elites: the Hausa-Fulani elites of Northern Nigeria, in particular. The internal politics at the time justifies this shift in focus. The narrow elite basis of the ethnic conflict is emphasized by the African scholar, B. J. Dudley:

> references to the Northern People's Congress (NPC), the National Council of Nigeria and Cameroons (NCNC), and the Action Group (AG) ... and so on are not the "total collective," the organizations which these symbols denote but rather to *"leaders* of the NPC, NCNC, etc" ... Thus interpreted, politics in Nigeria ... is not about *alternative policies* but about the *control over men and resources.* It is therefore incorrect to see politics in Nigeria, as in the other states of

[1] John Stuart Mill, *Considerations on Representative Government* (Indianapolis: Library of Liberal Arts Press, 1958), p. 232.
[2] The attempted withdrawal of the Republic of Biafra, the secession of Bangladesh from Pakistan in 1971, and the two instances of secessionist civil war in the Southern Sudan together constitute the case studies upon which rests the argument of how variance in the costs of membership can precipitate secession crises. These arguments constitute the body of Chapter 7.

Africa, as simply "tribalism" – the competition of one "tribe" against the other.[3]

Although political confrontations before independence took on a mass character, they resulted primarily from the actions of ruling ethnic elites. The main objective here therefore is to begin to unravel the interests, fears, and motivations of these traditional elites.

Separatist agitation in Nigeria

Like many colonies created during the nineteenth-century European imperial expansion, Nigeria can only be described as culturally heterogeneous. Although over 200 different ethnic groups inhabit its territory, the main division is among the three largest groups which each constitute a majority in its own region – the Hausa-Fulani in the North, the Yoruba in the West, and the Ibo in the East. Since the British divided the territory into separate administrative units and restricted contact among the different regional populations, the experience of colonialism affected each community differently. For example, under British rule, the Yoruba first, and later the Ibo, benefited directly from educational, professional, and commercial opportunities. By contrast, in the North, the British found willing allies for their system of indirect rule amongst the powerful Fulani emirs. In return, they helped protect this traditional society by restricting the modernizing influences from the South. In Northern society, birth dictated power, wealth, and status. The titled aristocracy – the *sarakuna* – ruled autocratically over the masses – the *talakawa*. Islamic doctrine and the system of clientage reinforced emir authority.[4]

Within six years of gaining independence in 1960, Nigeria suffered a bloody civil war as the federal government attempted to prevent the withdrawal of the Eastern Region. Even before independence, Nigeria's political institutions endured numerous instances of instability.[5] Scholars have proposed a number of theories to explain Nigeria's tendency toward political disintegration. Some argue that ethnic

[3] B. J. Dudley, *Instability and Political Order* (Ibadan: Ibadan University Press, 1973), p. 76. Emphasis in the original.
[4] B. J. Dudley, *Parties and Politics in Northern Nigeria* (London: Frank Cass, 1968), pp. 48, 54.
[5] For example, in 1953 controversy also raged over the future political position of the capital city of Lagos. See Tekena N. Tamuno, "Separatist Agitation in Nigeria Since 1914," *The Journal of Modern African Studies*, 8, 4 (1970), 569.

competition generated by socio-economic modernization caused political tensions.[6] Others indict the contradictions of the Westminster constitutional government imposed upon a rigid tripartite regional system which generated coinciding political and ethnic cleavages.[7] Still others blame the imperfect embrace of democratic principles by a society with little appreciation for "the conventions or rules on which the operation of Western democratic forms [of government] depend."[8] Although each theory provides insights into Nigeria's political crises, this section emphasizes regional traditional leaders and their role in contributing to the debilitating political rivalry. In adopting an elite perspective, the analysis owes a debt to the scholarship of Richard Sklar. From his research into the general experience of post-colonial Africa, Sklar argues that not only should "tribalism ... [be] viewed as a dependent variable rather than a primordial political force," but that ethnic conflict itself is generated specifically "by the new men in power in furtherance of their own special interests."[9]

Elite political competition in Nigeria, as in other countries in Africa, was largely a function of economic underdevelopment. More specifically, the scarcity of investment capital, foreign domination of private companies, and the pervasiveness of the poverty severely restricted economic opportunities. Consequently, the large state sector controlled most scarce resources. After the British began to devolve powers to indigenous government institutions in 1951, personal incomes, social status, and responsibility for the allocation of national wealth became increasingly dependent on access to the emerging state bureaucracy. The critical result was that society's new elite established themselves by wielding political power, not by leading commercial enterprises.

This high concentration of wealth in public institutions, Sklar argues, characterized the economic hierarchy of most developing

---

[6] Robert Melson and Howard Wolpe, "Modernization and the Politics of Communalism: A Theoretical Perspective," in Robert Melson and Howard Wolpe (eds.), *Nigeria: Modernization and the Politics of Communalism* (East Lansing: Michigan State University Press, 1976), pp. 1–42; Crawford Young, *The Politics of Cultural Pluralism* (Madison: University of Wisconsin Press, 1976), pp. 274–326.

[7] James O'Connell, "Political Integration: The Nigerian Case," in Arthur Hazelwood (ed.), *African Integration and Disintegration* (London: Oxford University Press, 1967), pp. 129–184.

[8] John P. Mackintosh, *Nigerian Government and Politics* (Evanston, IL, Northwestern University Press, 1967), pp. 617–618.

[9] Richard L. Sklar, "Political Science and National Integration – A Radical Approach," *The Journal of Modern African Studies*, 5, 1 (1967), 11.

countries: under such conditions, "dominant class formation is a consequence of the exercise of power," and "class relations, at bottom, are determined by relations of power, not production."[10] To illustrate Sklar's point, in Nigeria legislators, ministers, and civil servants could expect to earn from seven to thirty times the wages of a common public or private sector employee, even without considering the housing subsidies or car allowances.[11] Furthermore, government officials could accumulate further wealth through commercial patronage, since they were responsible for distributing export licenses, development projects, and appointments for the boards of public corporations. The reserves of the agricultural marketing boards which were controlled by the regional governments held the largest sources of finance capital. Although these funds were designed to facilitate economic development, they were frequently dispensed to businesses connected to the ruling parties under "criteria defying economic rationality."[12] The Eastern Region Marketing Board was threatened with bankruptcy several times. An official inquiry judged that the bankruptcy of the Western Region Marketing Board in 1962 was essentially a result of political favoritism in the allocation of its finances.[13] In his study of the Nigerian political system under the last years of colonialism, Larry Diamond concludes: "the achievement of this new [elite] status, and the accumulation of material wealth that marked it, came to depend to an extraordinary degree on political office, political connection, and political corruption."[14] The relative lack of economic resources in the private sector meant that, outside of politics, there was no other route toward upward mobility for the ambitious. "The desire to achieve elite status and to accumulate wealth thus motivated a fierce hunger for political power."[15]

The Northern emirs needed to control emerging political institu-

---

[10] Richard L. Sklar, "The Nature of Class Domination in Africa," *The Journal of Modern African Studies*, 17:4 (1979), 536–537.

[11] Richard L. Sklar and C. S. Whitaker, "The Federal Republic of Nigeria," in M. Carter (ed.), *National Unity and Regionalism in Eight African States* (Ithaca: Cornell University Press, 1966), p. 112.

[12] Larry Diamond, "Class, Ethnicity, and the Democratic State: Nigeria, 1950–1966," *Comparative Study of Society and History*, 5 (1983), 465.

[13] G. B. A. Coker, J. O. Kassim, and Akintola Williams, *Report of the Coker Commission of the Inquiry into the Affairs of Certain Statutory Corporations in Western Nigeria* (Lagos, 1962). The findings of the commission are reprinted in Larry Diamond, "Class, Ethnicity, and the Democratic State: Nigeria, 1950–1966," *Comparative Studies of Society and History*, 2 (1983), 465.

[14] Diamond, "Class," p. 462.

[15] Ibid.

tions to protect not only their commercial and clientele interests, but also their prestigious place within their community.[16] Autobiographical accounts reveal that their main fear lay in their potential subjugation by the more politically sophisticated and economically advanced Southerners. This fear surfaced as early as 1914, in the hostile reaction by Northern rulers to Governor-General Lugard's initiative to amalgamate under one colonial government the previously isolated administrative districts. Before 1914, British authorities operated completely separate governments to the east, west, and north of the Niger River.[17] To Ahmadu Bello, born the Sardauna of Sokoto and later to become a prominent Nigerian politician, the policy of amalgamation was no less than "the mistake of 1914". In his autobiography, Ahmadu Bello declared: "Lord Lugard and his Amalgamation were far from popular amongst us at the time. There were agitations in favor of secession; we should set up on our own; we should cease to have anything more to do with the Southern people; we should take our own way."[18] A Nigerian historian, Tekena Tamuno, argues that by "we" and "us" the Sarduana means his fellow emirs, since the *talakawa* had little influence over the politics of the period. Their opposition to unification was relatively successful, as each region still retained a separate secretariat until the 1920s, and its own lieutenant-governor until April 1939. The British in effect allowed the emirs to rule at their own discretion over the Northern population.[19]

The transition to independence fostered closer contacts with prominent Southerners and brought on electoral politics, both of which threatened Fulani dominance. The specific threat came in the form of an alliance between numerous progressive Southern leaders such as Chief Obafemi Awolowo, leader of the Yoruba-dominated political party, Action Group, and radical Northern *talakawa* organizations such as the Northern Elements Progressive Union (NEPU). Both advocated a sweeping reform of Nigeria, and specifically, the replacement of the regional structure with a federation of multiple autonomous states. They intended to dismantle what they perceived to be a feudalistic and unjust social system in the North.[20] No longer able to

[16] Tekena N. Tamuno, "Separatist Agitation in Nigeria Since 1914," *Journal of Modern African Studies*, 8, 4 (1970), 566.
[17] Ibid., p. 566.
[18] Ahmadu Bello, *My Life* (Cambridge: Cambridge University Press, 1962), pp. 133, 135.
[19] "Separatist Agitation," pp. 565–566.
[20] Diamond, "Class," p. 478.

rely on British protection, the Northern aristocracy quickly realised that their survival depended on control of the North's emergent political institutions, and preferably those of the Lagos federal government. In a democratic polity where victory at the ballot box meant control, the emirs allied with the Northern Hausa merchant class to found the Northern People's Congress (NPC). They tried to invoke a sense of regional loyalty amongst a diverse population. Their slogan emphasized: "One North, one people, irrespective of religion, rank, or tribe."[21] In a largely illiterate society suffering ethnic cleavages and poverty, the strongest electoral strategy was to play upon pride and fear. Election campaigns based on ethnic prejudice at times even resorted to far-fetched accusations and suspicions.[22] The NPC was not above the use of propaganda, the commercial privileges of incumbency, and even "ruthless and systematic repression" to secure electoral victories within its region.[23]

Significantly, when ethnic recriminations, mass mobilization, and coercion could no longer protect Fulani emirs from Southern reforming zeal, they contemplated secession to protect their position. In a revealing example, Ahmadu Bello recounts that the consensus during the 1953 constitutional controversy was for "the suggestion of secession from Nigeria, as it then was."[24] More precisely, Bello was describing the "self-government" debate in the colonial parliament in April, 1953. With 50% of the seats, the Northern delegation blocked the Action Group sponsored motion seeking independence for a federal Nigeria by 1956. Northern leaders postponed full independence to give their region time to catch up with the South in terms of education and political experience. The Northern members of parliament therefore voted for a more vague declaration seeking British withdrawal "as soon as practicable."[25] After a series of riots in Lagos

[21] Richard L. Sklar, *Nigerian Political Parties* (Princeton: Princeton University Press, 1963), pp. 338–349.
[22] In the 1959 elections, for example, major party newspapers and political elites accused each other of malicious intentions. The Action Group would supposedly ban the practice of Islam in the North, while the NPC would force it upon the South. The National Council of Nigeria and the Cameroons (NCNC) – an Ibo-dominated political organization with its base in the Eastern region was accused of planning "Ibo-imperialism" for positions in the federal bureaucracy. For an examination of the use of repression and propaganda during this election, see K. W. J. Post, *Nigerian Federal Election of 1959* (London: Oxford University Press, 1963).
[23] Diamond, "Class," p. 462.
[24] Bello, *My Life*, p. 114.
[25] Ibid., p. 118.

and Kano, in a tense emergency joint session of the Northern House of Chiefs and the House of Assembly in May, the Northern elites adopted an eight-point program which established a nearly indepen- dent regional government. This eight-point program restricted the Lagos government to a non-political executive agency which would administer only external defense, foreign affairs, customs, and the West African research institute.[26] Colonial officials invited all Nigerian leaders to London in July for a series of meetings. Under pressure from the British government, the Northern elites relented from their secessionist program and agreed to a federal constitution.[27]

To summarise, Nigeria's underdeveloped economy led to elite ethnic competition in politics and for scarce resources. Political office became the primary means of upward mobility. The 1951 introduction of electoral politics forced the traditional elites to win office to protect their vested interests. Mass mobilization of the electorate along com- munal divisions was the most effective way to do so. Nigeria's tragedy lies in the fact that after independence politics itself came to be viewed through the prism of ethnicity. Without the restraint of colonial rule, the elites of each community rapidly reassessed the benefits of membership in, or secession from, the new state. This process subsequently led to further separatist agitation after British withdrawal.

The economic, social, and political conditions which contributed to the enormous material incentives to dominate the governmental bureaucracy, although discussed here with reference to Nigeria, are in fact common to many post-colonial states. Elites have historically been willing to employ whatever methods necessary – propaganda, coercion, ethnic mobilization – to retain power. The Nigerian case demonstrates the way in which the Fulani aristocracy, once they lost the political initiative, contemplated secession to protect their position within Northern society, and so retain the financial and other advan- tages associated with power.

The principle of national self-determination

This section examines the appeal of self-determination as a force for political mobilization and secession, and hence, as the second category

---

[26] Tamuno, "Separatist Agitation," p. 568.
[27] Ibid., p. 569.

of the benefits of secession. It is commonly held that the principle refers to a people determining their own political destiny. As one authority remarked, "self-determination might mean incorporation into a state, or some measure of autonomy within a state, or a somewhat larger degree of freedom in a federation, commonwealth or union, or it might mean complete independence."[28] The following section has three objectives: first, to present a chronological survey of this principle's origins; second, to describe precisely the nature of the benefits involved so that its popular appeal becomes clear, and thus, differentiate this category from the political ambitions motivating elites; and third, to address some of the numerous reservations with its application. When some statesmen endorsed the principle of self-determination after World War I, they did not anticipate how its original meaning might metamorphosise. It has come to represent the means toward very different ends in different political contexts. Despite its ambiguity, however, the doctrine has established a firm link between a collective entity of people, territory, and legitimate self-government. Its widespread acceptance has made living with multiple levels of political and cultural loyalty increasingly difficult. The rigidity of this idealized connection has provoked many nationalist problems, and so necessitates an inquiry into its origins and influence. In its discussion of individual and group "rights," this inquiry into self-determination explicitly returns to one of the fundamental norms underlying both liberal domestic society and the international community. Although self-determination is somewhat difficult to accommodate within a strict cost/benefit analytical framework, understanding its power to both motivate and legitimate secession is essential to understanding its dynamic.

The origins of the principle

Rooted in the rationalism and universalism of Enlightenment thought was the belief that humanity was constituted by individuals who were, in all relevant senses, equal. The individual was thought to possess natural rights "to life, liberty, and the pursuit of happiness" from which derive certain political rights as well. As the French Revolution expanded the conception of democracy, the people were

---

[28] Clyde Eagleton, "The Excesses of Self-Determination," *Foreign Affairs*, 31, 4 (July 1953), 594.

empowered to decide the form and substance of their government. The ideal of self-determination therefore originally espoused the idea that a state's legitimacy must depend on the desires of the people and not the ruling monarchs. Revolutionary proclamations did not address questions of population size or the potential viability of the people. The French Declaration of Rights of 1795 described this novel conception of popular sovereignty: "Each people is independent and sovereign, whatever the number of individuals who compose it and the extent of the territory it occupies. That sovereignty is inalienable."[29]

During the nineteenth century, the ideal progressed from being concerned with participatory domestic political institutions to the proper structure of the international system. Specifically, it addressed the rights of nations as collective entities. As a consequence, the principle of self-determination became associated with the right of a people, if it did not constitute its own state, to establish one even at the expense of foreign rulers. Alfred Cobban argues, "the logical consequence of the democratization of the idea of the state by the [French] revolutionaries was the theory of national self-determination."[30] Writing in 1861, John Stuart Mill, for example, asserted in his essay *On Representative Government*: "When the sentiment of nationality exists in any force, there is a *prima facie* case for uniting all the members of the nationality under the same government – a government to themselves apart. This is merely saying that the question of government ought to be decided by the governed."[31]

The lack of both a simple definition of the nation and a single route to self-determination hindered the implementation of this novel doctrine. In this early context the "nation" possessed two possible meanings: first, that of a community based on a historic political tradition, like Britain, France, or Switzerland; and second, that of a community based on shared language and cultural attributes, like Germany or Italy. "Determination" assumed both the existence of such a community and more importantly, its ability to govern itself within an independent state. Although Walker Conner has dated the expression "the self-determination of nations" to the 1865 Procla-

---

[29] The Declaration of Rights of 1795 is quoted in Otto Dann and John Dinwiddy (eds.), *Nationalism in the Age of the French Revolution* (London: Hambledon, 1988), p. 34.
[30] Alfred Cobban, *National Self-Determination* (London: Oxford University Press, 1944), p. 5.
[31] John Stuart Mill, *Three Essays* (London: Oxford University Press, 1975), p. 381.

mation on the Polish Question endorsed by the London Conference of the First International,[32] the idea of self-determination gained its first practical political expression in Bismark's and Mazzini's policies. This led to the unification of numerous historic principalities into the powerful German Empire and to the Risorgimento to unify Italy.

Although the imperial ambitions of the Great Powers and the appeal of socialism in the late nineteenth century curtailed its ascendancy, a number of leading Entente statesmen during World War I returned this principle to prominence. President Woodrow Wilson was its most out-spoken and powerful advocate: "Self-determination is not a mere phrase. It is an imperative principle of action which statesmen will henceforth ignore at their peril."[33] For Wilson, as for many liberal thinkers in the West, this principle was a direct corollary of democratic government: the nation-state was regarded as the political expression of the democratic will of the people. Wilson strongly encouraged the Allied governments to recognize this principle officially. In the Allied reply of January, 1917, to President Wilsons's Peace Note, they included a demand for "the liberation of Italians, of Slavs, of Roumanians, and of Czecho-Slovaks from foreign domination" in their war aims, and subsequently, in their propaganda.[34]

Despite Wilson's influence, the decisive factor affecting Allied policy on the issue was, as Alfred Cobban correctly points out, the wartime alliance with tsarist Russia.[35] While the Entente maintained diplomatic links with the tsar, his imperial rule of numerous minorities and his foreign policy objective of pan-Slavism could not be effectively challenged. As a result, no general adoption of the principle was forthcoming. However, Britain, France, and the US always considered these issues because of the multinational character of the Central Powers. Clearly, the potential to exploit the enemy's discontented minorities was an opportunity that the Entente could not neglect. Within a week of the October Revolution, Lenin issued the Declaration of the Rights of the Peoples of Russia whose first principles stated: "(1) The equality and sovereignty of the peoples of

---

[32] Walker Connor, "National-Building or Nation-Destroying," *World Politics*, 24, 3 (April 1972), 331.
[33] Woodrow Wilson's speech of February 11, 1918 is quoted in S. Wambaugh, *Plebecites Since the World War* (Washington, DC: Carnegie Endowment for International Peace, 1933), p. 11.
[34] Cobban, *Self-Determination*, p. 13.
[35] Ibid., pp. 11–12.

Russia; (2) The right of the peoples of Russia to free self-determination including secession and the formation of independent states."[36] The revolution in Russia combined with the appeal of Wilson's Fourteen Points pressured the Allies to take an official stand on the issue. In order to regain the initiative from Russia and the US, the Inter-Allied Parliamentary Commission consisting of government representatives of France, Belgium, Italy, and Britain proclaimed in October, 1918, its acceptance of the principle of nationality and of "the right of people to dispose of their own destiny."[37]

Out of the wreckage of the defeated Ottoman, Hapsburg, and Romanov Empires, many distinct communities founded states which more closely, though imperfectly, followed cultural and linguistic lines. Through its territorial arrangement, the 1919 Versailles Peace Conference recognized national self-determination as the potential organizing principle of international relations. In an attempt to garner international support, the Lithuanians, Latvians, Estonians, Czechs, Finns, and Poles explicitly appealed to the principle of national self-determination. Its prominence predisposed Allied governments to recognize these newly created states in Central and Eastern Europe, although they tempered their support by insisting on treaties to protect ethnic minorities. However, fearing its potentially subversive impact on their empires, the Allies quickly limited its application to the defeated Central Powers. In its first metamorphosis then, the original values of national self-determination had been replaced. The principle initially justified the unification of numerous historic princi-palities into modern Germany and Italy. At the close of World War I, the same principle justified the dismemberment of historic political authorities such as empires into their constituent distinct commu-nities.

What is important here is that Wilson's dictum that "no people must be forced under a sovereignty under which it does not wish to live"[38] captured popular idealism in the immediate post-war era. The principle placed justice for nations at the foundation of international relations. Cobban argues that "world opinion regarded [national self-determination], along with the principles embodied in the League of

---

[36] Bohdan Nahaylo and Victor Swoboda, *Soviet Disunion: A History of the Nationalities Problem in the U.S.S.R.* (New York: Macmillan, 1989), p. 19.
[37] Cobban, *National Self-Determination*, p. 16.
[38] Woodrow Wilson quoted in Lee Buchheit, *Secession: The Legitimacy of Self-Determination* (New Haven: Yale University Press, 1978), p. 63.

Nations, as the moral foundations of the peace."[39] However, the Versailles territorial settlement failed to apply the principle in a systematic fashion. The resulting minority conflicts and border disputes revealed the inherent difficulties with the doctrine and its application. Having noted its powerful historical origins and widespread appeal, the discussion now turns to the advantages which the doctrine's implementation presented for formerly subject communities. These advantages define this second category of the benefits of secession.

The nature of the benefits

In a secession crisis, elite motivations are readily apparent. This second category is more difficult to specify as it rests on the popular political dream that mobilises a willing people to dedicate substantial effort toward the goal of independence. The mobilizing power of the dream is especially important since the material benefits of domi- nating state institutions may be negligible to the average citizen. Michael Walzer outlines three separate benefits associated with national self-determination in general, and secession in particular.[40] First, nations can best guarantee their own safety when they possess the medium of sovereign power. One has only to think of the suffering endured by the Armenians and the Kurds at the hands of foreign rulers described earlier to comprehend the claim that the possession of its own state would better equip a community to protect itself. Second, Walzer asserts that an additional benefit of sovereign state- hood is the opportunity to organize political life according to the community's values and culture. Finally, Walzer declares that nations aspiring to statehood on the first two grounds continue to disturb world peace as long as their aspirations are denied. Kenneth Waltz echoes this third point. He argues that the desirability of self-determi- nation lies in the eventual achievement of the optimal structure of the international system. Waltz asserts that an international system based on nation-states would minimise the incidence of conflict: "If each nationality were a separate nation, then each nation would be satisfied with its lot and wars would forever cease."[41] Policy debates within the

[39] Cobban, *Self-Determination*, p. 44.
[40] Michael Walzer, "The Reform of the International System," in Oyvind Osterud (ed.), *Studies of War and Peace* (Oslo: Norwegian University Press, 1986), pp. 227–239.
[41] Kenneth Waltz, *Man, The State, and War* (New York: Columbia University Press, 1959), p. 143.

British Foreign Office as early as the autumn of 1916 rested on similar concerns of the appropriate foundations for lasting peace. A Memorandum on Territorial Settlements declared:

> It is clear, moreover, that no peace can be satisfactory to this country unless it promises to be durable, and an essential condition of such a peace is that it should give full scope to national aspirations as far as is practicable. The principle of nationality should therefore be one of the governing factors in the consideration of the territorial arrangements after the war.[42]

Consequently, as Peter Calvert notes, the principle of self-determination in its nineteenth-century and twentieth-century manifestations has "given millions a chance of greater dignity in the collective enjoyment of the territories in which they live. We cannot believe that these benefits are completely outweighed by the sad stories of wars, massacres, atrocities, and torture."[43] In such ways, the aspiration for self-determination encapsulates the hopes for safety, cultural integrity, freedom from alien exploitation, and self-government. It represents a confluence of both a powerful catalyst for demands for change and one of the main arguments for the legitimacy of those demands. The last section discloses the way in which developments in the international system have qualified its potency.

The controversy surrounding the principle

Numerous World War I statesmen considered the possibility of such "sad stories." Particularly worrisome was the difficulty of circumscribing this "right," and thus, limiting its application. The fear was that its selective application could inspire the unrealisable aspirations of other communities. Reflecting the preferred policies of the British government, a memorandum of November 1918 from the Foreign Office warned:

> It would clearly be inadvisable to go even the smallest distance in the direction of admitting the claim of American Negroes, or the Southern Irish, or the Flemings, or Catalans, to appeal to an Inter-State Conference over the head of their own government. Yet if a right of appeal is granted to the Macedonians or the German Bohemians, it

---

[42] David Lloyd George, *The Truth about the Peace Treaties* (London, 1938), pp. 31–32.
[43] Peter Calvert, "On Attaining Sovereignty," in Anthony D. Smith (ed.), *Nationalist Movements* (London: Macmillan, 1976), p. 148.

will be difficult to refuse it in the case of other nationalist move-ments.[44]

Perhaps one of the most vocal critics of his president's proposals, the American secretary of state, Robert Lansing, described the principle as "loaded with dynamite."[45] He indicated the danger of raising the expectations of some peoples – such as the Southern Irish, Flemings, and Catalans mentioned in the Foreign Office Memorandum – beyond what the interests of the Great Powers could satisfy. Lansing argued that "considerations of national safety, historic rights, and economic interests" should have priority over the principle of self-determina-tion.[46] Certainly most leaders recognized that the principle could only be applied with regard to prevailing circumstances. Even Wilson, for instance, did not advocate the dismantling of the Austro-Hungarian Empire, believing it necessary to maintain stability in Central Europe.

The subsequent tragedy lies in the fact that while these leaders interpreted self-determination as representing a right circumscribed by other considerations, few explained the principle in such amended terms. Eduard Beneš, president of the Czechoslovak Republic and himself an early advocate of the right of self-determination, admitted: "It was misused and continues to be misused to an incredible degree. Everybody gives it the interpretation that serves his political interests and aims."[47] Having researched the documents of the period, Cobban concludes that, "it is difficult to find any public statement of the right of self-determination which is adequately qualified."[48] In the absence of leaders explaining its limitations, popular opinion accepted the principle at face value as an absolute right. As a result, every group which called itself a nation claimed self-determination as an absolute right and expected its application to further its own interests. As Beneš pointed out, this principle's implementation during the inter-war years was certainly far from perfect. The Versailles territorial settlement precipitated border disputes between the newly estab-lished states of Central and Eastern Europe and suffering among those minorities caught on the wrong side of an international border.

Despite these hardships, the principle of self-determination was not abandoned, but instead found expression in the policies of another

[44] Cobban, *Self-Determination*, p. 19.
[45] Robert Lansing, *The Peace Negotiations: A Personal Narrative* (New York, 1921), p. 97.
[46] Ibid., pp. 100, 103.
[47] Eduard Beneš quoted in Cobban, *Self-Determination*, p. 45.
[48] Cobban, *Self-Determination*, p. 46.

American president. During World War II, Franklin D. Roosevelt prodded the British government to accept self-determination as the future governing principle with respect to its colonies. While Roosevelt's motivations were certainly not devoid of self-interest, the British government ultimately acquiesced to the inclusion of self-determination for colonial peoples in the Atlantic Charter of 1941.[49] Although the British War Cabinet would later dispute the American interpretation of the Atlantic Charter, arguing that it did not concern the British Empire, US Secretary of State Cordell Hull considered that its provisos applied to "all nations and all peoples."[50]

Once the principle migrated beyond Europe, it underwent a profound second metamorphosis. As James Mayall points out, the principle of national self-determination effectively "[extinguished] the concept of empire as an acceptable political form."[51] With the passage of United Nations Resolution 1514, self-determination became the moral and political foundation for demands for decolonization. As the specific right of colonial peoples, the "self" of self-determination was restricted to colonial administrative units, despite their arbitrarily delimited territorial boundaries and despite the fact that many of these units had a greater variety of communities than the Austro-Hungarian Empire ever contended with. As the "self-determination of peoples" gained legal status but became restricted to the specific legacy of European overseas imperialism, it lost its original strength as a positive right. It no longer permitted a community to acquire a state, the borders of which would be coterminous to its own defining parameters and whose government would be subject to popular consent. It became the right to be free from rule by European colonisers. "Ironically, therefore, it is the colonial state under new indigenous management which is the embodiment of self-determination in the Third World. The population within its jurisdiction is formally the 'people' regardless of the substantive differences of tradition, language, religion, or opinion."[52] Self-determination ceased

---

[49] R. Hofstadter, "Franklin Roosevelt: The Patrician as Opportunist," in R. Hofstadter, *The American Political Tradition* (New York: Vintage, 1973), pp. 454–455.

[50] Cordell Hull quoted in A. N. Porter and A. J. Stockwell, *British Imperial Policy and Decolonization: 1938–1964*, vol. I (Cambridge: Cambridge University Press, 1987), p. 29; Hull also quoted in Robert Jackson, *Quasi-States: Sovereignty, International Relations, and The Third World* (Cambridge: Cambridge University Press, 1990), p. 88.

[51] James Mayall, *Nationalism and International Society* (Cambridge: Cambridge University Press, 1990), p. 150.

[52] Jackson, *Quasi-States*, p. 152.

to be a continuing process. Instead, laying the seeds for future ethnic turmoil, self-determination was the right of single populations under colonial rule, often of multiethnic character, to international recognition only once – at the time of their independence.

The controversy surrounding this principle therefore lies in the abyss between the aspirations it generates and the ability of the international system to accommodate those aspirations. On the one hand, with the widespread internalization of the doctrine among subjected peoples, it became both a catalyst for their numerous demands for independence and one of their primary justifications for those demands. On the other hand, the international community, in its efforts to maintain the stability of the system, discloses a hostility to the creation of new states through secession. Thus, self-determination has retained its power as a motivation for secession but lost its influence to legitimize the attempt. Harry Beran succinctly encapsulates the perceived injustice of the current international practice in this area. "In freezing the *status quo*, one generation which exercised its freedom of choice attempts to deprive later generations of the same freedom."[53]

However, despite the best efforts of international community to limit self-determination to specific circumstances and to emphasize the inviolability of existing borders, many communities have come to internalize the principle. In driving for secession, these communities act as if they believe they have a moral right to decide their own political future. The balance of power between the secessionist and the international community, nevertheless, clearly lies with the latter.

Such groups as the Karen, the Tamils, and the Southern Sudanese, although they controlled and administered territories and populations, have not attained the benefits of secession. Their territorial administrations have been denied international recognition, so leaving them to face repression, poverty and hardship in isolation.

In conclusion, given its continuing popular appeal, the principle cannot be relegated to the "scrap-heap of discarded illusions."[54] One can express reservations, as Sir Ivor Jennings has done, about the possibility of ever delineating an acceptable unit of people to whom self-determination is to be allowed: "On the surface it seem[s] reasonable: let the people decide. It [is] in fact ridiculous because the people

---

[53] Harry Beran, "A Liberal Theory of Secession, "*Political Studies,* 32 (1984), 25.
[54] Cobban, *Self-Determination,* p. 45.

cannot decide until somebody decides who the people are."[55] One can also legitimately question the existence of the "right" of national self-determination. But even if international relations academics, legal scholars, and political leaders agreed unanimously that self-determination does not constitute a right, this ideal would retain power as long as it inspired communities which do not presently possess sovereign statehood.

Most communities do not appear troubled by Jennings' reservations; they are able to distinguish their members internally, and thus, choose with whom to share the privilege of self-government. More importantly, if groups have accepted this doctrine's message of the integral connection between the community and legitimate government, have incorporated it into their world view, and then have acted accordingly, the consequences are such that it would appear that such a right existed. In numerous instances, deeply aggrieved people in culturally heterogeneous states have come to believe that they have a right to self-determination. The political elites of heterogeneous states ignore this doctrine's power only at their peril. Even though he was writing over sixty years ago, historian C. A. Macartney's assessment of its power remains appropriate in the present day: "In virtue of it, peoples weak, ignorant, and obscure, whose very existence was denied by their masters, have proved strong enough to send the world's mightiest empires tottering to the ground in order that they should build up their pigmy edifices on their ruins."[56] This principle that electrified popular idealism in 1919 retains power today as its repercussions after decolonization reverberate around the world, pervading the consciousness of numerous subjected communities. Although some peoples do disregard its appeal, its message has empowered numerous other communities in their efforts to change their political circumstances. Though not a sufficient condition on its own, the principle of self-determination has become a constant force for secession and for its legitimization.

Changes in the costs and benefits associated with membership and secession impact secession decisions. Evaluating the influence of a perceived rise in the benefits of secession, however, is difficult. Its effect on the secession dynamic revolves around a community's view of its own future prospects rather than on historical experience. The

---

[55] Ivor Jennings, *The Approach to Self-Government* (Boston: Beacon Press, 1963), p. 56.
[56] C. A. Macartney, *National States and National Minorities* (Oxford: Oxford University Press, 1934), p. 15.

purpose of Chapter 10 is to argue that a gradual but discernible shift in the normative foundation of relations between developed and developing countries has generated an unprecedented increase in the benefits of secession. Developed states have assumed a greater responsibility for ensuring the political and economic viability of fledgeling countries. Although as yet no attempt can be linked directly to the enhancement of such benefits, it has become a further incentive for secession.

III The dynamic of secession

7 "Last resorts": a rise in the costs of membership

What would tip the balance toward secession? On our metaphorical scales, the implicit and explicit restraints on secession – the benefits of membership and the costs of secession – counterbalance the motivations for secession – the costs of membership and the benefits of secession. But secession is change. It is a dynamic phenomenon. It can be thought of as the effect of motion on our metaphorical scales. Reduction in the barriers to secession could precipitate a secession crisis. Similarly, a rise in the forces for secession could also provoke a secession attempt. It is the balance between these costs and benefits that is critical. The next four chapters investigate each of the four possible cost or benefit shifts that can provoke a secession crisis. The purpose of this chapter is to unravel one of the most prevalent causal patterns. It traces outbreaks of secession to an objectionable rise in the costs of membership.

In these instances of rising membership costs, because the community regards the state as a threat, the decision to secede is one of "last resort." Such pressures for secession can be divided into two categories: first, threats to the community's safety, and second, threats to its unique cultural inheritance. A brief investigation of the events before the Nigerian civil war of 1966–1970 and those leading up to the Bengali declaration of independence in March, 1971, reveals how such threats to safety provided the impetus for these two secessions. The massacres of Ibos by their fellow Nigerians in 1966 secured wide support for secession, since many Ibos no longer believed that the Nigerian state could protect their interests. In fact, the Ibos went from being the strongest federalists to supporting secession in a very short period of time due to these suddenly rising costs of membership. Similarly, once the Pakistani army began shooting unarmed Bengali demonstrators, most Bengalis judged that not only could the Pakistani state no longer be trusted to promote their interests, it posed a serious threat to their lives.

State threats to a community's identity through callous policies of assimilation or discrimination can also trigger a secession attempt. An inquiry into the two Sudanese civil wars occurring after 1950 shows that the government's attempt to forcibly spread Islam and the Arabic language into the southern part of the country, thereby denigrating local cultures and faiths, perpetuated the conflict. The primary motivation behind the Southern Sudanese secessions was their judgment that they could no longer protect their languages and religions from the government's Islamic fundamentalism. Confronted by desperate circumstances, the Ibos, Bengalis, and Southern Sudanese chose secession as the only means of survival, even disregarding the likelihood of success. In each of these three cases, a change in the costs of membership provoked the secession crisis.

To analyze the secession dynamic, other potential influences need to be held relatively constant. For example, these three cases share a history of recent European colonialism, and thus, share an imbalance between relatively strong state institutions such as a centralized bureaucracy, police, and army, on the one hand, and precious little experience in the workings of political institutions such as political parties or elected parliaments, on the other. After gaining independence, these three societies fragmented into internecine factions; they no longer shared the common bond of opposing the imperial power. Economic underdevelopment further restricted the provision of essential services. Consequently, in each case, ethnic groups competed fiercely for political power to control limited resources. Significantly, because the elites of one distinct community dominated the central government, these states showed little concern for the needs of other less powerful members of society.[1] Hence, neither the Nigerian, Pakistani, nor Sudanese government attempted to foster a plural society. Clearly a number of other states disrupted by secession crises also fall into this analytical category. The continuing Tamil struggles in Sri Lanka and the Eritrean war for secession from Ethiopia provide two additional examples. The cases included in this chapter start

---

[1] At the time of the secession crises, parties representing the Hausa-Fulani of the North dominated the Nigerian state. West Pakistanis held a paramount position in the former Pakistan. The Northern Sudanese dominated the government in Khartoum.

beyond these contingent conditions; that is, the polarization of power is already clearly demarked.

Mortal threats to the distinct community

The *Declaration of Independence* pointed to the "unbearable tyranny of the state" as both the motivation and the justification for the withdrawal of the thirteen American colonies from the British Empire. Once the state employs coercive powers to threaten directly the safety of a distinct community, normal restraints on secession are no longer of primary concern. The community attempts to secede because the costs of remaining under the established political authority have become unbearably high. For instance, some states have systematically threatened and even killed many of their citizens. The distinct community, in an act of desperation, takes up arms to protect itself through secession. As victims of widespread violence, Ibos and Bengalis quickly concluded that their security was in peril. Nigeria and Pakistan could no longer guarantee their well-being. The massacre of members of their communities by fellow Nigerian citizens or by the Pakistani Army was a decisive factor in the decision of Ibo and Bengali leaders to seek secession.

The republic of Biafra[2]

After six years of independence from British colonial rule, the centrifugal forces of Nigerian politics overcame the centripetal ones with the effect that Nigeria suffered an exceptionally bitter secession crisis from 1967 to 1970. The purpose of this section is two-fold: first, to indicate the reasons behind the Ibo community's initial resistance to Nigeria's potential dissolution, and second, to describe the events which contributed to the Ibos' reversal and subsequent agitation for secession. The insecurity of the Ibo community after the massacres of their fellow countrymen in the North in 1966 and the betrayal of the agreements between the federal and regional governments in 1967

---

[2] Historical material for this section is drawn largely from A. H. M. Kirk-Green, *Crisis and Conflict in Nigeria: A Documentary Source Book, 1966–1970,* 2 vols. (Oxford: Oxford University Press, 1971); Tekena N. Tamuno, "Separatist Agitation in Nigeria Since 1914," *The Journal of Modern African Studies,* 8, 4 (1970), 563–584; Charles R. Nixon, "Self-Determination: The Nigeria/Biafra Case," *World Politics* (July 1972), 473–497; and Frederick Forsyth, *The Making of an African Legend: The Biafra Story* (London: Severn House, 1983).

provoked Biafra's secession from Nigeria. The suddenly rising costs of membership forced Ibos to abandon their formerly strong federalist position in support of secession.

In his model to determine the emergence of separatist movements in underdeveloped countries,[3] David Horowitz concentrates on the interaction between an ethnic group's economic and social position relative to other groups in the country and its relative regional position. Ibo economic achievements directly before and during the years after independence indicate that they were, what Horowitz would describe, a relatively advanced group in social terms residing in a backward region.[4] His model's implications for this type of group are that it would have much at stake in the state's perpetuation. As a consequence, such a group would endure much suffering before overcoming its early reluctance to secede, because secession would require sacrificing the economic and social advantages associated with integration in the existing state. The Ibos benefited from a strong economic position relative to the other two large distinct communities within Nigeria: the Hausa-Fulani in the North and the Yoruba in the West, and consequently, tried to salvage state institutions in 1966. None the less, it was the several instances of sustained violence and perceived betrayal which led the Ibos, Nigeria's "most modern, progressive, nationally-oriented people [to become] the country's tribal insurgents, leading the way to Nigeria's fragmentation."[5]

The heterogeneity of the Nigerian population complicated its politics. Even though there may be some 200 different ethnic groups, depending on the criteria for division, the three largest groups each dominated their respective regions. At the time of the secession crisis, the Hausa-Fulani comprised between 56% and 75% of the population in the North, Yoruba 90% of West, and Ibo 64% of the East.[6] As the discussion in Chapter 6 disclosed, through their overall larger

---

[3] Donald Horowitz, "Patterns of Ethnic Separatism," *Comparative Study of Society and History*, 23, 2 (April 1981), 165–195.
[4] This section focuses its analysis on the motivations and the actions of the Ibo community. In truth, the population of the Eastern Region, although predominantly Ibo, also included numerous smaller communities such as the Ibibio, Etik, Annang, Ijaw, Ogoni, Ekoi, Yalla, and Ukelle. The justification for this simplification lies in the fact that members of these smaller communities also suffered during the pogroms in the North and largely supported the Ibo leadership in its initiative to gain independence.
[5] Paul Anber, "Modernization and Political Disintegration: Nigeria and the Ibos," *Journal of Modern African Studies*, 5 (1967), 165–6.
[6] Alexis Heraclides, "Biafra," in *The Self-Determination of Minorities in International Politics* (London: Frank Cass, 1991), p. 82.

numbers the Hausa-Fulani dominated the federal government, but suffered from lack of social and economic progress. The Yoruba had achieved an enviable level of education and political sophistication under British rule. Before the discovery of oil reserves in the 1960s, the Ibo's Eastern region was by far the poorest of the three in natural resources. For economic advancement, the Ibo community relied on the British school system, resulting in an over-representation in professional occupations. Consequently, at the time of independence in 1960, the Ibos surpassed even the enterprising Yoruba community in terms of economic progress, and had left the feudal Hausa-Fulani far behind.[7]

Reluctant to sacrifice their advantageous position in commerce and civil service, the Ibos consistently avoided suggestions of separatism. By contrast, during the fifty years before the 1966 Biafran secession crisis, Yoruba politicians of the Western Region, Fulani aristocrats of the Northern Region, leaders of the Calabar-Onitsa-Rivers district in the southeast, and the small Tiv community in the Middle Belt, all seriously contemplated secession to alleviate dissatisfaction both with their unification into one large colony and then with the political paralysis and corruption of the Lagos government.[8] Even when Nigeria's disintegration appeared imminent after a series of coups, Ibo leaders continued to put forward federalist proposals in an attempt to maintain the integrity of the state. As the country stumbled from crisis to crisis in the early 1960s,[9] frustration with electoral manipulation and slow economic development engendered cautious support for the military coup of January 1966.[10] Commanding General Aguiyi Ironsi immediately set out to reverse the country's regional fragmentation. On May 24 with Decree No. 34, Ironsi established a unitary form of government. Because Northerners had dominated the federal government since independence, they felt particularly threatened by their loss of privilege and power in Lagos.[11] Since Ironsi was an Ibo, Northern leaders quickly accused his government of usurping

[7] Anber, "Modernisation," pp. 168–170.
[8] Tekena N. Tamuno, "Separatist Agitation in Nigeria Since 1914," *Journal of Modern African Studies*, 8, 4 (1970), 565–577.
[9] These crises include the political rivalry within the Action Group in the Western Region which led to the "state of emergency" in 1962–1963, the disputes surrounding the census also in 1962, the general labor unrest and strikes across the country in 1964, and the allegations of electoral impropriety in 1965. See Kirk-Green, *Crisis and Conflict*.
[10] K. W. J. Post, "The Crisis in Nigeria," *The World Today* (February, 1966), pp. 43–47.
[11] Tamuno, "Separatist Agitations," p. 578.

power for the exclusive pursuit of Ibo interests. Northern leaders responded with a coup in July 1966 and murdered Ironsi and other Ibo officers.[12] Widespread protests in the North following the proclamation of Decree No. 34 degenerated into violent pogroms directed against Ibos and other Easterners, and left many thousands dead.[13]

Significantly, even after this violence, the Ibos made yet one more attempt to maintain a united Nigeria. The new government under Lt. Col. Yakubu Gowon, the chief-of-staff, himself a member of a small minority group from the middlebelt region, convened an *Ad Hoc* Constitutional Conference on September 12, 1966. This conference was meant to resolve multiple grievances and thereby ease the level of tension in the country. During the debate on their country's future political structure, the Northern and Western delegations demanded a loose confederation with a constitutional "right" to secede. The North's original memorandum included: "Rights of Self-Determination: The right of self-determination of all peoples in the country must be accepted ... These rights include the right of any State within the country *to secede*."[14] Likewise, the Western delegation recommended: "Each state should have a right unilaterally *to secede* from the Commonwealth at any time of its own choice."[15] Although the right of secession was dropped by the second set of memoranda presented by Northern and Western representatives, there is no reason to doubt that the concept had considerable support in both regions.[16] Meanwhile the Eastern delegation actually presented the most federalist proposals.[17]

Directly after the inconclusive convention, a second wave of massacres, this time with the apparent complicity of state authorities, devastated Ibo and broader Eastern communities living in Northern cities. A. H. M. Kirk-Greene, a historian of Nigeria, estimates that some 30,000 predominantly Ibo civilians were murdered during the

---

[12] Charles R. Nixon, "Self-Determination: The Nigeria/Biafra Case," *World Politics*, 24, 4 (July 1972), 475.
[13] A. H. M. Kirk-Green, *Genesis of the Nigerian Civil War* (Scandinavian Institute of African Affairs Report No. 27 (1975), p. 21.
[14] "Form of Association for Nigeria. Paper by the Northern Nigeria Delegation," as printed in *The Ad Hoc Conference on the Nigerian Constitution* (Eastern Nigeria, 1966), pp. 3–4. Emphasis added.
[15] "Memorandum by the Western Region and Lagos Delegations to the Ad Hoc Committee on Constitutional Arrangements for Nigeria, 1966," as printed in *The Ad Hoc Conference*, p. 26. Emphasis added.
[16] Nixon, "Self-Determination," p. 478.
[17] Ibid., p. 478.

September-October violence, while more than 2 million refugees fled to the Eastern Region for safety.[18] After the killing of thousands of Ibos in the North in May, the murder of Ibo officers in July, and the even bloodier repetition in September and October, demands for secession became pronounced in the East. The Ibo community rapidly perceived its safety jeopardized. These threats to Ibo lives and property not only went unpunished, but uninvestigated.[19] Although negotiations among the military governors of the four regions continued during January, 1967, in Aburi, Ghana, the Eastern region had already achieved *de facto* independence in October. From that time on, Ibo General Odumegwu Ojukwu, military governor of the Eastern region, slowly appropriated many powers of the federal government to his regional government. He retained all taxes, used Eastern army regiments to secure the borders, and took responsibility for the resettlement of refugees.[20]

The Lagos government's rejection of efforts toward political compromise reinforced secession demands – a dynamic which had already been propelled forward by Ibo fears for their security. The Ibos' sense of betrayal arose from the central government's disavowal of the Aburi Agreement of January, 1967. The agreement had established Nigeria as a loose confederation of regions. One provision virtually guarantied the Eastern region interim independence, since from January, 1967 onwards all new laws anywhere in the country would require unanimous approval by the four military governors.[21] Within four months, however, the central government violated the Aburi Agreement. On May 27, it used a decree to abolish the regions, in effect creating twelve states.[22] This territorial division would have left the Ibo community with a diminished resource base from which to provide for its members. The declaration of independence of the Republic of Biafra on May 30 reveals that this decree became the specific trigger to their decision to secede:

> It became evident that each time Nigerians came close to a realistic solution to the current crisis, Lt. Col. Gowon unilaterally frustrated their efforts ... When in January, 1967, the Military Leaders agreed at Aburi on what the Federal Permanent Secretaries correctly

[18] Kirk-Green, *Genesis of the Nigerian Civil War*, p. 21.
[19] Nixon, "Self-Determination," p. 476.
[20] John J. Stremlau, *The International Politics of the Nigerian Civil War (1967–1970)* (Princeton: Princeton University Press, 1977), p. 39.
[21] Nixon, "Self-Determination," p. 484.
[22] Ibid., pp. 484–487.

> interpreted as confederation, he unilaterally rejected the Agreement to which he had voluntarily subscribed.[23]

The key points concerning the Biafran case can be summarized in the following manner: within an atmosphere of betrayal, disillusionment, and fear generated by the massacres of the previous year, the Ibos perceived the situation within Nigeria to be no longer tolerable. They judged that the costs of membership were rising rapidly. The central government's May decree precluded the accommodation of the Ibo community's interests. Crucially, this decision signaled an end to compromise solutions; the Lagos elites were willing to impose a military solution regardless of potential suffering. Consequently, the Ibo community chose secession as its "last resort" to protect its members from what they perceived as escalating threats to their safety. A bloody civil war ensued.

The Bengali secession[24]

The juxtaposition of the Biafran and Bengali secessions emphasizes their common denominator: a similar pattern of events which convinced both communities that they were the victims of massive violence. Disregarding their initial reluctance, both communities subsequently embarked upon the secessionist path. The crucial difference between these two secession attempts lies in foreign involvement. In the Nigerian civil war, both the federal authorities and the Ibos successfully obtained external assistance.[25] In contrast, the Bengalis received support from India without Pakistan obtaining countervailing foreign assistance. Therefore, we will return to the Bengali case again in Chapter 8 when we investigate how securing foreign allies can prove critical in the successful creation of a secessionist state.

Scrutiny of the Bangladesh example reveals that the Indian government's predisposition to support their struggle, although it may have been a facilitating factor, was not the primary motivation in the

[23] *Proclamation of the Republic of Biafra* (Enugu: Government of Biafra Press, 1967), pp. 5–6.

[24] Historical material for this section is largely drawn from *Bangla Desh Documents*, vols. I and II (Madras: B.N.K. Press, 1972); *Keesing's Contemporary Archives, 1969–1975*; and Richard Sisson and Leo Rose, *War and Secession: Pakistan, India, and the Creation of Bangladesh* (Berkeley: University of California Press, 1990).

[25] For an analysis of the assistance rendered to the Republic of Biafra and Nigerian central government from great powers, developing countries, and non-governmental organizations, see Heraclides, "Biafra," p. 82.

Bengali decision to secede. The purpose here is to investigate that primary motivating variable: how did peaceful demands for political change degenerate into a war of secession? Bengali grievances originally generated widespread protests but were inadequate to generate a secession crisis. A careful examination reveals that the declaration of independence of Bangladesh came only after the Pakistani army had launched a systematic massacre of unarmed Bengali civilians on the night of March 25, 1971.[26] Perceiving their lives to be in danger, many Bengalis took up arms to defend themselves. In effect, the Bengalis drew the same conclusion as the Ibos five years earlier. In both cases, the rapid and objectionable rise in the costs of membership triggered secession as the last resort for protection.

With the British departure from the Indian subcontinent imminent in 1947, Mohammed Ali Jinnah withdrew Muslims from the Hindu-dominated future India and created the state of Pakistan. However, East and West Pakistan were separated by over 1,200 miles of the Indian state and possessed different cultures and economies. Of the total population of 137 million in 1970, the 77 million who lived in the eastern wing were united by a common Bengali language and culture. Meanwhile, the population of the western wing was divided along ethnic and linguistic lines into several distinct communities such as the Punjabis, Sindis, and Baluchs. East and West Pakistan shared several unifying factors: Islam, anti-colonial sentiment, antagonism toward India, and a common history since 1947.

The Awami League served as the dominant political leadership of the Bengali community. Its political platform in 1970, as encapsulated in the Six Point Program, outlines the main sources of growing Bengali dissatisfaction. At their most basic level, Bengali grievances lay predominantly with the growing disparity of wealth between the eastern and western wings. Sheikh Mujibur Rahman, the leader of the Awami League, first introduced potential reforms in his 1966 pamphlet, "The Six Point Formula – Our Right to Live."[27] Designed to remedy these grievances, implementation of the Six Point Program would have empowered Bengali officials to administer their own economy. Of primary concern was the need to halt their community's slide into growing poverty. The central government's Planning Com-

---

[26] The Bangladesh Proclamation of Independence is reprinted in *Bangladesh – The Birth of a Nation* (Madras, 1972), a documentary sourcebook compiled by Nicholas Oldenberg and Philip Oldenberg. Also see *Keesing's Contemporary Archives*, 1971, p. 24567.

[27] For the exact list of the Six Points, see *Bangla Desh Documents*, vol. I, pp. 23–33.

mission's report of 1970 revealed an increasing gap in average income between East and West Pakistan. In 1959–1960, Western per capita income was 32% higher than that in the East.[28] Over the next ten years, the annual growth of West Pakistani income was 6.2%, while that of East Pakistan was only 4.2%. As a result, by 1969–1970, Western per capita income had grown to be 61% higher than that of the East.[29] The Six Point Program therefore recommended an extensive devolution of economic power to East Pakistan. Federal responsibilities would be limited solely to defense and foreign affairs.

By also pressing for their own currency, the Awami League hoped to end what they perceived as discrimination in the allocation of foreign exchange and investment funds which resulted in large capital transfers from East to West Pakistan. Although 56% of the population lived in East Pakistan, a majority of public investment was spent in West Pakistan. The same government report stated that East Pakistan's share of central government development expenditure ranged from a low of 20% during the five year plan of 1950 to 1955 to a high of 36% during the period 1965 to 1970.[30] As for private investment, East Pakistan received roughly 25% of the country's total since independence.[31]

The Six Point Program also recommended that the four provincial governments in West Pakistan and the Dhaka regional government should be able to conclude foreign trade agreements and keep the foreign exchange earned by their industry. This recommendation addressed another specific source of Bengali resentment: their lack of control over resource allocation to imports or investments within their own province. Through its exports of jute, hides and skins, East Pakistan's share of total Pakistani export earnings varied between 50% and 70%, while its share of imports ranged from 25% to 30%.[32] Until 1963, East Pakistan consistently earned significant surpluses on its foreign account. By contrast, the West's foreign trade was in chronic deficit; it had to be financed by using the East's export earnings and virtually all foreign exchange available through foreign aid. This system promoted the interests of Karachi business elites. The largely

---

[28] *Reports of the Advisory Panel for the Fourth Five Year Plan, 1970–1975*, vol. I (Karachi: Planning Commission, Government of Pakistan, 1970), Table 1, p. 2.
[29] Ibid.
[30] Ibid., Table 2, p. 6.
[31] Ibid.
[32] *Bangla Desh Documents*, vol. I p. 12.

inefficient industries in the West prospered by selling to the market in the East held captive by high tariffs. Over 49% of all "exports" of West Pakistan were sold in the East; in 1969 the West sold 50% more to the East than it bought from the East.[33]

One cannot but agree with historian S. Choudhury's characterization of economic relations between the two wings of Pakistan as disclosing "an unmistakable pattern of colonial exploitation."[34] The Six Points program was designed to halt the net transfer of resources from East to West Pakistan, which a panel of advisors for the central government's Planning Commission calculated to be, over the period from 1948 to 1969, between $2.6 and $3.0 billion.[35] What is significant for the purposes of the argument, however, is the fact that despite enduring discrimination and exploitation, the Bengalis channeled their initial efforts to reform the existing institutions of a unified Pakistan. Their "Six Points" posed a serious challenge to the vested interests of those in power, but they did not threaten the very territorial integrity of the country. The Awami League attempted to achieve the redistribution of domestic power according to democratic principles. The current regime's reluctance to negotiate a settlement did not shake the commitment of the Bengali leadership to peaceful political change. It was only the subsequent rejection of the democratic process by West Pakistan elites and the incidence of mass violence that forced the Bengalis to abandon such initiatives in favor of secession.

In fact, the Awami League leaders believed that the 1970 elections strengthened their demands that Bengali needs be addressed within the new constitutional arrangements for Pakistan. The genuine popularity of the Awami League turned these elections into a virtual referendum on the Six Point Program. Capturing almost 75% of the vote in East Pakistan, the Awami League won all but two of the province's total seats in the National Assembly.[36] Because East Pakistan had a majority of the population, the election results gave the Awami League an outright majority in the National Assembly, although not the two-thirds majority needed to approve constitutional amendments. Since the Assembly's first responsibility was to draft a

---

[33] Ibid., p. 12.
[34] S. Choudhury, *The Genesis of Bangladesh: A Study in International Legal Norms and Permissive Conscience* (Dhaka, 1972), p. 11.
[35] *Reports of the Advisory Panel*, Appendix 3.
[36] *Bangla Desh Documents*, vol. I, p. 13.

new constitution, Sheikh Mujib's optimism seemed justified. Expecting to assume power at the centre commensurate with the Bengalis' greater numbers, he claimed in the Karachi newspaper *Dawn*, on December 20, 1970, that "there can be no constitution except one which is based on the Six Point Program."[37]

Bengali confidence encountered West Pakistani intransigence. The military establishment and West Pakistani politicians formed an informal alliance to oppose those demands. Neither the head of the West Pakistani dominated army, General Yahya, nor the main West Pakistani politician and leader of the Pakistani People's Party (PPP), Zulfiqar Ali Bhutto, could condone a new administration dominated by Bengalis. Motivated by a combination of political ambition and the need to protect vested interests, Yahya and Bhutto together attempted to sabotage the redistribution of power.[38] The central government, the army, and the PPP collaborated first in trying to stall indefinitely the process of returning the country to democracy, then in interfering with the redistribution of political power according to the 1970 election results, and, finally, in trying to intimidate the Bengali community.

Despite such fierce opposition, Awami League leaders did not waiver in their firm commitment to a negotiated solution within the existing borders of Pakistan. A thorough investigation of Sheikh Mujib's and other Awami League leaders' campaign and post-election speeches, and of articles in the main Pakistani newspapers and magazines reveals neither secessionist threats nor desires for Bengali independence. In fact, Sheikh Mujib, in his pamphlet, "The Six Point Formula", adamantly declared: "[I] sincerely believe that the two wings of Pakistan are really two eyes, two ears, two nostrils, two rows of teeth, two hands, and two legs of the body-politic of Pakistan."[39] Even when the charismatic Mujib resorted to defiant rhetoric, he continued to work for reform of the established state. His protest plans revolved around starting a mass, non-cooperation movement, or *hartal*, within the tradition begun by Mahatma Gandhi on the subcontinent.

Because President Yahya subsequently justified his order to crack

[37] Sheikh Mujibur Rahman, *Bangladesh, My Bangladesh* (Dhaka, 1972), pp. 26–27.
[38] For more detailed study of the interplay of vested interests and Yahya's and Bhutto's personal ambitions, see *Bangla Desh Documents*, vols. I and II; and Sisson and Rose, *War and Secession*.
[39] *Bangla Desh Documents*, vol. I, p. 32.

down on Awami League supporters in his nation-wide broadcast on a breakdown in negotiations, it has become widely believed outside Pakistan that his actions resulted from such a breakdown in negotiations in Dhaka prior to March 25, 1971.[40] However, a careful inquiry into the sequence of events reveals that there was no deadlock in negotiations. In fact, there had apparently been much progress. Both sides agreed on how power should be transferred to elected officials in the short interim period before the convening of the National Assembly. M. M. Ahmed and Rehman Sobhan, two advisers intimately involved in the negotiations, agreed that the two sides had reached a compromise on all substantive points by March 25.[41] Both men expected to be called to a final session to formulate a joint draft of the Presidential Proclamation needed for the official transfer of power. Awami League representatives pronounced themselves satisfied with the result on March 25, characterizing it as the basis of an agreement on the long-term structure of the state.[42]

The optimism of the Awami League regarding a peaceful transfer of power, and the actual timing of the declaration of independence indicate that it was the Pakistani army's violent attack on Bengali civilians which provoked the secession crisis. Most likely in an attempt to negate both the negotiated compromises and the popular electoral verdict for future government, the central government ordered the attack. Bhutto's extreme antipathy to living under a Bengali-dominated administration as well as his complicity in the affair are revealed by his exclamation when hearing of the Pakistani army's attack on unarmed Awami League supporters on March 25, 1971: "Thank God! Our country is saved."[43]

It was only after the Pakistani army launched its surprise assault in Dhaka and other cities in East Pakistan that Sheikh Mujib gave his approval for the declaration of independence.[44] Under the command of General Tikka Khan, the attack began at Dhaka University and spread to the business and residential districts the following morning; it was followed by mass arrests of Awami League leaders and supporters, including Sheikh Mujib.[45] Given the Pakistani Army's

[40] *Keesing's*, 1971, p. 24568.
[41] Rehman Sobhan, "Negotiating for Bangla Desh: A Participant's View," *South Asian Review*, July, 1971.
[42] *Bangla Desh Documents*, vol. II, p. 20.
[43] Keesing's, 1971, p. 24568.
[44] Rahman, *Bangladesh*, p. 124.
[45] Ibid.

direct threat to their lives and livelihoods, many Bengalis took up arms to fight for independence. Once again a bloody civil war ensued.

In an attempt to garner support from the international community in general and from specific foreign governments in particular, Bengali leaders justified their secession with allegations of genocidal practices by the army. In a critical confluence, the attack by the army provided both the direct motivation for secession and its subsequent moral legitimation. Tajuddin Ahmed, prime minister of Bangladesh's government-in-exile, described the end of a unified Pakistan thus: "General Yahya ... unleashed the Pakistani Army with open license to commit genocide on all Bengalis. Pakistan is now dead and buried under the mountain of corpses. The hundreds and thousands of people murdered by the army in Bangladesh will act as an impenetrable barrier between West Pakistan and the people of Bangladesh."[46] External observers have substantiated the accusations of genocide. The International Commission of Jurists, in their study of events in East Pakistan in 1971, reached the conclusion that the Pakistani Army's violation of human rights was "on a scale which was difficult to comprehend ... The violation included indiscriminate killings of civilians, torture, rape, and targeted massacres of professionals, skilled labor and intellectuals."[47] On March 26, a clandestine radio broadcast declared the independence of the sovereign People's Republic of Bangladesh.[48] The motivation and justification of the Bengali decision to secede lay in the violence perpetrated by the Pakistani Army.

To conclude this section, the comparison of these two cases helps crystalize their subtle differences. The Ibos largely benefited from their integration in Nigeria because of the educational and economic opportunities that the larger country had to offer. By contrast, the pattern of relations between the two regions of Pakistan revealed official discrimination against Bengali interests. Yet, both distinct communities exhibited reluctance to press separatist proposals that might threaten the territorial integrity of their respective states. Before 1966, the representatives of Nigeria's Eastern Region tabled the strongest federalist proposals. The Bengalis dedicated many years of

---

[46] Tajuddin Ahmed quoted in Oldenberg, *Bangladesh – The Birth of a Nation* (Madras, 1972), p. 83.
[47] *The Events in East Pakistan, 1971* (Geneva: Secretariat of the International Commission of Jurists, 1972),pp. 22–23, 26–27.
[48] *Keesing's*, 1971, p. 24567.

effort to have their grievances redressed within Pakistan. The critical point here is that, even though the last hope of negotiations was dashed by ruling elites in Lagos and Islamabad, all earlier considerations paled once these communities were confronted by mass violence. In both cases, Ibos and Bengalis feared becoming the victims of mass violence, whether condoned by or actually perpetrated by the state. The escalation of these fears for their own security contributed directly to the Ibo and Bengali decisions to take up arms in an attempt to secede.

Cultural threats to the distinct community

The costs of membership manifest themselves in two forms. The first part of this chapter focused on how an increase in the mortal costs of membership can trigger a secession crisis. The second part focuses on how a rise in cultural costs, in the form of threats to religion, language, and culture, can provoke a similar response. Confronted with threats of forcible assimilation and cultural repression, subordinate communities face an unenviable choice of three options: first, assimilation into the dominant culture; second, acceptance of official discrimination and second-class status within the society; or third, opposition to the government's imposition of such policies. The examples cited here show that resistance to cultural, religious or linguistic threats can escalate into secessionist agitation, even when there may be no mortal threat.

Even the fear of such an impending deterioration can prompt secession as a response. Fears that the state could begin to threaten its unique traditional values can lead a community to attempt secession to pre-empt such a potential loss. In 1860, the election of Abraham Lincoln, as the candidate of the Northern anti-slavery Republican Party, to the presidency of the United States was sufficient grounds for eleven Southern states to secede from the Union. The South feared that the moral impetus behind the new administration would threaten its distinct culture – its way of life and institutions which depended on slave labor. South Carolina seceded even though prior to its secession no laws that might restrict the Southern way of life had ever been enacted by the federal government, passed by Congress, or even proposed by the president. The white community of South Carolina perceived that there was no alternative to secession because remaining within the United States would imply the inevitable erosion of its interests and way of life.

Such historical experiences have resonances in contemporary conflicts. In the years directly after Sri Lankan independence, the Sinhala-dominated central government ignored Tamil demands for recognition of their unique language and religion.[49] Tamil leaders have long protested against the Sri Lankan government's espousal of Buddhism as the official state religion, as it is anathema to the predominantly Hindu Tamils. The government's blatant discrimination in educational and civil service employment opportunities in favor of the majority Sinhalese community, specifically with the "Sinhala Only" language legislation and the "standardization" of university admissions, further alienated the Tamil community. In the Indo-Lanka Accord of 1987, the Sri Lankan government made concessions on many of these Tamil grievances. Pressure from extremist groups and the escalating cycle of communal violence have prevented their implementation.[50] In the future the Accord may still provide the basis for a settlement on the island, although it is premature to judge whether it will prove a sufficiently powerful instrument to convince the Tamil community to forgo their secessionist aspirations, renounce their support for the Liberation Tigers of Tamil Eelam, and begin the process of reintegration into Sri Lankan society. The fact that continued violence has bred extremism in both the Tamil and Sinhala communities has made the prospect of peace on the island recede further. The real tragedy is that the Sri Lankan conflict continues despite the fact that younger leaders of both sides can no longer recall the issues which led to the original disputes.

Comparison of these two sketches with the earlier discussion of the Ibos and the Bengalis reveals a remarkable similarity: the denigration of a community's unique identity can provoke a response comparable

[49] For an analysis of contemporary aspects of the Sinhala-Tamil crisis, see *The Indo-Sri Lanka Agreement: An Emerging Consensus, 1987* (Madras: ProTEG Publications, 1988); and a series of articles published in *Asian Survey*, 27–32 (1987–1992). For more historical material, see Virginia Leary, *Ethnic Conflict and Violence in Sri Lanka* (Geneva: International Commission of Jurists, 1981); and Walter Schwarz, *The Tamils of Sri Lanka* (London: Minority Rights Group, 1988).

[50] The main provisions of the Indo-Lanka Accord, were as, follows: (1) It affirmed that Sri Lanka was a multiethnic and multilingual state. Although Sinhalese was the "official" language, Tamil gained the status of being a national language of the state. (2.) It committed the Sri Lankan government to the establishment of a system of provincial councils with devolved powers. (3) It combined the northern and eastern provinces, where most of the Tamils reside, into one administrative unit. As a party to the agreement, India sent a peacekeeping force to the island to disarm the Tamil rebels. For more details, see *The Indo-Lanka Agreement: An Emerging Consensus* (Madras: ProTEG Publications, 1988), pp. 7–74.

to the fear of violence. Ralph Premdas' dictum is in some sense correct: "The forced loss of the values of a nation is the true meaning of being vanquished. It is the moral equivalent of genocide."[51] Secession crises can and do arise from an objectionable rise in the cultural costs of membership.

The Southern Sudanese: religious persecution[52]

The contemporary history of the Southern Sudanese provides a truly unique case study of secession. In the last four decades the Sudan has suffered two temporally separate secession crises. This unparalleled phenomenon allows us to pinpoint both the conditions which twice drove the Southern Sudanese to attempt secession, and crucially, the concessions for which they were willing to relinquish their secessionist aspirations. The primary motivation behind the Southern Sudanese decisions was their judgment as to whether or not they could protect their languages and religions from the central government's forcible spread of Islamic fundamentalism. The distinctive features of this case throw the actual dynamic of secession into relief. It reveals how distinct communities constantly re-evaluate their alternatives. Alterations in circumstances, in particular, changing government attitudes toward diversity and autonomy, can and do influence the decision to secede.

After achieving independence from Britain in 1956, the Northern-dominated central government of Sudan sought to consolidate control over the vast territory under its jurisdiction. Its objective was to reverse the former British policy maintaining a division between North and South. To this end, the central government decreed the universal introduction of Islam and Arabic in 1958. In a highly heterogeneous country, with a majority of the population practicing animist or Christian faiths and unaccustomed to direct rule from

---

[51] Ralph Premdas, "Secessionist Movements in Comparative Perspective," in R. Premdas *et al.* (eds.), *Secessionist Movements in Comparative Perspective* (London: Pinter Press, 1990), p. 15.

[52] Historical material for this section is largely drawn from Dunstan Wai, *The African-Arab Conflict in the Sudan* (London: Holmes and Meier, 1981); Douglas H. Johnson, *The Southern Sudan* (London: Minority Rights Group, 1987); and M. O. Beshir, *Southern Sudan: Background to Conflict* (London: C. Hurst and Co., 1966). Legal documents such as the Addis Ababa Agreement, the Southern Province Regional Self-Government Act, and the Permanent Constitution are quoted from Hurst Hannum, "Sudan," in *Autonomy, Sovereignty, and Self-Determination: The Accommodation of Conflicting Rights* (Philadelphia: University of Pennsylvania Press, 1990), ch. 15, pp. 308–327.

Khartoum, these twin policies generated much hostility. The reasons for both government policies and Southern Sudanese resistance are rooted in colonial history.

Like many states in Africa, Sudan is essentially an arbitrary creation of European colonialism. With its carving out of the Anglo-Egyptian condominium and its annexation of the independent sultanate of Darfur in the south as recently as 1916, the Sudan is a more recent creation than most of its African counterparts.[53] Possessing some 50 ethnic groups which speak 114 languages,[54] Sudan's main cleavage actually lies between the 40% of the population which resides in the North, follows the Islamic faith, and perceives its cultural roots within Arab civilization, and the remaining 60% of the population which lives in the South, belongs to Nilotic and Equatorian peoples, speaks African languages, practices Christianity or animist religions, and whose roots lie in black Africa.[55] Southern Sudanese resentment of Northerners pre-dates their annexation into the Anglo-Egyptian condominium. It originates specifically in the experience of the nineteenth-century Arab slave trade in black Africans.[56]

During their four decades of colonial rule, the British formalized the division between the two Sudanese societies; they ruled each as separate administrative entities. While allowing the development of two strong Islamic brotherhoods, as well as general political sophistication through some participatory government in the North, the British protected the less-developed South from Northern encroachments. For instance, the Arabic language was prohibited in the South, and after 1920 the languages of the six major groups – Dinka, Nuer, Bari, Latuka, Shilluk, and Zande – were actively encouraged in the predominantly Christian missionary schools in the South.[57] In 1922, the British introduced a pass system to restrict Arab movements in the colony. The required special visa for Northerners to travel in the South effectively prohibited most contacts between the two parts of the

---

[53] R. S. O'Fahey and J. L. Spaulding, *Kingdoms of the Sudan* (London: Methuen, 1974), p. 186.
[54] *Sudan Yearbook* (Khartoum: Ministry of Guidance and National Information, 1983).
[55] See generally, P. M. Holt and M. W. Daly, *The History of The Sudan* (London: Weidenfeld and Nicholson, 1979).
[56] Nelson Kasfir, "Peace-Making and Social Cleavage in Sudan," in V. Montville (ed.), *Conflict and Peace-Making in Multi-Ethnic Societies* (New York: Lexington Books, 1990), pp. 363–387.
[57] Charles Gourdon, "Instability and the State: Sudan," in Caroline Thomas and Paikiasotby Saravananuttu (eds.), *The State and Instability in the South* (London: Macmillan, 1989), p. 68.

colony.[58] The British also instituted a pluralist legal and judicial system. The *shari'a* was administered to Muslims in personal matters such as marriage and inheritance, while the general territorial legal system was based on British laws and covered most commercial concerns and personal matters for non-Muslims.[59]

Although they protected the Southern community relatively well from Northern encroachment, the British colonial administrators did not carefully consider Southern needs in the preparations for Sudanese independence. In the early 1950s, Southern Sudanese leaders were not even invited to participate in the negotiations for the potential post-colonial merger of Sudan with Egypt. British colonial officials did briefly consider detaching the South from the rest of the colony, but such plans were quickly abandoned due to intense Egyptian and Northern Sudanese pressure.[60] The severe under-representation of the Southern Sudanese in the colonial administration handicapped their ability to protect their interests after independence. In the formation of the post-colonial government in 1953, "the Sudanization Committee," Southerners received only 6 posts from some 800 available senior administrative positions.[61] Thus, Northern leaders dominated the newly independent government and single-mindedly used its machinery to further their Islamic agenda. Both the military government of General Abboud and the later civilian administration under Prime Minister Sadiq-el Mahdi ignored Southern protests. Prime Minister Mahdi clearly stated the character of the new Sudan: "The dominant feature of our nation is an Islamic one and its over-powering expression is Arab, and this nation will not have its entity identified and its prestige and pride preserved except under an Islamic revival."[62] According to Dustan Wai, a historian of the Sudanese civil war, as early as 1956 the North began to pursue a vigorous policy "of cultural integration of the South into the Northern fold through Arabization and Islamicization. Northern values were imposed on Southerners by the use of force, giving the system an internal colonial character."[63]

[58] M. O. Beshir, *Southern Sudan: Background to Conflict* (London: C. Hurst and Co., 1966), p. 51.
[59] Douglas H. Johnson, *The Southern Sudan* (London: Minority Rights Group, 1987), p. 4.
[60] Bona Malwal, *People and Power in Sudan – The Struggle for National Stability* (London: Ithaca Press, 1981), pp. 24–28.
[61] Kasfir, "Peacemaking and Social Cleavage in Sudan," Montville (ed.), *Conflict and Peace-Making* 369.
[62] Wai, *African-Arab Conflict*, p. 117.
[63] Ibid., p. 85.

What is significant about this case is that the Southern Sudanese leaders, in a pattern similar to secessions of the Ibos and Bengalis, initially sought to redress their community's fears within the framework of a unified Sudanese state. They confronted religious persecution with proposals for domestic reform rather than pressing for Sudan's territorial dismemberment. To illustrate, in the first general elections of 1958, the Southern Federal Party won 40 of the 46 seats allocated to the South in the parliament.[64] The party's widely supported platform certainly posed a serious challenge to existing authorities. The Southern Federal Party demanded a federal structure of government, equal status formally accorded for the English language and Christianity with Arabic and Islam, and a separate army for the South.[65] Nevertheless, these very demands also acknowledged the ultimate sovereignty of Sudan. In fact, Southern Sudanese leaders only began to contemplate secession after the Khartoum government had rejected a series of attempts to protect their community from further Islamicization. Their demands for Southern autonomy were ignored. Subsequently, the election results of 1958 were also ignored. Hostilities finally erupted once the central government attempted to restrict religious freedoms in the South.

The central government began by discouraging the use of indigenous languages and observance of African traditions and religions, and then expelled all Christian missionaries and closed their schools in February 1962. Although only 15% of all Southern Sudanese were Christians, a majority of the first generation of leaders had been educated in Christian schools and were themselves Christians;[66] the government's decree therefore provoked disproportionate indignation and effective resistance. With the army's indiscriminate attacks on protesters in Southern villages in late 1962, sporadic fighting and army mutinies in the South grew into a full civil war.[67] Though the secessionist group, the Anya Nya, suffered internal rivalries due to differences in ethnic loyalties to different leaders, it maintained nominal unity within a loose organizational structure in its struggle from 1958 to 1972. Despite its lack of a clear hierarchy of command, the Anya Nya managed to control large tracts of land in the Southern

[64] Anne M. Lesch, "Rebellion in the Southern Sudan," *University Field Staff Reports*, No. 8 (1985), p. 4.
[65] Ibid., p. 4.
[66] Gourdon, "Instability," p. 68.
[67] Hannum, "Sudan," p. 311.

region. From this base, its political wing called for independence for the South.[68]

The Southern Sudanese rebellion, although motivated by a number of domestic considerations, was in large part a reaction to the cultural threats posed by the inroads of Islam actively enforced by the central government. Southern resistance persisted as long as the Khartoum government was controlled by fundamentalist groups pursuing a purely Islamic vision of the country. The Southern Sudanese judged that a secessionist war was the lesser of two evils, because enduring escalating religious and cultural persecution within Sudan was an unpalatable option. The hostilities did not cease until nearly a decade later when the central authorities formally acknowledged the right of Sudanese citizens to practice Christianity and other religions and to speak English and other indigenous languages. These had been the fundamental demands first of the Southern Federal Party and later the justification provided by the Anya Nya for its struggle.

A combination of several fortuitous events in the late 1960s and early 1970s created an opportunity for negotiations between the Khartoum government and the Southern Sudanese rebels.[69] The product of those negotiations – the Addis Ababa Agreement of 1972 – was given legal status through the enactment of the Southern Province Regional Self-Government Act (SPRA) and through its incorporation into the Permanent Constitution in the following year. These initiatives engendered a period of relative peace. The general demobilization of guerrillas, their reintegration into Sudanese society, and their leaders' heavy participation in the South's regional government indicates a high level of acceptance by the community of the agreement's provisions. The Southern Sudanese still faced numerous economic and political difficulties, but their main efforts to address these difficulties were made within the framework of the Sudanese state.

[68] Ibid., p. 311.
[69] The fortuitous events were threefold: first, after the 1969 coup by Free Officers, the new president, Colonel Jaafar Numeiri proposed that the Sudan become a secular, socialist state, claiming that the Islamic state founded by Northern parties was directly detrimental to the maintenance of the territorial unity of the state. Second, bloody confrontations in 1971 between the army and the Umma Party and Ansar brotherhood temporarily eclipsed the influence and the power of Islamic fundamentalists who had consistently opposed a compromise solution with the South. Third, in 1970 due to his own strong leadership, the rebel leader Joseph Lagu overcame ethnic divisions and personal rivalries to consolidate the disparate guerrilla bands of the Anya Nya into a more centralised organization – the Southern Sudanese Liberation Movement.

The key concessions which contributed to the peace after 1972 were the central government's abandonment of its declared goal of establishing an Islamic state, its designation of English as an official language, and its recognition of the black African communities' contributions to Sudan. The Addis Ababa Agreement and SPRA both extended official recognition to Christianity and other indigenous religions. Although Article 9 of the constitution stipulated that Islamic customs were to remain the primary sources of legislation, it allowed non-Muslims to be governed in their personal matters by their own laws, thereby reinstating the British legacy of legal pluralism.[70] Even though Article 10 of the constitution made Arabic the official language of the entire country, the SPRA designated English as the principle language of the South. Crucially, Part I of the new constitution defined the Democratic Republic of Sudan as being constituted by Arab and African entities, thus recognising Southerners as partners in building the new country. The SPRA provided a special self-governing status to the Southern region created through the amalgamation of the three former provinces of Bahr El Ghazel, Equatoria, and the Upper Nile. The Addis Ababa Agreement's amnesty for Anya Nya guerrillas and their integration into the Sudanese Army led to a general cease-fire. These provisions, in particular those concerning religious tolerance, language rights, and regional self-government, addressed the long-standing grievances of the Southern Sudanese.

Through the creation of an executive and an elected legislature for the Southern region, the SPLA provided the Southern Sudanese with an effective apparatus of self-government to protect and promote their interests.[71] This legislation also provided the region with the necessary fiscal powers to administer its own affairs.[72] The Regional

[70] Relevant articles of the constitution of the Sudan are quoted in Hurst Hannum, *Autonomy, Sovereignty, and Self-Determination: The Accommodation of Conflicting Rights* (Philadelphia: University of Pennsylvania Press, 1990), pp. 317–319.
[71] Prior to a bill's passage in the National Assembly, a majority of the Regional Assembly could request that the national president withdraw it from consideration if it was deemed detrimental to the South's interests. Once the bill had been approved, with a two-thirds majority, the Regional Assembly could request the postponement of its implementation, although the acceptance or denial of both types of requests were left as a matter of presidential discretion.
[72] Article 10 of the SPRA vested in this new Regional Assembly the authority to pass laws for the "preservation of public order, internal security, efficient administration, and the development of the southern region in cultural, economic, and social fields." To these ends, it had the right to legislate on the protection of native customs, and on matters concerning prisons and the penal code, public schools, health care, and land control. Article 6 of the Addis Ababa Agreement was very specific about entrusting the

Assembly successfully employed these safeguards to protect Southerners' interests during the following decade, on matters concerning the development of the South's oil resources and the redrawing of the Southern region's boundaries.[73]

In spite of the subsequent conflict, there are reasons to substantiate the hypothesis that the political structure created by the SPRA could have formed the basis of lasting co-existence of Northerners and Southerners within the same country. The establishment of an effective regional government generated widespread participation among members of the Southern Sudanese community.[74] The Regional Assembly became the focus of political competition between former Southern Sudanese guerrillas and civilian leaders. In an example of the fiercely contested regional elections, in 1974, the first Regional Assembly elected the Southerner Abel Alier as president, in preference to Joseph Lagu, the former rebel leader.[75] As the central government's chief negotiator of the Addis Ababa Agreement, Alier had worked for years within the Sudanese civil service. His administration made significant progress in establishing the basic government institutions, to which he appointed many former Anya Nya members. Part of Alier's success lay in his ability to build on the preexisting infrastructure, since the Anya Nya had organized rudimentary local councils, courts, schools, and clinics in the territory under its control.[76]

The potentially destabilizing ethnic rivalries dividing the Southern Sudanese community did not derail the democratic political process. The 1978 elections signaled the smooth constitutional transfer of power from President Alier to his rival, Joseph Lagu.[77] Economic disagreements between the regional and central governments were

South's regional government with the responsibility for its economic development. Article 25 of the SPRA gave the regional government the right to raise taxes, while the National legislature was required to approve funds "in accordance with the requirements of the Region."

[73] Johnson, *Southern Sudan*, pp. 5–6.
[74] The SPRA left the lines of hierarchy and accountability between the regional High Executive Committee and the central government vague. While Article 16 stipulated that the HEC should act on behalf of the national president, Article 20 made the HEC responsible to the Regional Assembly and the regional president. This conflict created an awkward arrangement in which commissioners were accountable to the Regional Assembly while working on matters directly relating to the welfare of Southerners, but were required to report to the central government's ministries in Khartoum.
[75] Johnson, *Southern Sudan*, p. 5.
[76] Ibid., p. 5.
[77] Ibid., p. 6.

also settled through domestic political channels. During the 1970s with its special regional status, the South overcame official intransigence to protect its interests regarding irrigation, infrastructure projects, refugee resettlement, finance of government expenditures, and natural resource development.[78] Moreover, Southern Sudanese politics evolved to become more accommodating of different ethnic insecurities. After the 1982 elections, the Regional Assembly divided the three main offices among the three main rival groups, with James Tempura, an Equatorian, as president; Dhol Acuil, a Dinka from Bahr El Ghazel as vice-president; and Matthew Obur, a Shilluk from the Upper Nile, as speaker of the Assembly.[79] However, the Khartoum government intervened by arresting Acuil and Obur in 1983 before it became clear whether such a grand coalition of diverse interests could have provided effective government. Although various Southern accusations of economic neglect contributed to the suspicion with which Southern leaders viewed the central government's policies, in and of itself this discontent was insufficient to generate a secession crisis. Southerners remained convinced that their regional government remained the best alternative for improving their livelihood.

The main cause of the second civil war therefore lay in the North's explicit reinstitution of Islam as the governing principle of the country. President Numeiri, after slowly appropriating near dictatorial powers in the late 1970s,[80] still could not balance the contradictory pressures for greater regional autonomy by the Southerners with the agitation for the *sharia* by powerful Islamic groups in the North. To gain the support of influential religious groups, and thereby save his unstable regime, Numeiri was gradually forced to sacrifice the South's interests.[81] Islamic fundamentalists opposed the Addis Ababa Agree-

---

[78] For discussion of disputes over regional budget financing, the Joint Egyptian–Sudanese Jonglei Canal project, the transfer of the Bentin oil fields from South to North, and the location of the country's first oil refinery, see Lesch, "Rebellion in the Southern Sudan"; and Johnson, *Southern Sudan*.

[79] Johnson, *Southern Sudan*, p. 6.

[80] Mohammad Beshir Hamid, "Confrontation and Reconciliation within an African Context: The Case of Sudan," *Third World Quarterly*, 5 (April 1983), 320–329.

[81] Numeiri's incremental betrayal of the Addis Ababa Agreement, which he had played an instrumental role in negotiating, must be understood in terms of Khartoum politics. In the Sudan, changes in the central government are effected mainly by the minority urban population, leaving the majority in rural areas with little say in politics. For Numeiri, who suffered and survived coup attempts in 1971, 1975, and 1976, the retention of power increasingly became a matter of life and death. As he distanced himself in the late 1970s from his former allies in the armed forces and among the socialists, he developed closer relations with Islamic fundamentalist groups. These

ment in principle, since their oft-stated goal was the creation of an Islamic Republic. As the new powerbrokers, these groups demanded religious concessions. By satisfying the religious groups with his incremental rejection of critical elements of the Addis Abba Accord, Numeiri alienated Southerners. In the late summer of 1983, he announced that Sudan would once again become an Islamic state.[82] Southerners objected fiercely.

Particularly objectionable to the Southerners was a series of presidential decrees later known as the September Laws, in which Numeiri made the *sharia* the foundation of Sudanese law.[83] The new codes of penal law, civil procedure, and commercial law were based on Islamic jurisprudence, as demanded by the Muslim Brotherhood, and were to apply equally to both Muslims and non-Muslims alike. Special courts were established to hear cases in which people were accused of impeding the enforcement of the *sharia*. Expecting resistance to these new decrees, the Khartoum government sent the army into the South to enforce the September Laws. With this troop deployment, the central government ended its conciliatory policy of having former Anya Nya soldiers guarding the South. Khartoum's intervention culminated in the redivision of the South into its previous three provinces without prior consultation with the Regional Assembly.[84]

The promulgation of the *sharia* and its enforcement in the South by the army threatened the social bonds which maintained the Southern community's coherence. Such central government decisions and actions raised the potential cultural costs of membership for Southerners in Sudan. As a consequence, they engendered much hostility in the South, contributed to the mass desertion of Southern soldiers and civil servants, and led to the re-emergence of violent protests. In the end, religious and cultural intolerance by Islamic fundamentalist leaders in Khartoum precipitated the second secessionist war in late 1983.

relations were cemented by the "National Reconciliation" of 1977 in which Numeiri made an informal alliance with such conservative Muslim groups as Hassan al-Turabi's Muslim Brotherhood, and Sadiq al-Mahdi's Ansar, the very movement he had bloodily suppressed six years earlier. See Johnson, *Southern Sudan*, p. 6.
[82] *The Return to Democracy in Sudan* (Geneva: International Commission of Jurists, 1986), pp. 38–39.
[83] Marina Ottaway, "Post-Numeiri Sudan: One Year On," *Third World Quarterly*, 9 (1987), 891, 893.
[84] Johnson, *Southern Sudan*, p. 9.

To summarize, the Addis Ababa Agreement and the SPRA were imperfect legal documents, but they contributed directly to peace in the South. Southerners could practice Christianity and other animist religions and speak English and other indigenous languages without fear of persecution. Southerners also used the wide latitude granted to their regional government to promote their own economic interests. The Regional Assembly became the new focus of loyalty and aspiration for the community. Nevertheless, given the pressure of Islamic fundamentalism in the North, and given the wide powers wielded by President Numeiri, it was perhaps inevitable that the authoritarian central government would eventually perceive the secular, democratic, autonomous regional government as a threat and that it would seek to control its junior regional partner. With the abrupt end in 1983 of official accommodation of diverse interests, the patterns of Sudanese politics returned to their original forms. Full citizenship once again depended upon an individual holding Islamic beliefs. Northern Muslim campaigns for the expansion of Islam into non-Muslim areas in the South provoked Southern resistance and the fierce civil war which plunged Sudan into chaos again.

By way of a conclusion, an understanding of both the nature of ethnic demands and the types of central government reactions is critical to understanding the bitterness of these three secession crises. First, using the helpful distinction suggested by Ralph Premdas in his comparative study of Asian secessions, ethnic demands can be separated into those concerning either "primordial" factors or "secondary" ones.[85] Demands arising from primordial factors refer "to those cleavages in a society that are deep and serve the very identity of a group. Primordial variables are usually part fact and part myth ... [and] include language, religion, race, values or culture."[86] Such demands are usually stated in absolute terms, making it difficult to reach a compromise. A language either is or is not recognized as an official tongue of the country. The state either does or does not institutionalize a particular religion. Two confrontations arising from primordial claims include Southern Sudanese demands for formal equality of Christianity and animist religions against Northern Sudanese intentions of establishing an Islamic Republic, and Tamil

[85] Ralph Premdas, "Secessionist Movements in Comparative Perspective," in R. Premdas *et al.* (eds.), *Secessionist Movements in Comparative Perspective* (London: Printer Press, 1990), pp. 12–31.
[86] Ibid., p. 22.

demands for a secular state against the deeply ingrained Sinhalese mission to protect Buddhism. As these demands touch upon the characteristics which form the basis of the distinct community, they become nearly non-negotiable.

Premdas also describes the secondary factors which can fuel distinct community discontent. "Secondary factors can be equally fabricated as well as primordial ones ... [and] include neglect, exploitation, domination and internal colonialism, repression and discrimination."[87] This type of complaint, although also very sensitive, could provide the basis of compromise, as long as leaders of both sides enter negotiations in good faith. Bengali demands for greater economic autonomy for their region within Pakistan, as encapsulated by the Awami League's Six Point Program, did initially lend themselves to negotiation after the 1970 elections.

Second, reconciliation rests not only on the nature of ethnic demands, but also on the type of reaction they generate amongst those in power. Through his study of ethnic conflict, mainly in the developing world, Donald Horowitz argues that such demands can be divided into those which are made at the expense of the central government and those which are at the direct expense of another distinct community, giving them a mutually exclusive character.[88] In the first case, society rests on the profusion of communities. This profusion prevents the formation of fixed patterns of ethnic rivalry, thereby enabling the central government to intervene in ethnic conflicts as a reasonably neutral arbiter. The central government's flexibility then permits it to accommodate demands from one distinct community without harming the interests of others. The Indian government helped resolve the Naga secession crisis by accommodating their grievances by creating an autonomous Nagaland within the Union, without directly encroaching upon the interests of other communities living in the subcontinent.

In the second case, society revolves around a small number of distinct communities. Rapid economic growth can at times accommodate the growing expectations of these different groups. However, in the absence of a rapidly expanding economy, the economic and political demands of one community, therefore, are often met at the expense of another community's interests. In the resulting intense

[87] Ibid.
[88] Donald Horowitz, "Three Dimensions of Ethnic Politics, *World Politics*, 23 (January 1971), 232–244.

competition for scarce resources, members of each community measure their social attainments against those of the other groups. Such a description fits closely the Bengali–Pakistani rivalry for political power and the zero-sum game nature of the Tamil–Sinhalese conflict. Compromise proves increasingly difficult as separatist pressures mount.

Premdas' and Horowitz's insights help explain the potential sources of a distinct community's underlying discontent with its current political situation and the government's potential response to ethnic protest. However, what is important to remember here is that discontent, although one of the necessary elements for a secession crisis, is on its own not sufficient to motivate a decision to secede. Furthermore, strong forces serve to maintain the integrity of the state. Beyond the specific benefits of membership and the costs of secession, as captured within the analytical framework, one should not underestimate the always present less tangible restraints on secession in the form of convenience and force of habit. Harry Beran asserts that people are unlikely to undertake the demanding process of secession on a momentary whim. Tradition and sheer inertia would probably keep a relatively secure distinct community within the established state. The Declaration of Independence eloquently described the reluctance of most communities to break the ties that bind them together. "Prudence, indeed, will dictate that Governments long established should not be changed for light and transient Causes; and accordingly all Experience hath shown, that Mankind are more disposed to suffer, while Evils are sufferable, than to right themselves by abolishing the Forms to which they are accustomed."

Nevertheless, even though people may in fact be "disposed to suffer," certain "Evils" are clearly insufferable. An escalation in the dual threats of mass violence and enforced cultural or religious assimilation fall into this category. In the cases of the Ibo, Bengali, and Southern Sudanese secession crises, those who dominated the state valued neither the lives nor the cultures of these distinct communities. The ruling elites did not respect these communities as equal partners in the construction of their respective countries. These three communities, in return, were unwilling to respect the legitimacy of those elites to continue to rule them. Confronted with escalating threats to their physical or cultural security, they chose to try to withdraw from the state itself.

8 "Opportune moments": a reduction in the costs of secession

Despite numerous restraints on secession, secessionist struggles continue to ravage many countries around the world. The purpose of this chapter is to trace how a reduction in the costs of secession affects the secession dynamic. More specifically, the discontented community is more likely to attempt secession when the perceived likelihood of success has been enhanced; in other words, at an "opportune moment." State opposition and international hostility toward secessions constitute these costs. Although there has not necessarily been a noticeable decrease in international hostility toward secessions in general, effective state opposition in specific cases can be reduced in two ways. Domestically disruptive circumstances such as war, or social upheaval, can curtail the government's effective authority over its territory. External intervention in support of a discontented community can also impede government efforts to suppress a secessionist movement. On our allegorical scales, a secession crisis would arise because the distinct community has experienced a marked reduction of this particular cost.

The weakening of the central government or foreign intervention on behalf of the distinct community have historically provided just such opportune moments for secession attempts. One stark example of how the central government's collapse can precipitate secession crises lies in the Russian revolution. Numerous peripheral communities took advantage of this opportune moment to secede from tsarist Russia. The new Bolshevik government was confronted with a deluge of secessionist activity by at least fifteen distinct communities.

The previous chapter cited the Bengali case to illustrate the way a rapid increase in the perceived costs of membership can generate a secession crisis. This chapter returns to the Bengali case to investigate the significant role foreign allies can play in such crises. The Indian Army's intervention in the Bengali war for secession in 1971 and the Turkish military involvement in Cyprus in 1974 proved instrumental in the creation of Bangladesh and the autonomous authority of Northern Cyprus. The comparison of these two contemporary secession crises which share similar terms of foreign involvement permits a few observations about both the nature of external assistance to secessionist communities and the international community's role in the creation of new states.

Collapse of the central government

If long-standing oppression, exploitation or neglect has bred discontent, the distinct community could use the opportunity provided by the central government's weakness to press for independence, the risk of repression having declined. Much internal turmoil caused by revolutionary activity, war, or natural disaster, can curtail the central government's effective authority within its borders and provide such a window of opportunity for secession. Tibet enjoyed independence from the late nineteenth-century until 1951 due to the decline of the Q'ing Dynasty, the rise of war-lordism, the war against Japan, and the level of general social disorder and national disintegration within China.[1] The spread of revolutionary fervor across Europe in 1848 encouraged the Hungarians to rebel against the Hapsburg Dynasty. When Allied troops soundly defeated the Iraqi Army in the spring of 1991, Kurdish *pashmergas* attempted to capitalize on the Iraqi government's momentary weakness to liberate Kurdish areas in northern Iraq. None the less, the collapse of a central government precipitates the most spectacular consequences leading to secessions. The 1974 overthrow of Emperor Haile Selassie's regime in Ethiopia prompted much secessionist activity on the part of the Oromo, Afar, Somali, Tigrayan, and Eritrean communities. Before 1991, from the sheer scale of the phenomenon, the descent of tsarist Russia into revolution in 1917 precipitated the greatest myriad example of successful and unsuccessful secession attempts.

---

[1] Tibet was nominally, although not formally, independent during this period with the exception of four years, 1907–1911, when it was under direct control from Beijing, through imperial troops dispatched to the region as a result of the Younghusband expedition in 1904. Having consolidated their victory in China, Communist Party leaders sent the People's Liberation Army to occupy Tibet in 1951.

Russia, 1917–1922: a deluge of secession crises[2]

The causes of discontent with the established regime are not necessarily the same as the causes behind the decision to secede. There are certainly cases in which the factors for both are one and the same. To illustrate, the Southern Sudanese secession attempts described in chapter 8 provide one example in which the roots of discontent and the motivations for secession were the same: the escalating threat to the Southerners' religions and cultures posed by expansionist, state-sponsored Islamic fundamentalism. In the case of imperial Russia, by contrast, tsarist policies of repression and forced cultural assimilation during the second half of the nineteenth century generated discontent, while the weakening of the tsar's regime provided the opportune moment and impetus for many peripheral communities to choose secession as the means to alleviate their grievances. This section therefore touches only briefly upon some of the reasons for discontent with tsarist rule. It also only mentions the way that, once the Bolsheviks had successfully reasserted centralized authority, this signified the end of independence aspirations for most rebellious communities in the border regions. The main body of this section focuses on the way in which many communities took advantage of Moscow's weakness to unburden themselves of objectionable rulers, establish their own autonomous administrations, and declare independent republics. The search for independence was in no way limited to those communities which had previously experienced some form of sovereignty. What is fascinating about this case is that among the disparate peoples of the former Russian Empire who shared little in terms of religion, language, culture, or education, the secession dynamic was so pervasive and similar.

Before the turn of the century, many distinct communities had nursed long-standing grievances regarding their treatment by the Russian government. The gradual escalation of cultural repression during tsar Alexander III's reign and, in particular, the prohibition of

[2] Historical material for this section is largely drawn from Bohdan Nahaylo and Victor Swoboda, *Soviet Disunion: A History of the Nationalities Problem in the U.S.S.R.* (New York: Macmillan, 1989); Robert Conquest, *Soviet Nationalities: Policy and Practice* (London: Bodley Head, 1967); Albertas Gerutis (editor, translated from Lithuanian by Algirdas Budreckis), *Lithuania: 700 Years* (New York: Maryland Books, 1969); Bohdan Nahaylo and C. J. Peters, *The Ukrainians and the Georgians* (London: Minority Rights Group, 1980); and David Marshall Lang and Christopher J. Walker, *The Armenians* (London: Minority Rights Group, 1987).

many peripheral languages in the 1860s and 1870s exacerbated these grievances.[3] For example, in 1863 the minister of the interior, Count Vuluyev, banned the publication of all educational and religious books in the Ukrainian language, including those intended for elementary education.[4] This restriction was extended to the Polish and Baltic languages as well. Further, Prince Golitsyn, in his capacity as governor-general of the Caucusus, closed all Armenian primary and secondary schools.[5] Before their declarations of independence in 1917–1918, several distinct communities had already reacted to increasing repression through wide-scale revolts against Russian rule; the Lithuanian and Polish rebellions in 1831, 1863, and 1905 being but a few examples.

Secessionist leaders articulated and justified their aspirations both to their fellow citizens and the outside world in a number of ways. Many pointed either to particularly onerous repression suffered under the tsars or to some historic expression of autonomy, however brief. Further, many tried to organize some democratic manifestation of their community's desire for independence, and thus, legitimate new republics and gain external recognition and support based on the prevailing international excitement and embrace of the Wilsonian principle of national self-determination. The Cossaks, for example, justified their demands for independence by recalling their *hetman* Bohdan Khmelnytsky's historic role in unifying Ukraine in the mid-seventeenth century, before its fateful union with Russia in 1654.[6] Possessing a cherished historic attachment to their sovereignty, the Lithuanians and Poles grounded their claims for independence in 1918 in the Lithuanian-Polish Commonwealth, which ruled vast territories for several centuries before finally disappearing due to its partition among Prussia, Russia, and Austria in 1797.[7] Many other distinct communities which fought for independence, beginning in 1917, however, had previously displayed little or no separatist inclinations.

No matter what the unique moral justifications for each declaration of independence or the different sources of discontent, it was in fact

---

[3] Hugh Seton-Watson, *Nations and States: An Inquiry into the Origins of Nations and the Politics of States* (London: Methuen, 1977), pp. 77–87.
[4] Nahaylo and Peters, *Ukrainians and Georgians*, p. 6.
[5] Lang and Walker, *The Armenians*, p. 6.
[6] Nahaylo and Peters, *Ukrainians and Georgians*, p. 5.
[7] Jakstas, "Lithuania to World War I," in Gerutis, *Lithuania: 700 Years*, pp. 43–122.

the upheaval of World War I and the subsequent Russian civil war which effectively disrupted Moscow's authority over its territories and, thus, provided both the impetus and the opportunity for many communities to achieve meaningful autonomy. Accurate accounts of the time are difficult to obtain, but there seems to have been no fewer than fifteen autonomous authorities functioning during the early 1920s. At first, local organizations, such as the national councils of the Finns, Poles, Lithuanians, Latvians, Estonians, Ukrainians, Georgians, Armenians, Azerbaijanis, Bessarabians, and Cossacks, and the Muslim councils, Kuraltais, of the Bashkiris, Crimean Tatars, Kazakhs, and Turkestans were established to provide rudimentary government.[8] Because the border regions suffered the indiscriminate ravages perpetrated by various armies, whether foreign ones like those of the Germans and Turks, or of the White Russians and Bolsheviks who were engaged in a bloody civil war, these local organizations provided much needed protection and other basic services. As the authority of the Provisional Government in Petrograd evaporated, these national councils appropriated for themselves correspondingly greater powers for trade, communications, the maintenance of law and order, and defense.[9] Into the political vacuum created by the Bolshevik coup strode these national councils declaring their independence.

In a representative example, the Ukrainian Central Council, Rada – created by the All-Ukrainian National Congress in March, 1917 – enjoyed wide-spread support within the Ukrainian community.[10] Though socialist in outlook, the Rada resisted Bolshevik control; when Kievan Bolsheviks attempted to seize power, troops loyal to the Rada defeated them.[11] Even though its original demands in March, 1917, concentrated on winning far-reaching autonomy from the Provisional Government, by November, the Rada proclaimed the independent Ukrainian People's Republic. The Byelorussian Rada followed suit with its own declaration of independence in February, 1918.[12] Polish, Finnish, Lithuanian, Latvian, and Estonian declarations of independence followed in quick succession in early 1918.[13] The Transcauca-

[8] Conquest, *Soviet Nationalities Policy*, p. 25.
[9] Bohdan Nahaylo and Victor Swoboda, "1917 Revolutions: The Empire Breaks Up," in Nahaylo and Swoboda, *Soviet Disunion*, pp. 18–24.
[10] Nahaylo and Peters, *Ukrainians and Georgians*, pp. 6–7.
[11] Ibid., p. 6.
[12] Nahaylo and Swoboda, "1917 Revolutions," in *Soviet Disunion*, pp. 23–24.
[13] For an account of the events in the Baltic during World War I, see Gerutis, *Lithuania*, pp. 135–160.

sian Sejm composed of the national parties of Azerbaijan, Armenia, and Georgia proclaimed the independent Federation of the Transcaucasus in April, 1918. The pressure of internal disputes, however, quickly led to the division of this federation into its constituent units: the independent republics of Azerbaijan, Armenia, and Georgia.[14]

Secessionist fervor was not restricted to the European areas of Russia. With the hopes of one day creating a pan-Islamic political entity, many of Russia's Muslims mobilized their communities in late 1917 for self-government and ultimately for secession. For instance, organized by Alash-Orda (the Kazakh National Party) in December, 1917, the Third All-Kazakh National Congress proclaimed an autonomous Kazakh–Kirghiz state under its own guidance. Simultaneously, the Bashkir Consultative Council, Kuraltais, proclaimed Bashkiri independence.[15] Composed of elected adult male and female Tatars, the Crimean Tatar Kuraltais formed a national government, drafted a constitution, and proclaimed its independence in November, 1917. In December, 1917, northern Caucasian Muslims founded the Alliance of United Mountaineers of the Caucusus and elected Nadzhmuddin as its chief mufti. Nadzhmuddin called for a mass uprising to create a Muslim *shari'at* regime and was able to extend his rule over Chechen and Daghestan territories.[16] Bitter at their complete exclusion from the newly organized soviets in Turkestan, Muslims convened an Extraordinary Congress, which formed a government in Kokand and proclaimed an independent Turkestan in November, 1917.[17]

Most local councils inspired fierce loyalty. By accumulating arms and funds, by organizing resistance to foreign armies, and by successfully soliciting external assistance, some distinct communities successfully established their own states. Once the new Bolshevik government consolidated power in Moscow, it was faced with multiple secession crises. The creation of numerous little states was anathema to both Lenin and Stalin, yet they were confronted with the reality that some national councils could control and defend their territories and would not easily be coaxed into a union with Soviet Russia.[18] Due to the failure of Sovietization and the Red Army's

[14] Nahaylo and Peters, *Ukrainians and Georgians*, p. 16; and Lang and Walker, *The Armenians*, pp. 8–9.
[15] Nahaylo and Swoboda, *Soviet Disunion*, pp. 32–34.
[16] Ibid., p. 36.
[17] Conquest, *Soviet Nationalities Policy*, p. 25.
[18] Nahaylo and Swoboda, "1919: Sovereign Soviet Republics," in *Soviet Disunion*, pp. 15–31.

defeat in some regions, political expediency forced Lenin to grant diplomatic recognition to the areas clearly beyond Soviet influence. In the first such agreement, the Peace of Tartu, Russia officially granted Estonia its independence on February 2, 1920: "Russia unreservedly recognizes the independence and autonomy of the State of Estonia, and renounces voluntarily and for ever all rights of sovereignty possessed by Russia over the Estonian people and territory."[19] Russia signed similar treaties with Lithuania, Latvia, and Georgia quickly thereafter. By 1921 Western powers had extended diplomatic recognition to a few of these newly-created political authorities. The fortunate few became members of the League of Nations and exchanged ambassadors with other established states. The Russian civil war disrupted Moscow's rule over its former territories; as a direct consequence Lithuania, Latvia, Estonia, Poland, Finland, and for a certain time Georgia, were admitted into the international community of states.[20]

By way of a conclusion to this section, it is important to emphasize the limited and specific thrust of the arguments thus far. Numerous discontented communities shared a common belief that Moscow's temporary weakness provided an unparalleled opportunity to escape from the "prison" of tsarist rule.[21] The public pronouncements of Lenin, Stalin, and the Bolshevik party provided further encouragement. Lenin, in particular, argued that nationalist movements among oppressed peoples should be encouraged as a means toward socialist progress. In his *Report on the National Question* in 1917, Stalin supported a "right" to secession: "The oppressed nations forming part of Russia must be allowed the right to decide for themselves whether they wish to remain part of the Russian state or to separate and form an independent state."[22] Nevertheless, once the Bolsheviks gained control of the Kremlin, the pressures of government forced the disavowal of their earlier policies regarding the rights of small communities. Such pressures included the threat of encirclement by newly created states on Russia's borders which were hostile to the

[19] Nahaylo and Swoboda, *Soviet Disunion*, p. 44.
[20] Lithuania's admission to the League of Nations was delayed until September 1920 due to its border dispute with Poland. See Albertas Gerutis, "Independent Lithuania, " in *Lithuania*, pp. 170–174.
[21] Bzrezinski described the tsar's empire as a prison of nationalities. See Nahaylo and Swoboda, *Soviet Disunion*, p. 353.
[22] Stalin's report is quoted by Alfred Cobban, *National Self-Determination* (London: Oxford University Press, 1944), p. 105.

socialist revolution. The new Bolshevik government also judged that it could ill afford to lose the valuable raw materials, fuel, and food furnished by the peripheral regions.

Thus, the construction of the new Soviet state and the reassertion of centralized authority proved incompatible with the aspirations for autonomy of numerous communities. For most, consequently, freedom from Russian rule would only last a matter of months, not years or decades. Having established administrations, only a few possessed the resources required to defend them against the on-slaught of the more powerful Red Army. In a revealing statement of Soviet policy objectives, Zinoviev declared before the Petrograd soviet in 1920, that Russia "cannot do without the petroleum of Azerbaijan or the cotton of Turkestan. We take these products which are necessary to us."[23] As a result, the Red Army occupied the Turkestan region administered by the Kokand Muslim regime. Lacking arms and funds, the Kokand forces were defeated, with over 14,000 Muslim soldiers slaughtered and their ancient city burnt to the ground.[24] In order to regain access to oil, natural gas, and fertile agricultural areas, the Red Army subsequently reconquered the Transcaucasus and Ukraine. In another representative example, Russia honored its treaty commitments with Georgia for only ten months before this territory was occupied by Soviet military units under the command of General S. Ordzhonikidze.[25] Within five years of the fall of tsar Nicholas II, the Bolsheviks had not only consolidated their power in the Kremlin, but also re-annexed most of the tsar's possessions "by means of bay-onets."

External support

On occasion foreign powers have assisted the central government in domestic struggles against separatists. At the Hapsburgs' request, the Russian Army quelled the Hungarian secession attempt in 1848. Far more frequently, strategic opportunism leads foreign powers to cham-pion secessionist causes; hence, the state's ability to resist secession can be restricted not only by domestic turmoil, but also by external intervention. Neighboring states have assisted secessionist move-ments to weaken their rivals' stability, and thereby extend their own

[23] Ibid., pp. 107–108.
[24] Nahaylo and Swoboda, *Soviet Disunion*, p. 39.
[25] Nahaylo and Peters, *Ukrainians and Georgians*, p. 16.

influence. In the relatively unstable Horn of Africa, multiple govern-ments have interfered in their neighbors' domestic conflicts:

> In the early 1970s, for example, the Libyan government was fur-nishing assistance to the separatist movement across the southern border in Chad. While deploring this intervention, the Chad govern-ment was offering aid and sanctuary to black insurrectionists in the southern Sudan. While trying to suppress this movement, the autho-rities at Khartoum were simultaneously supporting a separatist movement within the Eritrean sector of Ethiopia. Ethiopia, which was fighting a number of separatist movements in addition to that of the Eritreans, was countering by joining Chad (as well as Uganda) in aiding the blacks of the Southern Sudan.[26]

External intervention has on occasion tipped the internal balance of power toward the seceding community. French military and naval pressure on the distressed British government contributed to the thirteen American colonies winning their independence. Panama seceded from Colombia in 1902 with American help, but not before the United States had reassessed its foreign policy interests in Latin America and decided that an independent Panama served those interests better than a strong Colombia. Secessionists have also misjudged the interests of potential supporters. Confederate leaders expected Britain to assist their secession attempt because of British industrial dependence on the South's raw material exports, in par-ticular "King Cotton." The expected British assistance was not forth-coming; Southern leaders gravely miscalculated in this instance.

In the era of Cold War ideological rivalry, the superpowers provided covert assistance to separatist movements to extend their own influ-ence. Rarely did this imply that the United States or the Soviet Union judged independent statehood for the separatist group to be in its interests. In one example, in the early 1970s the CIA assisted the Kurdish opposition to the Iraqi regime. A Congressional intelligence report in 1975 revealed the limited objectives of this CIA operation. The preferred policy of the United States was: "that the insurgents simply continue a level of hostilities sufficient to sap the resources of our ally's [Iran] neighboring country [Iraq]. This policy was not imparted to our clients [the Kurds] who were encouraged to continue fighting."[27]

[26] Walker Connor, "The Politics of Ethno-nationalism," *Journal of International Affairs* 27–28, 1 (1973–1974), 15.
[27] James Mayall, *Nationalism and the International System* (Cambridge: Cambridge University Press, 1990).

There is an important distinction here. On the one hand, foreign patronage is often an essential element for success in creating a sovereign state through secession, even though the likely attraction of external assistance may not be the decisive variable in the original decision to secede. On the other hand, many historic examples exist where the distinct community decides to secede only once it is assured of specific allies willing to support its struggle, in which case external patronage does become the significant variable in the decision. The following section returns to the events surrounding the third Indo-Pakistani War in 1971 and investigates those in the eastern Mediterranean following the Turkish invasion of Cyprus in 1974. It discloses the way in which India and Turkey assisted in establishing an independent Bangladesh and a quasi-independent Northern Cyprus enclave, respectively. It is unlikely that the Bengali and Turkish-Cypriot communities would have achieved these impressive results of state-building without some external assistance. Chapter 7 argued that the combination of the Pakistani ruling elites' rejection of the political negotiations and of the Pakistani army's violent attack on unarmed Bengali citizens provided the primary motivating factors in the Bengali decision to secede. The likelihood of potential Indian involvement, although relevant, did not play a prominent part in the initial decision to secede. In contrast, guaranteed Turkish military protection and financial assistance did heavily influence the declaration of independence of the Turkish Republic of Northern Kibris. This comparison of two instances of foreign aid to secessionist communities also indicates the limits of foreign influence on secession.

India: midwife to the birth of Bangladesh[28]

Confronted by the Pakistani Army's well-coordinated and powerful attack in March, 1971, it is generally accepted that the Bengali forces did not command the resources required to achieve independence. It is therefore critical to examine the influence of external allies in the establishment of Bangladesh. After investigating foreign involvement in the Bengali crisis, this section argues that Bengali independence

[28] Historical material for this section is largely drawn from *Bangla Desh Documents*, vols. I and II (Madras: B.N.K. Press, 1972); *Keesing's Contemporary Archives, 1969–1975*; and Richard Sisson and Leo Rose, *War and Secession: Pakistan, India, and the Creation of Bangladesh* (Berkeley: University of California Press, 1990).

was not the goal, but rather a by-product of the Indian government's pursuit of other strategic interests.

Although demands for political reform generated an impressive show of Bengali solidarity, mass mobilization could not be translated into effective power against the Pakistani Army. Awami League negotiators believed that the tripartite agreement between representatives of the military government, the largest political party of West Pakistan – Z. A. Bhutto's Pakistan People's Party – and themselves on March 25, 1971 would serve as the basis for a satisfactory settlement of their demands.[29] Motivated by vested interests, however, West Pakistanis opposed the peaceful transfer of power to elected officials, which would have given Bengalis the leadership of the central government. They judged that a military solution would be the only way to negate the election results. General Tikka Khan soon earned the name of "the butcher of Dhaka." The Pakistani army launched a surprise attack on Bengali demonstrators in Dhaka and other main cities in East Pakistan.[30]

Faced with this vicious army assault, many Bengalis took up arms to defend themselves and their new state, which was proclaimed the following day. As argued in Chapter 7, their secession was one of "last resort." The Mukti Bahini, Bangladesh's guerrilla force, began almost immediately to harass Pakistani troops. Nevertheless, the impact of the Mukti Bahini in the spring of 1971, though romanticized in the Indian and international press, was minimal.[31] Lacking the training to launch effective raids, also lacking arms and ammunition, the guerrillas proved little match for the Pakistani army's efficiently executed operation.[32] By the end of April, the army had succeeded in reestablishing the central government's authority in East Pakistan.[33] The Awami League, although not eliminated, was a severely diminished force, with most of its leaders including Sheikh Mujib arrested or in exile. One might speculate that the violent suppression of widespread discontent and of such a popular organization as the Awami League might have eventually led to difficulties for the Pakistani government. However, in the short term, the army's "Operation

[29] Rehman Sobhan, "Negotiating for Bangla Desh: A Participant's View," *South Asia Review,* July, 1971.
[30] *Keesing's,* 1971, p. 24567.
[31] Sisson and Rose, *War and Secession,* p. 182.
[32] M. Rashiduzzaman, "Leadership, Organization, Strategies, and Tactics of the Bangla Desh Movement, " *Asian Survey* 12 (1972), 186–192.
[33] *Keesing's,* 1971, p. 24569.

Searchlight" had protected West Pakistani political and economic interests from forceful Bengali demands for regional economic autonomy and for political power at the centre commensurate with their larger population.

The Indian government's initial reaction to the violent confrontation in neighboring East Pakistan was cautious. While the Lok Sabha (Lower House) condemned the Pakistani actions on March 26 and extended "whole-hearted sympathy and support" for the struggle in "East Bengal" for "a democratic way of life,"[34] the government of Prime Minister Indira Gandhi was more guarded and chose to recognize the conflict as an internal matter of Pakistan.[35] India neither recognized the secessionist entity of the People's Republic of Bangladesh nor publicly approved Pakistan's disintegration. India did, however, assist the Bengali government-in-exile to organize itself in Calcutta, set up Radio Bangla, and helped it to appear as a credible alternative to the military regime.[36] In the spring of 1971, India also provided the Mukti Bahini with sanctuary, some military and other technical advice, training, funds, and other material support on a limited scale.[37] There seems to be no real substance, however, behind Pakistani accusations that Indian intrigue generated the conflict.

Through their careful reconstruction of the events of 1971, historians Richard Sisson and Leo Rose conclude that the escalation of Indian involvement in the conflict progressed from "concern to crisis."[38] Numerous pressures forced India to play a more active role in the Bengali secession. To begin with, India was ill-equipped to deal with the mass flight of refugees from East Pakistan, which had reached several million by the summer and nearly 10 million by November, 1971.[39] Further, Sisson and Rose point out that such a mass migration threatened to upset the precarious balance of ethnic, religious, and ideological forces in India's north-eastern states, not to mention placing an enormous financial burden on the federal government to house and feed these refugees. The first priority for the Indian government became to assure a political solution in its neighbor which would facilitate the return of all refugees. By May, 1971, the

---

[34] Ibid., pp. 24568–24569.
[35] Sisson and Rose, *War and Secession*, p. 156.
[36] Rashiduzzaman, "Leadership," p. 190.
[37] *Keesing's*, 1971, p. 24802.
[38] Sisson and Rose, *War and Secession*.
[39] *Keesing's*, 1971, p. 24990.

decline of armed Bengali resistance and the Pakistani government's
intransigence convinced the government in New Delhi that its preferred resolution to the conflict would be unrealizable without intervention.

India's involvement in this secession crisis progressed through a
number of stages, initially emphasizing diplomatic pressure while
later undertaking military action. The original moral support expressed by the Lok Sabha thus gained momentum. India first
attempted to convince the international community to pressure Pakistan to modify its recalcitrant stance toward the Awami League.
India's diplomats championed the Bengali cause in world capitals.[40]
Although Bengali representatives were barred from United Nations
debates on their plight, their case was well represented by the Indian
government. Foreign Minister Swaran Singh's high level meetings
with Soviet, European, and American foreign policy officials during
the summer months were followed by an impressive tour of six
Western capitals by Prime Minister Gandhi in October and November,
1971.[41]

The Indian government gradually abandoned concerted international pressure once its futility in changing Pakistani attitudes
became readily apparent. Mrs. Gandhi then deftly prepared international opinion for the subsequent Indian intervention. She emphasized the international community's duty to the elected government
in East Pakistan and its responsibility to the millions of refugees.
While Mrs. Gandhi was in Washington, DC in November, she
declared: "We have acted with patience, forbearance, and restraint.
But we cannot sit idly by if the edifice of our political stability and
economic well-being is threatened."[42]

Meanwhile, Indian preparations for total military intervention
began in mid-July with the decision to make the Mukti Bahini into an
effective fighting force, and escalated after the monsoon season in late
September.[43] Indian military personnel began to direct the guerrilla
operations so that by mid-October, with Indian artillery support, the
Mukti Bahini could claim tenuous control of substantial, though

[40] Ibid., pp. 24990–24991.
[41] Ibid., p. 24992.
[42] Indira Gandhi quoted in Chris N. Okeke, *Controversial Subjects of Contemporary
International Law* (Rotterdam, 1979), p. 146. Also quoted in Sisson and Rose, *War and
Secession*, p. 157.
[43] *Keesing's*, 1971, p. 24802.

scattered, territory within East Pakistan.[44] In the interim, India turned the refugee crisis to its own advantage. While publicly stressing this human tragedy, the Indian government opposed the plan of the United Nations High Commissioner for Refugees (UNHCR) to establish "reception centers" in East Pakistan to facilitate their return. India argued that no refugees would return until a "climate of security" was created by the establishment of an Awami League-led government. India also would not permit UN observers to visit refugees camps within its own borders, for it wanted to avoid international publicity for its now extensive military assistance to the Mukti Bahini.[45] India even rejected UN Secretary General U Thant's offer of "his good offices" to mediate escalating Indo-Pakistani hostility. India successfully focused international attention on the search for an internal political solution satisfactory to the Bengali community.[46]

During the first three weeks of November, the Indian Army placed its troops in strategic positions to the north, east, and west of Dhaka for an assault on the capital city. The date cited for the formal commencement of the third Indo-Pakistani war is December 3, when the Pakistani air force launched a pre-emptive strike on major Indian installations. The war in effect began after November 21, when the Indian army fought its way to occupy important areas in East Pakistan. It was an unequal contest, the Indian army possessed overwhelming advantages: a larger army with greater mobility, better arms, and control of both air and sea. By December 6, when India extended formal diplomatic recognition to the People's Republic of Bangladesh, the outcome of the war was no longer in doubt.[47]

To summarize, through a combination of deft manipulation of world public opinion, diplomatic negotiation, and military victories, India achieved its initial policy objective – the return of Bengali refugees. Although India's assistance did not play a significant role in this secession of "last resort," it proved essential for its subsequent success. With the Pakistani army's surrender, the midwife presented the rest of the world with a *fait accompli*, the birth of the independent state of Bangladesh.

---

[44] Ibid., p. 24994.
[45] Ibid., p. 24993.
[46] Ibid., p. 24993.
[47] Ibid., pp. 24994–24995.

Turkey's creation: the Turkish republic of northern Cyprus[48]

The glaring difference between the Indian intervention in East Pakistan and the Turkish intervention in Cyprus is in their results. While international recognition was accorded relatively quickly to the fledgeling republic of Bangladesh,[49] the Turkish-Cypriot enclave continues to suffer from effective diplomatic isolation. A brief exposition of Turkey's involvement in Cyprus and its instrumental role in the secession of Northern Cyprus precedes discussion of these issues of international recognition and isolation.

Cypriot society suffers the perfect coincidence of linguistic, religious, and economic cleavages dividing it between the wealthier Greek Orthodox community and the poorer Turkish Muslim one. The 1960 census revealed that nearly 80% of the population was Greek, about 16% Turkish, with the remainder made up of various minorities.[50] The highly interspersed, although not integrated, residential patterns of the two communities prevented territorial division.[51] With the approach of independence, the elaborate and rigid 1960 constitution prescribed a detailed political system, which Arend Lijphart has called the epitome of "consociational democracy."[52] Grand coalitions were assured by the election of a Greek-Cypriot president and a Turkish-Cypriot vice-president, and by the allocation of seven Cabinet portfolios to the Greek community and three to the Turkish community. The seven-to-three ratio was maintained for the House of Representatives and the civil service, although its extension to six-to-four for the army and police signified a double over-representation of Turkish-Cypriots. The dual nature of the government was further

---

[48] Historical material for this section is largely drawn from Polivios Polyviou, *Cyprus: Conflict and Negotiations, 1960–1980* (London: Duckworth, 1980); Necati Munir Ertekun, *The Cyprus Dispute and the Birth of the Turkish Republic of Northern Cyprus* (Nicosia, 1981); Michael Attalides, *Cyprus, Nationalism, and International Politics* (London: Q Press, 1979); and Keith Kyle, *Cyprus* (London: Minority Rights Group, 1984).

[49] By the end of 1972, over eighty states had established formal diplomatic relations with Bangladesh. See *Keesing's*, 1972, pp. 25113, 25196, 25212, 25444.

[50] The results of the 1960 census are cited in Arend Lijphart, "Consociational Failure in Cyprus, 1960–1963," in *Democracy in Plural Societies: A Comparative Exploration* (New Haven: Yale University Press, 1977) p. 158.

[51] Unlike most distinct community conflicts which culminate in secession, the Turkish community in Cyprus originally was not territorially concentrated anywhere on the island. Instead Greek villages were located next to Turkish ones. The villages themselves were not integrated with Turkish and Greek families.

[52] Lijphart, *Democracy*, p. 159.

reinforced by the election of communal chambers with exclusive legislative powers over religious, educational, and cultural matters and the creation of separate municipal councils in the five largest towns. Moreover, all legislative decisions concerning taxation, municipalities, and electoral reform required the concurrent majorities of Greek and Turkish representatives.[53]

While Greek-Cypriot leaders only reluctantly accepted the 1960 compromise, Turkish-Cypriots insisted on its rapid implementation to bolster their weak position. With a population of about 110,000, Turkish-Cypriots sought opportunities for social advancement through the civil service since they were poorly represented in commerce and other professions and suffered high illiteracy rates. Turkish members of the House of Representatives utilized their constitutional powers with respect to tax legislation to pressure the bureaucracy to implement quickly the seven-to-three provisions in government employment. The first three years of independence witnessed a precarious balance between Greek and Turkish interests and patience. The Greek president of Cyprus, Archbishop Makarios, in a letter to the Turkish vice-president, Dr. Fazil Kucuk, dated November 30, 1963, proposed a series of constitutional amendments designed to eliminate the presidential and vice-presidential vetoes, concurrent majorities on legislation, separate municipal governments, and Turkish over-representation in the civil service, police and armed forces. Turkish-Cypriot leaders and Turkey both rejected these proposals. Civil war broke out in December.[54]

Though active hostilities subsided within a few weeks, reconciliation between the two communities has remained beyond their grasp. Despite US and UN involvement, including mediation by Secretary of State Dean Acheson in 1964–1965 and UN-sponsored intercommunal talks between the Greek president of the House of Representatives, Glafkos Clerides, and the Turkish-Cypriot leader, Rauf Denktas, from 1968 to 1974, tensions persisted across the island.[55] In 1974 the Greek

[53] For a more complete description of the consociational features of government, see Stanley Kyriakides, *Cyprus: Constitutionalism and Crisis Government* (Philadelphia: University of Pennsylvania Press, 1968), pp. 53–71; and T. W. Adams, "The First Republic of Cyprus: A Review of an Unworkable Constitution," *Western Political Quarterly*, 19, 3 (September 1966), 475–490.

[54] For a discussion of the Greek-Cypriot proposals and the subsequent events leading to a descent into civil war, see Thomas Ehrlich, *Cyprus: 1958–1967* (Oxford: Oxford University Press, 1974), pp. 36–60.

[55] For the Greek-Cypriot viewpoint of these negotiations, see Polivios Polyviou, *Cyprus: Conflict and Negotiations, 1960–1980* (London: Duckworth, 1980); for the Turkish-Cypriot

military junta's fomentation of a conspiracy against the president of Cyprus, Archbishop Makarios, culminated in a coup organized by the National Guard and led by its 650 Greek officers, which installed a more pliant president.[56] Under the Treaty of Guarantee, which along with the Treaties of Alliance and Establishment transferred sovereignty from Britain to the Republic of Cyprus, Britain, Greece, and Turkey promised to uphold Cyprus's independence and constitution.[57] In the event of a breach in these conditions, the British, Greek, and Turkish guarantors would "consult together" about "measures necessary to ensure observance." Article IV of the Treaty, however, stated that if a coordinated response proved impossible, "each of the three guaranteeing powers reserves the right to take action with the sole aim of re-establishing the state of affairs created by the present Treaty."[58] After hasty consultations with British officials who made it clear that Britain would not become involved in the dispute, Turkey, under the legal cover of the Treaty of Guarantee, launched an assault on July 20. Though it encountered fierce resistance, the Turkish Army occupied the northern 36% of the island.[59] The consequent mass migration of Turkish-Cypriots and Greek-Cypriots led to enormous refugee problems, but also to increasingly homogenous populations in the two separated zones. Having created an autonomous region in Northern Cyprus, the Turkish army relinquished its administration to the civilian government dominated by Rauf Denktas and his National Unity Party. It proclaimed the Turkish Federated State of Cyprus the following year.[60] Once again, UN-sponsored intercommunal negotiations languished for years until the declaration of independence of the Turkish Republic of Northern Cyprus on November 15, 1983.

Guarantied Turkish economic assistance and military protection bolstered the continued separatism of Turkish-Cypriots. Only Turkey extended diplomatic recognition to the new administration. The Turkish lira has been the official currency of Northern Cyprus since 1983, confirming its reliance on the Turkish economy. Northern Cyprus has become a large drain on scarce Turkish resources; the

perspective, see Necati Munir Ertekun, *The Cyprus Dispute and the Birth of the Turkish Republic of Northern Cyprus* (Nicosia, 1981).
[56] Kyle, *Cyprus*, p. 14.
[57] Adams, "The First Republic of Cyprus," pp. 475–490.
[58] Kyle, *Cyprus*, p. 8.
[59] Ibid.
[60] Ertekun, *Cyprus Dispute*.

Ankara government subsidises about two-thirds of Northern Cyprus's total budget, including the entire development budget and half of the operating budget.[61] Turkish-Cypriot leaders consistently resisted Archbishop Makarios' conciliatory proposals designed to reunite the island.[62] A formal resolution of hostilities would provide Turkish-Cypriots with access to international loans for development projects, enhanced trade relations, opportunities in shipping and tourism, and ultimately potential membership within the European Union, which have all been closed off due to their diplomatic isolation; however, for the civilian administration of Rauf Denktas the "Cyprus problem" had essentially been resolved. As historian David Souter points out: "While residual problems of international recognition and intercommunal relations could be resolved by a comprehensive settlement, they have little incentive to pursue this so long as Turkey provides full military, political, and economic backing for the Turkish-Cypriot regime."[63] In these ways, Turkey has played an instrumental role in the creation and survival of Northern Cyprus as an autonomous entity – an achievement that the small, economically and politically weak Turkish-Cypriot community could not have managed on its own.

In conclusion to this section, the Bangladesh and Northern Cyprus experiences are anomalies in two separate senses: first, rarely do the interests of the community seeking secession and of the foreign state considering intervention coincide perfectly; and second, rarely does one side in such a conflict enlist external assistance without the other side obtaining countervailing support from another foreign power.

Any state's involvement in its neighbor's domestic strife rests on the pursuit of multiple objectives. These objectives may in fact either be indifferent to or even lie in opposition to the distinct community's aspirations of independence. In the case of Bangladesh, for example, India's requirements for an acceptable solution to the crisis did not include an independent Bangladesh. Basing their argument on detailed scrutiny of the available government documents, Sisson and Rose assert that Indira Gandhi's Cabinet decided in the summer of 1971 that the fundamental policy aim must be the return of all refugees.[64] Any resolution to the crisis which did not ensure this

---

[61] Kyle, *Cyprus*, p. 18.
[62] Polyviou, *Cyprus*.
[63] David Souter, "The Cyprus Conundrum: The Challenge of Intercommunal Talks," *Third World Quarterly*, 11 (April 1989), p. 78.
[64] Sisson and Rose,*War and Secession*, pp. 148–157.

objective would be unacceptable. In settling on this clear goal, Gandhi's government specifically resisted early calls for military intervention from prominent Indians such as the director of the Institute of Defence Studies and Analysis in New Delhi, K. Subrahmanyam. In an article for the newspaper, *National Herald*, Subrahmanyam argued forcefully that the crisis presented India with "an opportunity the like of which will never come again."[65] The government in effect disregarded his argument that by dismembering its traditional enemy and creating a friendly and dependent neighbor, India would establish itself as the undisputed regional power in South Asia. It was judged that the best means toward the more limited end of repatriating Bengali refugees was the transfer of power in East Pakistan to a politically moderate Awami League government. India did not insist that Pakistan concede full independence to East Pakistan. The Awami League's Six Points Programme could have served as the basis of a satisfactory settlement. When it became clear that pressure by either the international community or the Mukti Bahini would be insufficient to force the Pakistani government into a more conciliatory approach and when it was calculated that a full scale military intervention would prove cheaper than feeding the increasing numbers of refugees, only then did the Indian government begin preparations for direct military intervention and contemplate recognising an independent Bangladesh.

The expediency of the Cold War usually precluded the definitive resolution of a secession crisis in favor of independence. Although the distinct community could often gain support from one superpower, the central government could enlist counterbalancing support from the other. Frequently such rivalry was mirrored in the competition between regional powers, as between India and Pakistan in South Asia and between Turkey and Greece in the eastern Mediterranean. The bipolar global balance of power further reinforced by traditional regional antagonisms prevented the resolution of many secessionist conflicts. Neither the superpowers nor the regional actors could afford to lose an ally through secession.

Nevertheless, in the Bengali secession, India was able to break this usual course of events. Significantly, India carefully enlisted Soviet diplomatic and material assistance through the quick conclusion of the Indian–Soviet military alliance in the summer of 1971. It then

[65] Ibid., p. 149.

sought assurances that Pakistan would not gain offsetting support from its allies, the United States and the People's Republic of China.[66] Pakistan was notably less successful in its maneuvering. When it attempted to enlist support from China, the Chinese government condemned India as the "naked aggressor."[67] Due to Soviet pressure on its northern border, however, the Chinese position was deemed too weak to accede to Pakistan's request. The birth of independent Bangladesh was the byproduct of India's pursuit of its own interests, not an end in itself.

The glaring divergence of consequences of these two comparable instances of foreign intervention in secession also indicates the international community's influence on the outcomes of such conflicts. Bangladesh succeeded in obtaining international recognition. By contrast, with the exception of a few diplomatic ties, the Turkish Republic of Northern Cyprus has been relegated to international isolation. Part of the explanation lies in James Crawford's and Rosalyn Higgins's description of the creation of states in international law. Crawford argues that the creation of states has become increasingly regulated by international norms and conventions such as self-determination.[68] Higgins argues that the application of self-determination has been restricted to the exercise of power by the majority within diplomatically recognized borders.[69] The rapid process of decolonization in 1947 divided the new state of Pakistan into two geographically segmented parts. Within these anomalous circumstances, the Bengali community not only formed an overwhelming majority within the eastern wing, but also constituted an outright majority of the entire population of Pakistan. The claims of the Bengali community fit the requirements which the international community implicitly prescribed and Higgins rendered explicit. Thus, it earned the right of self-determination. By contrast, the generally accepted boundaries of Cyprus appear to be co-extensive with the island itself. The international community has not recognized the Turkish-Cypriots, constituting less than 20% of the island's population, as a legitimate self-determining unit, therefore international recognition has not been

---

[66] *Keesing's*, 1971, p. 24992.
[67] *Keesing's*, 1972, p. 25069.
[68] James Crawford, *The Creation of States in International Law* (Oxford: Clarendon Press, 1979).
[69] Rosalyn Higgins, *The Development of International Law Through the Political Organs of the United Nations* (Oxford: Oxford University Press, 1963).

forthcoming. Although foreign patronage is certainly an asset for the distinct community struggling to secede, in and of itself, such patronage cannot guarantee success in achieving sovereign statehood.

India's manipulation of the crisis also reflects the inherently weak position in which secessionist movements often find themselves. Many Bengali officials in the Mukti Bahini and the government-in-exile in Calcutta certainly resented India's domineering attitude toward them. When struggling for survival, the distinct community does not have the luxury of choosing its allies. In most cases it must accept aid from any source, and hope that its provider's interests coincide with its own and remain limited. New developments in regional politics may convince the seceding group's former ally that it is more expedient for it now to begin supporting the state. In the shifting alliances and strife in the Horn of Africa foreign supporters have frequently reassessed their interests and then pursued policies to the direct detriment of their former clients. Heavily reliant on external assistance, secessionists seldom retain the momentum necessary to achieve their aspirations.

The aims of this chapter, then, have been as follows: to demonstrate that the collapse of the central government and the prospect of foreign assistance can influence the decision to secede. Under such circumstances, the discontented community identifies an "opportune moment" to seek independence. Nevertheless, these opportunities often prove fleeting. In the numerous cases cited here, the re-emergence of a strong central government often signaled the end of bids for autonomy or independence. Once the Communists consolidated central government control over war-torn and fragmented China in 1949, they sent troops to end Tibet's secession and reoccupied the province by 1951. After overthrowing Emperor Haile Selassie, the Dergue was able to suppress most separatist activity within Ethiopia's borders by 1978, with the exception of the Eritrean and Tigrayan liberation movements. Had it not been for American, British, and French intervention after the Gulf War in 1991, it is likely that its superior firepower would have enabled the Iraqi Republican Guard to subjugate the rebellious Kurdish population. In the most prominent case study used here, under the direction of the new Bolshevik government, the Red Army defeated most secessionist movements, dismantled their territorial administrations, and incorporated most of the lands of imperial Russia into the new Soviet Union.

165

Although external intervention is not a necessary feature of secession, foreign powers have throughout history played decisive military, diplomatic, or economic patronage roles in the creation of new states through secession. Many more instances exist, however, where changing perceptions of geostrategic interests have made foreign states an unreliable source of assistance. Even though Indian aid to the Bengalis and Turkish assistance to the Turkish-Cypriots proved crucial in these communities' struggles, examples of inconsistent commitment on the part of external allies such as the experiences suffered by the many communities in the Horn of Africa are far more prevalent. A reduction in the costs of secession may provide the impetus for a secession crisis; it does not necessarily provide the momentum for the seceding community to realise its aspirations.

9   A reduction in the benefits of membership

The Ibo, Bengali, and Southern Sudanese communities investigated earlier responded to the state's escalating threat to their lives and culture with secession. By contrast, for the numerous distinct communities embedded in developed Western societies, the motivation for secession decisions lies not in state-sponsored threats to their way of life, but rather in the perceived "mere" reduction in what they have come to expect as the normal security, economic, and social benefits of membership. The purpose of this chapter is to explore how fundamental changes in these benefits can result in the same consequences – a secession crisis.

The secession dynamic here differs from the secessions arising from "last resorts" or "opportune moments" described earlier. Reduction in the benefits of membership often occurs almost unnoticed. Historically such gradual changes have motivated fewer responses because they are frequently overshadowed by other essential factors which constitute the costs of both membership and secession. Whereas Chapter 7 disclosed that all other considerations become irrelevant once the distinct community is confronted by escalating violence or worsening forcible cultural assimilation, in the cases here the fact that the benefits of membership play the primary role in generating support for secession in itself implies the absence of mortal or cultural costs. Furthermore, in the following cases no external circumstances like war, social upheaval, or the material assistance by foreign allies to the secessionist group have combined to weaken the central government's effective authority over its territory; in other words, there have been no "opportune moments" for secession similar to the collapse of tsarist Russia described in Chapter 8. Perhaps the most significant contrast between the Ibo, Bengali, and Southern Sudanese cases and the multiple secessions during the Russian revolution cited earlier and this category of secession dynamic lies in the stability of political institutions which govern the society. Community demands are mediated by democratic institutions in which individual civil and political rights are deeply entrenched. That more secure governments no longer define all opposition as treason further facilitates the process of accommodation. In other words, although in each case the state still opposes the endeavor, community leaders contemplate secession under a dramatically decreased prospect of mortal opposition to their challenge.

Since awareness of the not insubstantial benefits of integration can act as a restraint on secessionist aspirations, this chapter examines two different types of situations in which a reduction in these benefits precipitates a secession decision. In the first section, investigation of Norway's independence from Sweden in 1905 illustrates the way that the government's negligence in discharging its duties can generate a secession. Specifically, once the Swedish government's inflexibility on what had become a key foreign policy issue became clear, Norwegian leaders abandoned their efforts to reform the Union's institutions. Popular opinion in Norway united behind demands for outright withdrawal.

The second section investigates how international considerations impact upon the secession dynamic. International influences on secession crises can take two forms. There is a clear distinction between first, the existence of specific external allies willing to assist a secessionist movement as described in Chapter 8, and second, developments in the international system which may moderate earlier restraints on the decision to secede. By reducing the security and economic benefits of membership, and thus, improving the potential viability of independence for many distinct communities, this latter crucial factor has influenced the secession dynamic.

Although this category of cases has not precipitated nearly so many outright secession attempts thus far, it has generated vigorous secessionist politics. To varying degrees the Scots, Welsh, Basques, Catalans, Bretons, Corsicans, Flemish, and Quebecois have all engaged in public debate on separatist proposals. In two counterbalancing trends, while representative government provides an established mechanism to vent grievances, and thus, tempers potential separatist confrontations, the continued evolution of international society in terms of security requirements and economic integration could raise the probability of future secession attempts. Such reductions in the benefits of membership, although falling short of directly triggering a secession attempt now, could create circumstances more conducive to secession in the future. The change would occur when distinct communities perceive that the state has ceased to be the primary provider of advantages they were unwilling to forfeit earlier.

The Catalan and Quebecois cases elucidate the possible secession dynamic in Western democratic societies. Although a similar history of mistreatment has alienated some Catalans and Quebecois from their respective states, in both cases, recent federal governments have treated these communities with sensitivity. Furthermore, both communities have now secured extensive autonomy to administer their own affairs. Recent events nevertheless display a gradual escalation in demands by both communities. Even though domestic issues continue to play a significant role, the study of domestic politics is inadequate to explain the persistence and even escalation of Catalan and Quebecois separatist demands. Secession need not rest exclusively on domestic factors; international considerations play a crucial role in the decision to secede.

State policies

The Norwegian secession

The roots of Norway's secession from Sweden lay not in the "unbearable tyranny" of the state.[1] Norway's secession was not predominantly one of "last resort" nor one due to an "opportune moment." Support for secession arose at the turn of the century from the conviction that the Swedish kingdom was not upholding the duties its Norwegian subjects deemed vital. Norway's secession crisis arose from that fact that, although Norwegian interests were not actively threatened, many Norwegians believed they were increasingly being neglected. Institutionalized discrimination, exploitation, and repression need not characterize a state's treatment of its distinct commu-

---

[1] Material for this section has been drawn mainly from Karen Larsen, *A History of Norway* (Princeton: Princeton University Press, 1950); T. K. Derry, *A History of Modern Norway: 1814–1972* (Oxford: Clarendon Press, 1973); Ingvar Andersson (translated from Swedish by Carolyn Hannay), *A History of Sweden* (London: Weidenfeld and Nicolson, 1957); and T. K. Derry, *A History of Scandinavia: Norway, Sweden, Denmark, Finland and Iceland* (London: George Allen & Unwin, 1979).

nities. Neglect could also characterize such a relationship. Since Sweden no longer provided the benefits of membership expected by Norwegians, this dispute ultimately generated a secession crisis.

The Norwegian secession was certainly facilitated by other factors. Capable and visionary leaders, such as the minister of state, Christian Michelsen, and his colleague, the Norwegian representative in Stockholm, Jorgen Lovland, handled the actual act of secession with speed and tact. The military plans begun in 1898, which included the building of defensive fortifications that were designed to enable Norway to repel an attack, were completed by 1903, thereby further strengthening the Norwegian leaders' negotiating position.[2] The Japanese defeat of the tsar's army and the White Sea fleet in 1904–1905 temporarily eclipsed Russian power and diminished the potential threats to a newly independent, though weak, Norwegian state. Due to their preoccupation with the simultaneously occurring Moroccan crisis, the British, French, and German governments had little interest in a war in the North and exerted diplomatic pressure for a peaceful settlement of the dispute.[3]

Regardless of these facilitating factors, Norwegians for many years tried to redress their grievances within the framework of Swedish institutions. Norway's high level of self-government, as embodied in its elected legislature, the Storting, meant that the Swedish kingdom posed few direct threats to its well-being.[4] Ever since their incorporation into Sweden, in 1814, most Norwegian leaders retained the belief that the union was advantageous for their community and favored moderation in addressing disagreements.[5]

The most contentious issue concerning Swedish rule over Norway consistently revolved around the provision of consular services. In the nineteenth century, with few employment opportunities besides subsistence farming and fishing, many Norwegian men turned to the sea. Having far surpassed the shipping industry of their Swedish neighbors, they created the third largest merchant marine in the world. The Norwegian people therefore required more extensive and frequent

---

[2] Larsen, *Norway*, p. 488.
[3] When the Norwegian minister of state, Christian Michelsen, sent Polar explorer Nansen to England on an unofficial mission, Nansen found English public opinion supportive of Norwegian claims. Prime Minister Balfour professed to Nansen to regard a war in Scandinavia as "a 'folly' so great as to make it outside the limits of practical politics." Quoted in Derry, *Scandinavia*; p. 273.
[4] Andersson, *Sweden*, p. 395.
[5] Larsen, *Norway*, p. 486; Derry, *Modern Norway*, p. 118.

assistance overseas than their Swedish counterparts.[6] Their divergent trading objectives necessitated different types of consular services abroad. While no legal statutes restricted the appointment of members of either community to fill diplomatic posts, in practice most officials were Swedish and were responsible to the Swedish foreign minister.[7] Although it was accorded extensive self-government, Norway was never allowed to nominate its own foreign minister. This was important because discontent arose from Norwegian perceptions that the foreign ministry gave primary consideration to Swedish needs, at times to the detriment of Norwegian ones. Recurring grievances included the accusations of Swedish interests dictating the location of consulates and of Swedish officials mistreating Norwegian sailors. Consular officials had little understanding of their problems or even of the Norwegian language.[8] Norwegian businesses protested that the Swedish foreign ministry had not promoted their exports abroad, and was not willing to delegate such responsibility to Norwegians. The Swedish historian, Ingvar Andersson, acknowledges that diplomatic service "was a question on which the Norwegians, in view of their recent advances in trade and navigation, were naturally particularly sensitive."[9] It is not surprising that Norwegian ship-owners, captains, and seamen provided the most vocal agitation for the creation of a separate consular service.[10] Given their prominence within the community, their demands carried much weight with the Norwegian provincial government.

Even though requests for equal privileges in diplomatic representation had been mooted in the Storting as early as 1831, efforts to settle this disagreement began in earnest in the 1880s and lasted for two decades.[11] The successes and setbacks of twenty years of negotiations need not be detailed for the purposes of the argument. What is significant is that while the Norwegian delegation proposed various reforms of the foreign ministry, it consistently sought a solution within the union's institutions. It was not until the perceived rejection of these efforts by the Swedish government in 1904 that the Norwe-

[6] Larsen, *Norway*, p. 486.
[7] Ibid., p. 485.
[8] Ibid.
[9] Andersson, *Sweden*, p. 396.
[10] Larsen, *Norway*, p. 487.
[11] Derry, *Modern Norway*, p. 70.

gians became convinced that their needs would be best served by achieving independent statehood.

Although the king formulated foreign policy, he relied for its implementation on the foreign service. Since 1835, the Norwegian minister of state had been summoned to participate in foreign policy discussions only when they related directly to Norwegian interests.[12] When their petitions for more equal involvement were ignored, many Norwegians judged that there was no recourse but to establish their own service to assist their seamen abroad. The Storting addressed this issue by passing a bill in 1891 designed to establish a separate consular service; the king refused his sanction.[13] The Swedish government argued that since consular service was so intimately connected with the department of foreign affairs, the Norwegians had no right to act independently.

After the elections of 1894, the new Storting adopted a resolution declaring its intention to enter into negotiations on the whole state of the union.[14] Nearly a decade of negotiations made little progress, until the confluence of several factors in 1903 facilitated the rapid settlement of differences. Based on Sigurd Ibsen's report on how separate consular services could be harmonized within one foreign policy department, the liberal Swedish foreign minister Alfred Lagerheim, and the more conciliatory Norwegian government directed by Francis Hagerup signed a general agreement in December, 1903.[15] Identical laws passed by the Storting and the Swedish Parliament, the Riksdag, were to direct its implementation. This agreement could only be modified by mutual consent.

At this point, when compromise appeared imminent, the Swedish government withdrew from some of its commitments. Indignant at this breach of faith and subsequent Swedish intransigence, Norwegians rapidly came to view secession as the only means to remedy their plight. Specifically, to the shock of most Norwegians, once the new Swedish prime minister Erik Gustaf Bostrom, forced his colleague Lagerheim to resign from the foreign ministry in 1904, he honoured neither the letter nor the spirit of the agreement reached in the previous year.[16] After long delay, the Swedish draft of the "identical laws"

---

[12] Ibid., pp. 70–71.
[13] Larsen, *Norway,* p. 487.
[14] Ibid., pp. 487–488.
[15] Ibid.
[16] Derry, *Scandinavia;* p. 271.

imposed six extra provisions relegating Norway once again to dependency status.[17] Bostrom refused to yield to Norwegian protests and declared the negotiations officially closed on February 7, 1905. The "dependency clauses" did not significantly alter Norway's former position within the union. They were motivationally relevant because they were not negotiated, but unilaterally imposed. This *de facto* rejection of extended negotiations reinforced Norwegian suspicions that the Swedish government would repeatedly fail to address their needs. The dependency clauses implicitly emphasized Norwegian subservience in relation to an issue long understood by both sides to be one of paramount interest to Norwegians, and so predictably touched their newly fortified pride. Consequently, the Norwegian government under the inspired direction of Christian Michelsen and Jorgen Lovland quickly embarked upon the process of gaining sovereign statehood. The official Norwegian challenge to Swedish rule came on June 7. On August 13th a referendum organized by the Storting allowed Norwegians "to answer the question whether or not they approve the dissolution of the union which had taken place." With a turnout of over 84%, the voters approved the secession by 368,208 to 184.[18]

Why did the Swedish government adopt the dependency clauses? In fact, there are several layers of explanations. First, whereas the expansion of their mercantile marine was fueling Norwegian economic growth, by contrast, Swedish shipping had declined by the late nineteenth century. The growing prominence of iron and steel, pulp and paper, textiles, and other manufacturing industries replaced shipping in the Swedish economy.[19] During the final two decades of the nineteenth century, Norwegian vessels already conveyed about half of the trade of their Swedish neighbors.[20] Further, although they did not believe an expensive network of consulates was imperative, Swedish ministers were also reluctant to bestow such a privilege on the Norwegians. Therefore, the second and more deeply rooted source of friction, as Norwegian historian Karen Larsen argues, had its origins not in economic rivalry, but rather in conflicting conceptions of the union itself.[21] Larsen's research reveals that: "In some circles in

---

[17] For a detailed citing of these six provisions, see Larsen, *Norway*, p. 488.
[18] Larsen, *Norway*, p. 491.
[19] Eli F. Heckscher (translated by Goran Ohlin), *An Economic History of Sweden* (Cambridge, MA: Harvard University Press, 1954), pp. 209–233, 244–246.
[20] Derry, *Scandinavia*; p. 118.
[21] Larsen, *Norway*, p. 484.

Sweden, Norway had been looked upon ever since 1814 as a dependency received as compensation for the loss of Finland." Even if some
Swedish leaders did not ascribe to this extreme view, most did
subordinate Norway to an inferior position. By contrast, despite their
smaller size, Norwegians consistently strove to be recognized as equal
partners within the Union. They sought to construct an efficient
representative government both to look after their domestic interests
and gradually to gain some of the privileges of sovereign statehood.
The request for separate consular services was simply the next logical
step in the gradual construction of a Norwegian state, but a step that
became too controversial for Swedish leaders to accept. The inability
to reach a compromise solution was thus in large part due to the fact
that neither Swedish nor Norwegian leaders were willing to relinquish their own unique vision of the Union.

In a unanimous resolution, the Storting both explained the motivations for secession and justified the dissolution of the state in the
following manner. Since the primary duty of the constitutional
monarch was to form a responsible government which administered
to the needs of his subjects, once the king was unable to fulfill these
duties, his royal power ceased to have jurisdiction over Norway.[22] The
Norwegians dissolved the union because the king's government could
no longer provide the specific and unique benefits of membership
required by their community.

In summary, Norway seceded peacefully from Sweden and was
recognized by its European neighbors once the union's dissolution
had been finalised. The peaceful nature of its political transition from
province to full sovereignty distinguishes it from most other secession
crises before 1991. Although numerous considerations entered into
the calculations of Swedish leaders at the time – the difficulty in
conquering Norwegian territory, the potential loss of life, the financial
drain and economic disruption of such a military campaign – it was
the restraint of King Oscar II which was the most "potent influence for
peace."[23] In the end, the actual secession caused little disruption in
the public life of either country. Furthermore, in contrast to numerous
examples of ongoing hostilities between the former sovereign and the
seceding community, Sweden and Norway have succeeded in culti-
vating close, friendly relations.

[22] Ibid., p. 490.
[23] Ibid., p. 491.

"Mature anarchy" and economic integration: developments in the international system

In some cases, detailed dissection of solely domestic factors cannot explain the persistent appeal of separatism. The Catalan and Quebec secession movements, for example, initially appear enigmatic because there has been neither a recent acceleration in state repression nor an impairment of the state's ability to oppose secession – two factors which Chapters 7 and 8 demonstrated were critical to the secession dynamic. Using the Catalan and Quebec cases, this section argues international developments have motivational power as well.

Before considering these two cases in detail, the context must be defined. The structure of the international system inherently influences the security and economic challenges to the states competing within it, and therefore also to the communities within each state. Through the development of institutions of domestic government and international diplomacy, states have addressed these challenges, thereby providing the benefits of membership for their inhabitants. The political evolution of the international system and unprecedented global economic integration modify the relations among states and the specific challenges faced by any particular state. Such systematic developments, by reducing real or perceived external security threats and by diminishing government control over its domestic economy, can reduce for a distinct community the advantages previously obtained only by integration in an existing state.

Separate categories of communities, however, must be distinguished depending on the type of state to which they belong as this would impact on their contemplation of political alternatives. For example, optimal tariff structure theory indicates that "large" countries with vigorous exporting economies may be able to influence positively their terms of trade as a result of their strong bargaining positions *vis-à-vis* their trading partners. For the secessionist community to avoid losing valuable trade advantages, the country from which it is seceding would have to be either relatively "small," and therefore unable to influence positively its terms of trade, or otherwise, a part of a larger entity such as a free trade area. Thus it is not sheer level of interdependency that is significant, but the relative position of the existing state and the distinct community within the interdependent global economy.

This argument therefore distinguishes between the cases of the

Bretons, Corsicans, and Romansch and those of the Quebecois and the Catalans. Secession for the former three would present greater economic disadvantages – even under high levels of interdependency. This is because France and Switzerland can protect their vital national interests since they still command comparatively influential positions *vis-à-vis* their trading partners. Moreover, Switzerland continues to remain outside the European Union. By contrast, the latter two examples belong to Spain and Canada – two states which can affect their terms of trade only moderately and which belong to larger free trade areas. Under such circumstances, dissatisfied communities such as Catalonia and Quebec may be more willing to consider secession because it no longer entails similar sacrifices.

A few words of caution are necessary. Specifically, an important distinction must be made between a secession crisis and a secession movement. A secession crisis occurs when the leaders representing a territorially concentrated and distinct community within a larger state translate discontent into demands for secession, and possess the power, either through sufficiently strong internal community mobilization or through the use of force, to compel the central government to react to those demands. In contrast, a secession movement may represent the desires for independence among a substantial portion of the distinct community, but its leaders cannot compel the state to react to their demands because their power may be limited. Either they do not possess the support of a majority of a mobilized community or they do not command the resources to force the state to react. Thus far, Catalonia and Quebec have only presented secession movements. But secession movements can, of course, grow into secession crises.

Because the secession dynamic is incomplete, it is difficult to isolate the main motivations for the decision to secede. The purpose here is not to explain definitively Catalan and Quebecois separatism, but rather to suggest a theory for continued separatist agitation in advanced Western societies. That is, as members of the Catalan and Quebecois communities begin to perceive that evolution of the international system diminishes both external security threats and the economic benefits of membership, secession slowly becomes a viable political alternative. Thus, the erosion of the state's previous absolute jurisdiction could precipitate a secession crisis without the central government actually changing specific policies towards its communities. An examination of Catalan and Quebecois separatism sets the stage for a detailed exploration of these international factors.

Catalan separatism[24]

Current Catalan assertiveness persists in an anomalous political context. Its current power and prosperity contrasts sharply with the ill-treatment suffered under General Francisco Franco. Demands for ever greater sovereignty come when the Catalans already benefit from extensive devolution. These demands persist despite the fact that the central government not only no longer actively threatens Catalan culture, but even encourages its development.

Before 1980 Catalonia suffered numerous centralizing initiatives by the Madrid authorities, beginning in the seventeenth century with the reign of King Philip IV. The only exception was a brief expression of fully functioning autonomy from July, 1936 to May, 1937. The Catalans suffered the most systematic repression under the authoritarian government of Franco, as it attempted to suppress all manifestations of regional distinctness. Catalonia's autonomous government, the *Generalitat*, was abolished, while its leader was extradited from France during World War I and executed.[25] Legal statutes made the public use of the Catalan language illegal. Education and worship in Catalan were prohibited. The well-established Institute of Catalan Studies was closed.[26] The mass media was "castilianised", which meant the closure of all Catalan newspapers and magazines.[27] As Spain's principal industrialized region, Catalonia attracted many working-class immigrants in the post-war era. While much of this movement can be ascribed to economic necessity, Catalans consistently accused Madrid of encouraging it in order to dilute their community's cohesiveness.[28] Regional officials were frequently recruited from outside the region, and thus possessed little understanding of local

[24] Historical material for this section is drawn mainly from David D. Laitin, "Linguistic Revival: Politics and Culture in Catalonia," *Comparative Study of Society and History*, 31 (1989), 297–317; Kenneth Medhurst, *The Basques and the Catalans* (London: Minority Rights Group, 1987); P. Preston (ed.), *Spain in Crisis* (London: Harvester Press, 1976); legal documents such as the Spanish Constitution of 1978 and the Catalan Autonomy Statute are quoted in Hurst Hannum, "Spain – The Basque Country and Catalonia," ch. 13 in *Autonomy, Sovereignty, and Self-Determination: The Accommodation of Conflicting Rights* (Philadelphia: University of Pennsylvania Press, 1990), pp. 263–279.
[25] Medhurst, *Basques and Catalans*, p. 4.
[26] N. L. Jones, "The Catalan Question Since the Civil War," in P. Preston (ed.), *Spain in Crisis* (London: Harvester Press, 1976), pp. 236–241.
[27] Medhurst, *Basques and Catalans*, p. 5.
[28] Hannum, "Spain," p. 267.

needs and rarely spoke the local language. "At worst, local inhabitants could acquire the sense of living in occupied territory."[29]

Nevertheless, because of the scale of Catalan resistance, their community maintained its social cohesion during the years of repression and was strategically placed to benefit rapidly from constitutional changes following Franco's death in 1975.[30] The 1978 constitution reformed the formerly subordinate relationship between the Catalans, Basques, Galicians, Andalucians, and the central government by devolving extensive powers to the "four historic regions" of Spain.[31] Articles 143 through 158 enshrined both the mechanism by which autonomous status could be attained and the division of jurisdiction between the regional and central governments. The autonomy statutes were legally entrenched and superior to any state law. Once adopted, they can only be amended by absolute majorities in both the regional assembly and the Cortes, and by a referendum in the autonomous community.

The Catalan government, the Generalitat, has been accorded wide-ranging rights. Article 148 of the constitution stipulates that autonomous governments have exclusive jurisdiction over local civil law, allocation of natural resources, regulation of local transportation, industry, and communications, urban planning, public works, infrastructure, and social programs for health, unemployment, welfare, and culture. Given the Franco regime's abuse of police powers, the Catalans insisted on permission to establish an "autonomous police force." Article 156 guaranteed "fiscal autonomy" to the regions. They possess the right to raise local taxes and to receive a portion of national taxes as well. Finally the Catalan president, although formally appointed by the king, is responsible only to the regional assembly. "Thus, to a meaningful extent, the highly centralised Spanish government has become significantly decentralised in less than a decade."[32]

The Generalitat has ambitiously employed its new powers to

[29] Medhurst, *Basques and Catalans*, p. 4.
[30] David D. Laitin, "Linguistic Revival: Politics and Culture in Catalonia," *Comparative Study of Society and History*, 3 (1989), 297–317. Medhurst even asserts, "Catalonia was the largest single source of opposition to (Franco's) regime ... (M)ass gestures of defiance pointed to the re-emergence of a certain communal self-confidence (which) lay behind a renewed and sometimes spectacular campaign in support of Catalan culture." See Medurst, *Basques and Catalans*, p. 10.
[31] Hannum, "Spain," pp. 268–269.
[32] Ibid., p. 269.

achieve nothing short of a transformation of Catalan life. Through interventionist policies, the regional government both reduced the threat of dilution by migration and assured pre-eminence for the Catalan language. Under Article 3 of the constitution, it passed the Law of Linguistic Normalization, thus reinstituting Catalan as the official language of the region and of education.[33] Although secondary schools are bilingual, all university education is in Catalan, thus making this language a prerequisite for social mobility. The government is committed to purchase a sufficient number of books in Catalan to assure Barcelona publishers a moderate profit.[34] Television programing in Catalan prospers due to heavy subsidization. Speaking Catalan has become *de rigueur* not only in regional government and business offices, but also in federal agencies located in Catalonia.[35] In 1983, the Generalitat requested the federal government to alter the language of its services such as railways, telephones, expressways, and the courts of law from Spanish to Catalan. The Spanish state complied.[36] Besides language legislation, the coalition government of Convergencia i Unio (CiU)[37] since 1980, under the direction of Catalan President Jordi Pujol, has also pressed ahead with reform of the formerly protectionist and highly regulated economy. From 1980 to 1995, the Catalan government consistently outstripped the socialist government in Madrid in its reforming zeal.[38]

Some disputes remain. Disagreements frequently arise about the allocation of federal taxes to the regions. The central government prefers to negotiate financial arrangements annually to retain its leverage. The *Generalitat* and other regional governments press for a more permanent settlement of this issue. Taken as a whole, however, the process begun in 1978 has significantly empowered the Catalans to administer their own affairs.

Despite these achievements of self-government, or because of them, the Catalans continue to demand greater rights. Catalonia does not suffer the type of violence perpetrated by the Euskadi ta Askatasuna (Basque Homeland and Freedom). Nevertheless, the central government must accommodate escalating claims emanating from Barcelona.

---

[33] For details of this legislation, see Laitin, "Linguistic Revival," pp. 314–315.
[34] Ibid., p. 314.
[35] "Spain: A Survey," *The Economist*, April 25, 1992, p. 22.
[36] Laitin, "Linguistic Revival,"p. 314.
[37] CiU is an alliance of two conservative parties, Convergencia Democratica de Catalunya and Unio Democratia de Catalunya.
[38] "Spain: A Survey," p. 22.

For example, the Generalitat is demanding the right for its representatives to speak their own language in the Cortes in Madrid.[39] Its representatives in Brussels lobby the European Commission directly on Catalan issues, no longer relying on the Spanish government to protect its interests. It has joined the German *Länder* to press for greater regional representation in Commission decision-making.[40] The controversy over the official language of the 1992 Summer Olympics in Barcelona proved embarrassing to the Spanish government. Since no common ground could be reached between the central government's demands for Spanish and the Barcelona government's insistence on Catalan, the opening ceremonies were announced in French.

Although there is only anecdotal evidence of growing Catalan assertiveness, what is intriguing is its timing. Many factors motivate continuing Catalan dissatisfaction and demands. Alienation from Spain lingers due to memories of Franco's oppression. Pride in the efficient functioning of their regional government encourages greater self-confidence among Catalans. Yet such domestic considerations, in and of themselves, are not sufficient to influence Catalans to support a separatist agenda. Separatist sentiment persists just at the time when Catalans have secured more control over their own affairs than ever before in their history, and when Spain itself does not pose any immediate costs of membership. The post-war political and economic changes in the international system to be discussed below play an important and growing role in generating support for separatist proposals. The gradual realization that, due to international systematic shifts, the Spanish state is no longer the appropriate political authority to provide certain security and economic services for its citizens enhances the perceived viability of an independent Catalonia.

Quebecois separatism

The juxtaposition of Catalan and Quebecois separatism emphasizes their common elements. Both communities perceive themselves as victims of earlier political and linguistic discrimination, leaving the Quebecois with an almost traditional alienation from the rest of Canada. In contrast with its earlier subordinate position, Quebec, like Catalonia, is at the zenith of its provincial powers. Like Spain's

[39] Ibid., p. 22.
[40] Ibid., p. 23.

180

current support for Catalan culture, Canada also promotes the French language and Quebecois culture. Yet the appeal of separation grows in Quebec. The following section explores the Quebecois' three main grievances with Canada, describes how Canadian society and the Quebec provincial government have sought to remedy those grievances, and then chronicles the persistence of secession as a viable alternative within Quebec politics and public opinion.

With the defeat of French forces on the Plains of Abraham in 1759, Britain gained control of the colony of New France. Through the Quebec Act of 1774, the British parliament granted these subjugated people the right to their Catholic religion, seigneurial system, and civil legal code in return for loyalty to the British crown.[41] Although they possessed these formal privileges, in practice the French Canadians consistently perceived themselves as relegated to a subordinate position. The threat of forced assimilation, the central government's reticence to redress their concerns, and the discrepancy in advancement opportunities reinforced their historic discontent with Canada.

First, although its widely adopted policy in the eighteenth century was to assimilate colonized populations into British culture, the difficulties it suffered in governing New France after 1763 convinced the government to discard its usual approach in favor of the compromise encapsulated in the Quebec Act.[42] After the suppression of Papineau's rebellion in 1838, however, Lord Durham's Report on the revolt brought the assimilation issue back into the debate on the colony's governance. When the earl of Durham came to Canada to investigate the causes of the rebellion, he had expected to find a contest between the government and the people. Instead he reported that he encountered "two nations warring in the bosom of a single state."[43] His report strongly recommended that the only way to avoid future disturbances was to forcibly anglicize the Francophones.[44] To this end, the Act of Union of 1840 rejoined the two Canadian colonies (Ontario and Quebec) into a single province; the political aspirations

[41] For a complete list of the rights granted to the French community in Canada under the 1774 act, see Rudy Fenwick, "Social Change and Ethnic Nationalism: An Historical Analysis of the Separatist Movement in Quebec," *Comparative Studies of Society and History*, 23 (1981), 200–201.
[42] Camille Legendre, *French Canada in Crisis* (London: Minority Rights Group, 1980), p. 6.
[43] Ramsay Cook, *Canada, Quebec, and the Uses of Nationalism* (Toronto: McClelland & Stewart, 1986), p. 45; Lord Durham's Report is also quoted in "For Want of Glue: A Survey of Canada,"*The Economist*, June 29, 1991, p. 5.
[44] Cook, *Canada, Quebec*, pp. 45–50.

of the French Canadians were no longer to manifest themselves in their own exclusive public institutions.[45] To a certain extent, Lord Durham's recommendations have been achieved. The rate of Francophone assimilation in provinces outside Quebec is high. Only isolated pockets of French-speakers around Canada remain. As the only unilingual French political entity on the continent, Quebec remains the sole custodian of French language and culture in North America.[46]

Second, many in Quebec judge that the central government addresses injustices against French speakers much more slowly than those against English speakers. For instance, in the Manitoba School Act of 1890, the Manitoba legislature restricted the use of French in the province and abolished public aid for Catholic, mainly French language, schools. By 1905 New Brunswick, Alberta, and Saskatchewan also abolished French and Catholic educational rights within their provincial jurisdictions. In 1913 the Ontario provincial government followed suit.[47] The Supreme Court of Canada declared these laws unconstitutional ninety years after their initial implementation.[48] The fact that the legal system had changed a great deal during this century makes the Quebecois no less indignant that, when Quebec's legislature passed comparable restrictions on the use of the English language in the 1970s, they were struck down as unconstitutional within three years of enactment.[49]

Third, Quebecois leaders have long asserted that a cultural division of labor has developed within their province, with members of their own community filling the lower-skilled, lower-paid jobs. During most of the twentieth century, over 80% of Quebec industry has been owned by English speakers. In 1961, the proportion of manufacturing enterprises owned by Quebecois businessmen was estimated at 15%.[50] The findings of the Royal Commission on Bilingualism and Bicultur-

[45] For a description of the political institutions of the United Province of Canada, see William Ormsby, "The Providence of Canada: The Emergence of Consociational Politics," in Kenneth D. McRae (ed.), *Consociational Democracy: Political Accommodation in Segmented Societies* (Toronto: McClelland & Stewart, 1974), pp. 271–279.
[46] For a discussion of the problems regarding linguistic assimilation in Canada, see Richard J. Joy, *Languages in Conflict* (Toronto: McClelland & Stewart, 1968).
[47] Richard Von Loon and Michael Whittington, *The Canadian Political System: Environment, Structure, and Process* (Toronto: McGraw-Hill, 1976), pp. 66–67.
[48] "For Want of Glue: A Survey of Canada,"*The Economist*, June 21, 1991, pp. 9–10.
[49] Legendre, *French Canada*, p. 14.
[50] Thomas Sloan, *Quebec: The Not So Quiet Revolution* (Toronto: Ryerson, 1965), p. 49; Von Loon and Whittington, *Canadian Political System*, p. 63; Ramsay Cook, *The Maple Leaf Forever* (Toronto: Macmillan, 1967), p. 3.

alism (RCBB), based on analysis of data from the 1960 census, reinforced these allegations. On average, those of British origin earned 110% of the national average income, while those of French origin earned 86%. In Quebec, the income disparity was even greater. Those of British origin earned 140% of the national average while those of French origin earned only 91%. The report also revealed that, with the exception of the Maritime provinces, Quebec consistently suffered the highest unemployment in the country, predominantly among French speakers.[51]

The Canadian federal government and the Quebec provincial government have sought to redress some of these grievances. Yet within the unique character of Canadian federalism, Quebecois demands for greater privileges should be distinguished from the more general transformation of Canadian politics. Since the 1960s, Ottawa has devolved numerous powers to the provinces. Although the new federalist arrangements inherently apply to all provinces, Quebec has taken the fullest advantage of the flexibility of the Canadian federal system. It has used the redistribution of domestic authority to promote its unique vision for Quebec through what has become known as "the Quiet Revolution." It is a testimony to the flexibility and sensitivity of the Canadian government that Quebec was allowed and even assisted in its efforts to achieve its objectives.

Specifically, in the 1960s, the newly elected Liberal Party provincial government implemented a set of remarkable reforms designed to modernize Quebec's conservative social institutions in order to provide a foundation for a dynamic and increasingly outward looking economy.[52] To this end, the newly created Ministry of Education removed schools from the control of the Catholic Church and established a number of business schools and junior colleges for continuing education.[53] It also extended provincial programs to handle health and welfare concerns. The nationalization of eleven power companies to form Hydro Quebec and the creation of the Quebec Pension Fund enabled the provincial government to give preferential treatment to Quebec companies either through provision of investment funds or through allocation of engineering and con-

---

[51] *Report of the Royal Commission on Bilingualism and Biculturalism*, book III (Ottawa: Queen's Printer of Canada, 1969).
[52] Fenwick, "Social Changes and Ethnic Nationalism," 204–207.
[53] Graham Spry, "Canada: Notes on Two Ideas of Nation in Confrontation," *Journal of Contemporary History*, 6 (1971), 147–158.

struction contracts.[54] Moreover, the associated expansion of the provincial civil service itself extended employment opportunities to those students emerging from the reformed educational system.

Such ambitious programs required additional funding, thereby also necessitating reform of national fiscal arrangements. Due to the near bankruptcy of many provinces during the 1930s, the federal government had concentrated taxation powers within its own jurisdiction. Projects within exclusive federal jurisdiction were closely regulated by the Ottawa government. Federal grants in areas of provincial jurisdiction also became conditional on provincial governments opting in to federally directed, shared-cost initiatives. The provinces retained the right to opt out of these projects but with the associated sacrifice of federal funding. Historically, Quebec had not joined any of these social programs or accepted conditional grants.[55] After exerting much pressure for decentralization, the Liberal provincial government won a significant concession from the federal government in 1965: it could opt out of shared-cost social programs without the associated fiscal penalty. Thus the Quebecois government retained more tax funds to implement its novel social agenda.[56] As part of the bargain, the federal government retained the right to prescribe the objectives of provincial programs. After the 1968 elections, Prime Minister Pierre Trudeau's federal administration further reformed the taxation system so that Quebec secured more discretion over its taxes. In 1968, Quebec provided about 25% of federal taxes, but only received 16% of federal spending. By 1976, federal taxation and spending in Quebec had reached an equilibrium of about 22%.[57] The substantial degree of fiscal autonomy permitted the Quebec government to finance programs in health, education, pensions, unemployment, and youth projects.

Finally, with the series of recent language laws, French speakers no longer face the same disadvantages in terms of advancement opportunities. A product of the Royal Commission on Bilingualism and Biculturalism's Report, the 1969 Official Languages Act proclaimed Canada as officially bilingual. This decree reinforced the policies Trudeau had begun the previous year: those of increasing the propor-

[54] Donald V. Smiley, *Canada in Question* (Toronto: McGraw-Hill, 1972), pp. 147–148.
[55] Von Loon and Whittington, *Canadian Political System*, p. 205.
[56] Smiley, *Canada in Question*, p. 343; Von Loon and Whittington, *Canadian Political System*, p. 221.
[57] "For Want of Glue: A Survey of Canada," *The Economist*, June 29, 1991, p. 5.

tion of French speakers in the federal civil service, and, in particular, of promoting them to higher positions. In marked contrast to the trend toward bilingualism, on November 15, 1974, French was made the sole official language of Quebec.[58] With the election of the Parti Quebecois two years later, the provincial government further entrenched the position of the French language with Bill 101.[59] This bill was designed as a charter for the French language. By requiring all business in Quebec to operate in French, its intention was to create new opportunities for French speakers in commerce and industry in a similar fashion to the 1974 legislation, which had generated new openings in government employment. Of the numerous reactions to Bill 101, at least two had significant consequences. First, Bill 101 precipitated the migration of many Anglophone professionals and corporations from Montreal to Toronto.[60] Second, it naturally caused resentment in other parts of Canada. Whereas the Canadian government was expending scarce resources to create a bilingual society, the Quebec government was engaged in making its province unilingual. When the Canadian Supreme Court declared Bill 101 to be a breach of the new Charter of Rights and Freedoms, the Quebec government under Robert Bourassa's direction quickly introduced Bill 178 in its place.[61] By invoking the "notwithstanding clause" in the new constitutional agreements, the provincial legislature approved Bill 178, thereby reaffirming the primacy of the French language. Even the display of business signs in any language but French became illegal.[62]

In spite of these federal and provincial efforts to establish a new and mutually satisfactory place for Quebec embedded in Canada, the Quebecois continue to perceive threats to their culture. Furthermore, cultural threats need not reach extreme levels – like the religious and linguistic persecution in the Southern Sudanese rebellion – in order to mobilise a community to seek change. Perhaps most importantly for this case, with a population of only 7 million, the Quebecois constitute a small minority within a predominantly English speaking continent. Extrapolations of current demographic trends into the next century

[58] Legendre, *French Canada*, p. 13.
[59] Ibid.
[60] "For Want of Glue," p. 9.
[61] Ibid.
[62] Ibid. Exception is made in those areas of Quebec where the majority of residents are native-English speakers. In such areas bilingual signs are permitted.

project a falling Francophone population not just in relative terms but in absolute ones as well.[63]

At a more fundamental level, political disagreements between the central government, the other provinces, and Quebec, persist because the members of these separate constituencies hold two vastly differing conceptions of Canada itself. This conflict is, in some sense, inherently insoluble. As Jane Jacobs argues, separatist and federalist Quebecois both cling to the belief that Canada was created by two "founding peoples" – the English and the French.[64] They demand that the constitution recognize this duality and make it functional.[65] To place both founding peoples on equal footing and to enforce their equality, however, would imply that Quebec, with only about a quarter of the total population, should be provided with virtual veto powers over certain constitutional amendments proposed by the English speaking majority. These claims directly conflict with the conception of Canada held in most other provinces – that of a federation of equal provinces with equal duties and equal privileges.

The evolution of federal institutions has served both to reinforce and to accommodate such Quebecois claims. Quebec has achieved greater influence in national affairs than its population would merit and extensive autonomy to administer its own affairs both because of conciliatory arrangements offered by Canadian leaders and because of its own particular efforts and voting patterns. The roots of Quebec's influence in national politics can be traced to the nineteenth-century practice of according equal representation to the French and English communities in the colonial legislature of Upper and Lower Canada (1842–1867). The political institutions of that period revolved around an informal system of twinned prime ministers and twinned minis-terial portfolios for the two communities.[66] This system of concurrent majorities evolved into the informal rotation between Anglophones and Francophones of the country's five most important offices: those

[63] Quebec's current fertility rate is 1.5, while it would need 2.1 to replace its population. It is estimated that by 2040, the Francophone population will decrease by 1% per year. Given the Anglophone migration rate into Quebec, the French speakers fear the loss of their prominent position within the province.

[64] Jane Jacobs, *The Question of Separatism: Quebec The Struggle Over Sovereignty* (New York: Random House, 1980),pp. 78–82.

[65] See, for example, the 1980 proposals of the Quebecois federalist, Claude Ryan, for procedures to amend the constitution in Jacobs, *Question of Separatism*, p. 82.

[66] Kenneth D. McRae, "Consociationalism and the Canadian Political System, in McRae (ed.), *Consociational Democracy: Political Accommodation in Segmented Societies* (Toronto: McClelland & Stewart, 1974), pp. 251–260.

of prime minister, chief justice of the Supreme Court, speaker of the House of Commons, leader of the Liberal Party, and governor-general. In addition, the Quebec caucus's strength in the federal government has also been a crucial factor in securing a disproportionate share of influence. Since the Quebecois have historically tended to vote *en masse* for one party or another,[67] the Quebec representation consistently represents a unified and large block of votes in the federal parliament. Significantly, during the post-war era, the prime minister has been from Quebec for over two-thirds of the time.[68]

In their 1976 study of the Canadian federal system, two Canadian political scientists, Dale Postgate and Kenneth McRoberts, concluded that the Quebec government has secured "a greater range of powers and resources than is exploited by any other provincial government."[69] Through the continuing process of political decentralization within Canada, the Quebecois have been empowered to protect the French language and culture, to pursue their own unique vision of social progress, and to regulate their own economy.

Herein lies the anomaly: despite substantial progress on many fronts, the debate on secession has persisted as a priority in Quebec politics. In referendums in 1980 and again in 1995, Quebec citizens had the opportunity to vote on secession. In 1976, the Parti Quebecois (PQ) was elected to the provincial government on an avowedly separatist platform. The election had numerous undertones, but the consequences were that in 1980 the provincial government organized a referendum, as it had promised, on the question of whether Quebec should begin negotiations with the federal government on some new form of "sovereignty-association."[70] Although the Parti Quebecois

[67] Before 1984, Quebecois mostly voted for the Liberal Party in federal elections. Since 1984 support has shifted more toward the Conservative Party.
[68] For a more detailed analysis of the Canadian political system in terms of its consociational elements, see Arendt Lijphart, "Semi-Consociational Democracy: Canada," in *Democracy in Plural Societies: A Comparative Exploration* (New Haven: Yale University Press, 1977), p. 119–129.
[69] Dale Postgate and Kenneth McRoberts, *Quebec: Social Change and Political Crisis* (Toronto: McClelland & Stewart, 1976), p. 205.
[70] Text of the referendum question (reprinted in Legendre, *French Canada*, p. 17:
  The Government of Quebec has made public its proposal to negotiate a new agreement with the rest of Canada, based on the equality of nations; this agreement would enable Quebec to acquire the exclusive power to make its laws, levy its own taxes and establish relations abroad – in other words "sovereignty" – and at the same time, to maintain with Canada an economic association including a common currency; no change in political status resulting from these negotiations will be effected without approval by the people through another referendum; on these terms, do you give the Govern-

worded the referendum in a vague manner, its leaders' intent was to begin a gradual process of disengagement from the Canadian political system with the final goal of independence for Quebec. They strove to achieve sovereignty while retaining the many existing economic ties. In the end, the Parti Quebecois was not forced to specify its understanding of "sovereignty-association" because the electorate rejected its proposal by a vote of 60% to 40%. No doubt an understanding of the balance of benefits associated with remaining within Canada influenced Quebec voters in rejecting it.

Fifteen years later, the Quebecois were faced with a second referendum on secession. This time, the recently elected Parti Quebecois government tempered its proposed declaration of sovereignty with an offer to negotiate with the rest of Canada a form of political and economic partnership modeled on the European Union. On October 31, 1995, the secessionist proposal was defeated by the narrowest of margins: 50.5% to 49.5%.[71]

Nevertheless, what is interesting is not that separatist referendums were defeated twice, but that a full 40% of the voters in 1980 and then 49.5% in 1995 expressed a desire for secession. Since the Anglophone 20% of the population voted nearly unanimously in each referendum to defeat the proposal, this means that 50% of the Francophones voted in favor of secession in 1980 and 62% in 1995. This recurring desire for separation appears anomalous given the federal government's numerous efforts to address specific Quebec grievances and the growing confidence, affluence, and security of this distinct community. In a potent yet contradictory evolution, Quebec's gradual acquisition of greater provincial powers seems to have both fed and tempered the demands for secession. The process has encouraged a belief among Quebecois leaders that they can better control their community's destiny while at the same time it made them more sensitive to the negative impact of the decision to secede.

To summarize the main propositions, domestic factors such as demographic pressures, a history of past mistreatment, economic ties, and changing cultural values are certainly relevant in generating a desire among Catalans and Quebecois for change. These factors are all closely intertwined, which precludes any straightforward or simple

ment of Quebec the mandate to negotiate the proposed agreement between Quebec and Canada? Yes. No.
[71] "Shaking Canada," *The Economist*, October 21, 1995, pp. 41–42; "That's that, until Quebec tries again," *The Economist*, November 4, 1995, pp. 45–46.

generalizations concerning either case of separatism. Taken together, however, these cases suggest an additional complexity to the secession dynamic. The next section, therefore, introduces the way in which developments in the international system, by eroding previously pressing defense requirements and weakening the state's ability to provide economic benefits for its citizens, can influence secession decisions. As these changes permit a new level of demands without the previously associated risks, distinct communities reappraise their political options. This reappraisal in effect lends credibility to secessionist claims. The effects of changes in security requirements and economic integration have not been limited to discontented communities in the West but have also encouraged other communities in their aspirations for independence.

Security requirements

Turning now to the crucial matrix of established inter-state relations which impinge on any secession aspirations, the purpose of this section is to outline how the post-war evolution in security arrangements has enhanced the potential viability of small distinct communities in North America and Western Europe. This analysis of the international system must differentiate between its structure and its character. The international political system is, as Hedley Bull described, "an anarchical society."[72] Its primary distinguishing feature is that its constituent units, the states, refuse to acknowledge any overarching authority higher than themselves. All states participate in relationships on the basis of sovereign equality. If anarchy defines the international system's structure, it does not necessarily define the character of interactions among states. A whole spectrum of relations is possible. At one extreme lies what Barry Buzan refers to as an "immature anarchy"[73] – a situation in which states do not recognize each other's sovereignty, and thus, struggle for dominance over one another. At the other extreme lies what Buzan calls a "mature anarchy" – where international law regulates conduct among states.

Under conditions of anarchy, then, the constituent units are the

[72] Hedley Bull, *The Anarchical Society: A Study of Order in World Politics* (London: Macmillan, 1987).
[73] Barry Buzan, *People, States, and Fear: The National Security Problem in International Relations* (London: Harvester Wheatsheaf, 1983), pp. 121–123.

sources of threats to each other. States are forced to defend their independence and integrity in a number of ways. Buzan distinguishes two broad defense strategies: first, reducing domestic vulnerabilities, and second, addressing the international climate of threats.[74] For the first, national security strategies attempt to improve a country's position independent of relations with neighbors. Large size and a strong economy have historically tended to facilitate defense since security provisions including the military are produced under conditions of increasing returns to scale. By contrast, conditions including scarcity of natural resources, economic underdevelopment, and the lack of social cohesion have frequently impaired a country's ability to defend itself. The effective mobilization of military resources was, and still is, considered essential to statecraft. This is because states waged war as an instrument of policy – as an acceptable extension of diplomatic initiatives – often to achieve limited objectives. For the second, international security strategies attempt to address the source of threats: the relationship among states. Diplomatic initiatives, alliances, and international treaties would reduce the level of threats which are inherent in the very interactions among states.

Anarchy may still define the system's structure but its character has been altered by evolution in the interaction among states. Once Napoleon displaced professional armies, introducing *levée en masse*, statesmen could no longer conceive of war as essentially a limited activity isolated from domestic politics. The growth in casualties, the disruption of trade, commerce, and domestic life, and the spread of popular franchise forced political elites to provide greater public justification for their war aims. Due to the growing destructiveness of war in general, ruling elites began to establish conventions for avoiding conflicts. International institutions developed to mitigate the competitive anarchy. Such moderating mechanisms in international relations as the balance of power, international law, diplomacy, and great power crisis management have their origins in nineteenth-century European statecraft.[75] Hedley Bull and Adam Watson describe the evolution of such conventions as progress toward an international "society," which they define as: "a group of states ... which not merely form a system, in the sense that the behavior of each is a necessary factor in the calculations of others, but also have

[74] Ibid., pp. 73–75.
[75] Bull, *Anarchical Society*, p. 287.

established by dialogue and consent common rules and institutions for the conduct of their relations, and recognize their common interest in maintaining these arrangements."[76]

This evolution in the character of the international system is most clearly visible in the more stable relations in Western Europe and North America in the post-World War II era. Some elements of statecraft which contribute to this evolution are already widely accepted, such as the mutual recognition of sovereign equality.[77] Others are accepted in principle, such as the respect for non-intervention and inviolability of territorial boundaries, although in practice they restrain the behaviour of states less frequently. Perhaps most importantly, the settlement of disputes has gradually moved away from the battlefield and into the realm of diplomatic negotiations. Karl Deutsch argues that in the North Atlantic context the closely allied countries have incorporated stabilizing mechanisms in their relations with one another, and thus, have established "pluralistic security communities."[78] Within these security communities, Buzan argues, "the consensus ... is that wars ... are no longer a desirable or fruitful way of settling differences."[79]

The experience of World War I and the invention of nuclear weapons motivated this evolution toward a "mature anarchy." World War II revealed that national defense strategies had become outdated. Due to their limited size in terms of population, territory, and economic strength, many European states were defeated and devastated. By the end of World War II, the advances attained in military technology undermined the view that security could effectively be achieved through a reduction of domestic vulnerabilities. In fact, the North Atlantic Treaty Organization (NATO) implicitly acknowledged the inability of individual states to protect their own security. Furthermore, the advent of nuclear weapons and "the fear that victory and defeat will be indistinguishable"[80] compelled leaders to search for new international security alternatives to modify interactions among states, and thereby reduce the threat of war.

[76] Hedley Bull and Adam Watson, *The Expansion of the International Society* (Oxford, Oxford University Press, 1984), p. 1.
[77] Buzan, *People, States, and Fear*, pp. 93–101; Karl Deutsch, *et al.*, *Political Community and the North Atlantic Area: International Organization in the Light of Historical Experience* (Princeton: Princeton University Press, 1957).
[78] Deutsch, *et al.*, *Political Community*, pp. 3–21.
[79] Buzan, *People, States and Fear*, pp. 171–172.
[80] Ibid., p. 170.

This unprecedented search for new norms is slowly becoming entrenched in international law. Despite imperfections, some elements such as sovereignty, mutual recognition, and legal equality are gradually becoming the foundation of international relations. For instance, as James Mayall argues, the consequence of the international community's attempt after World War I to restrict the legitimate use of force only for self-defense against aggression – a principle enshrined in the United Nations Charter – has been to remove war from its previous place as an acceptable means to effect change within international society. The United Nations stands both as a model for more mature anarchy in the future and as a concrete embodiment of the progress already achieved. In some regions of the world, state practice still lags behind the development of international law, but in Western Europe and North America, war is now regarded as clear evidence of the breakdown of international society.[81]

As a result, within "pluralistic security communities" the size of a country's territory, population, and economy has ceased to have a close relationship to its security. With the help of NATO and other alliances, smaller states could now guarantee their inhabitants a level of security which they were unable to do before the post-war era. The American nuclear umbrella extends protection to its militarily stronger and weaker allies in Europe and North America equally. Constrained by a web of diplomatic commitments, most states pursue policy objectives, protect their interests, and settle their disputes through diplomatic channels in which military strength possesses diminished significance. Morever, in the Western European context, other traditionally domestic security concerns such as immigration, and law and order, have receded from the exclusive jurisdiction of the state. The European Union's recent progress in setting new parameters of inter-governmental cooperation on issues regarding police work further challenges existing conceptions of state authority.

The American security guarantee, the generally peaceful relations among neighbors, and the pooling of security responsibilities within the European Union have created the international climate in which Catalonia, Quebec, and other communities can contemplate secession with fewer security ramifications. These changes have enhanced the potential political viability of smaller distinct communities as inde-

---

[81] James Mayall, *Nationalism and International Society* (Cambridge: Cambridge University Press, 1990), p. 146.

pendent entities. It is no longer likely that a smaller, military weaker seceding community will be forcibly annexed by a more powerful neighbor. The contrast between the security challenges associated with the early-twentieth century versus the post-war era is stark.[82] At the turn of the century, Czech aspirations were limited to the creation of a Bohemian Kingdom within the Austro-Hungarian Empire due to fears of worse subjugation under German imperial expansion. In the late twentieth century, by contrast, the Catalans, Quebecois, Flemish, or Scots would not face security threats similar to those which the Czechs feared. They could confidently expect to ensure their security through membership in NATO and the European Union and reliance on their neighbor's respect for the principles of sovereignty, non-intervention, and inviolability of territorial borders. Independent Scotland, Quebec, Flanders, or Catalonia would be born into an international society which does not threaten states of similar size such as Denmark, Luxembourg, and the Netherlands.

Economic integration

The dramatic nature of this evolution toward international society notwithstanding, it does not affect the vertical division of the international system into its component states. Even in a maturing anarchy, sovereign states remain the basic units. By contrast, the powerful forces of economic integration and the emergence of the global market serve to counterbalance the division of the international system into national economies. Patterns of trade, production, financial flows, communications, transportation, and the interests of multinational corporations transcend national borders. The purpose of this section is to describe how post-war international economic integration has reduced most states' independent ability to control their domestic economy by limiting the effectiveness of fiscal and monetary instruments. This unprecedented integration has eroded most states' economic sovereignty. As a consequence, citizens can obtain the economic advantages hitherto only associated with membership in large and prosperous states from alternative sources.

Historically, community prosperity depended on self-reliance. The strength of Western European state-building initiatives in the

---

[82] Walker Connor, "Nation-Building or Nation-Destroying," *World Politics*, 24, 3 (April, 1972), 332.

eighteenth and nineteenth centuries laid the foundation for the subsequent industrialization and urbanization of their economies.[83] Central governments played an integral role in providing a common system of currency, taxation, law, regulation, and administration. Many states used their legislative and executive powers not only to regulate their domestic economies, but also to provide a certain measure of social welfare for their citizens. Adopting corporatist strategies, some states have also intervened at the microeconomic level to direct the growth of certain sectors.

In the post-war era, deregulation of capital markets and the growth of free trade regions and supra-national organizations have impaired self-reliance. In fact, these trends fostered a high degree of economic interdependence. First, deregulation of domestic capital markets and abandonment of international capital controls in many advanced economies since the 1970s have spurred international investment. In terms of cross-border financial flows, the market for investment opportunities has arguably become global.[84] This substantial integration restricts the room to maneuver in terms of monetary policy. With the exception of a few states in the West with particularly strong economies or key currencies such as Germany, Japan, and the United States, most countries can no longer pursue autonomous monetary targets at odds with the predominant monetary policy of the key currency countries, without suffering drastic economic consequences. Moreover, stock market jitters, currency fluctuations, and interest rate adjustments are transmitted across the increasingly global economy. The synchronised stock market crash across the major bourses in October 1987 provides but one example. It would appear then, that many "small" states are increasingly unable to protect their economies from such financial shocks.

Second, the rapid growth of international trade has also transformed those economies open to it by further limiting states' ability to pursue economic priorities. In theory, international trade on the basis of comparative advantage increases the efficiency and welfare of participants. It also creates complicated patterns of interdependence, using Joseph Nye and Robert Keohane's distinction, in terms of "sensitivity and vulnerability." Under an open trading regime, tech-

---

[83] Karl Polanyi, *The Great Transformation* (New York: Rinehart, 1944; reprint Boston: Beacon Press, 1985).
[84] Richard O'Brien, *International Financial Integration: The End of Geography* (London: Pinter, 1992).

nological innovations in one part of the global economy transmit pressures for emulation and competition by other producers. For instance, cheaper and more efficient production of electronics or automobiles in Japan affects the ability of American and European companies competing in the same market to continue to produce. The recurring opposition to each successive round of GATT[85] negotiations indicates that the international economy cannot yet be characterized as a free trade system. Nevertheless, integration into the global trading regime has restricted many states' ability to protect their domestic industries from decline due to external competition.

Third, the gradual development both of supra-national organizations such as the European Union and of free trade regions such as the European Free Trade Association (EFTA) and the North American Free Trade Association (NAFTA) has gone some way to providing the citizens of small countries with the same economic advantages that have previously been enjoyed only by citizens of larger and more prosperous countries. For example, for smaller states the economic benefits of membership in such organizations represent access to a larger market for their products, access to capital markets for investment, some protection against financial instability, and opportunities for geographic mobility for their professional classes.

For instance, Catalan industry grew rapidly under the Franco regime, to a significant extent because it produced for the protected Spanish market. Ongoing implementation of the Single Market Project with its consequent free movement of goods, services, people, and capital, has enabled Catalan industries to produce for the entire Western European market. In fact, the original twelve European Community governments voluntarily relinquished sovereignty over specific fields of cooperative activity and joint decision-making in the Single European Act of 1987 to enable the European Commission to pursue this goal of a single market. Under such conditions, therefore, prosperity is no longer strictly a function of empire or of a large domestic market. The significance of regional economic integration initiatives lies in their provision of guaranteed markets and sources of finance. A newly independent distinct community integrated into such a larger economic system would not be forced to fight the winds of economic competition isolated and alone.

[85] GATT is the acronym for the General Agreement on Tariffs and Trade, negotiated at Geneva in 1947.

In another example, for a number of reasons Slovenia's economic position has improved since its secession from Yugoslavia. Slovenia has achieved greater credit-worthiness outside Yugoslavia, and thus, Slovene businesses now find it easier to compete in the global capital market and attract foreign direct investment. With preferential access to the EU, Slovene industries now produce goods and services for a much larger marketplace than the small, highly regulated Yugoslav market. Moreover, unencumbered by Yugoslavia's high inflation, unemployment, and economic mismanagement, Slovenia is in a stronger position to achieve stable economic growth. Ultimately, its objective is to join the European Union. Indeed, secession has enhanced Slovenia's bargaining power versus its Western trading partners due to the expectation that it will move toward full membership within the European Union.

These three separate developments of financial integration, global trade, and supra-national organizations and free trade regions may not provide a direct incentive for a secession attempt. However, they have established international conditions which would be more supportive of the economic viability of many smaller distinct communities as independent entities. A number of caveats remain. First, these trends currently affect mainly advanced industrialised societies. Second, it is important to take into account the special characteristics of the state to be seceded from. Third, one must also make a distinction between intra-regional and extra-regional issues.

In the case of Catalonia, the advantages of belonging in Spain, which is judged to possess a relatively weak bargaining position within the European Union, are not enormous. Spain possesses little leverage in trade and other negotiations either with its EU counterparts or with the United States and Japan. Consequently, if Catalonia were to secede, it would lose little in terms of international economic leverage. The situation of Catalonia, however, contrasts sharply with that of Corsica or even Bavaria, if they were to contemplate secession. This is because Germany and, to a certain extent, France can still influence in their favor both intra-regional and extra-regional negotiations, such as those with the United States within the Uruguay Round of the GATT. Secession for the Corsicans or any of the German *Länder* would imply the sacrifice of the international weight which Bonn and Paris retain to defend their citizens' interests.

Nevertheless, the EU decision-making process provides disproportionate influence to smaller states in the drafting of directives. Under the current institutional structure, an independent Catalonia would be entitled to its own representatives in the European Commission and the Council of Ministers. Consequently, Catalonia most certainly would be able to protect its own interests in EU debates better with independent statehood than through indirect pressure. The incentive here is that this community would move from a subordinate position to one of formal equality.

So, how do these complex international factors affect the secession dynamic? They have made secession more likely by reducing the security and economic benefits of membership, and hence, reducing the previous restraints on secession. To summarise, the progressive transformation of international political and economic relations has altered the challenges for both established states and those contemplating independence. In Western Europe and North America, security from potential military intervention by a neighbor is no longer as pressing a concern as it was even half a century earlier, due mainly to the progress toward a more "mature anarchy". The emergence of a global economy with its characteristic features of large cross-border trade and financial flows has seriously impaired the effectiveness of economic policy instruments wielded by many governments. Few European states, with the possible exception of Germany, can be considered masters of their own estates. These trends, however, lead to complex responses. They have generated pressures in Europe both for greater federalism – in the form of Economic and Monetary Union (EMU) – and for continued separatist agitation.

Members of distinct communities continuously calculate the balance of costs and benefits associated with integration in a larger political entity. Similar calculations are made with reference to independence. In his investigation of the problems associated with migration and minority integration, Maurice Zinkin quotes a Scottish colleague in the Indian civil service more than fifty years ago, well before the more recent rise of Scottish nationalism: "We Scots make a calculation. Just now we think it pays to be united with England. If the calculation came out differently, we would all be nationalists."[86] This "calculation" necessarily varies over time and even from person to person. The constituent elements of the costs and benefits vary. An individual's assessment of them is necessarily

---

[86] Maurice Zinkin, "Minorities, Immigrants, and Refugees: The Problems of Integration," *International Relations*, 10, 3 (May 1991), pp. 268–269.

subjective. Nevertheless, the international systemic changes outlined thus far affect the decision to secede, because they reduce the benefits of membership for many distinct communities who are currently members of small states or who participate in larger, more integrated economic systems such as the European Union. In fact, these changes have already reinforced the convictions of some discontented communities, within Western Europe and beyond, that independent statehood is both a credible and desirable alternative.

To illustrate, Zinkin himself outlines the way in which a growing proportion of Scots could conclude, through a similar calculation as the one outlined by the Scottish civil servant, that it no longer "pays to be united with England":

> The advantages which the United Kingdom can offer Scots, Welsh and Ulstermen are diminishing because all are part of a European Community which is taking over some of the functions which previously all four nations agreed it was to their advantage that the United Kingdom should perform. The European Community now provides a common market, for instance, and foreign policy is more and more made in concert in Community.[87]

One can legitimately question Zinkin's optimism about future progress toward a common European foreign policy. In terms of regulation of the common market and monetary policy, none the less, Zinkin has on the whole correctly identified the underlying trend. His argument about Britain can be extended to include the advantages that Spain has traditionally offered to the Catalans, or Basques, but which have also diminished due to EU membership. The leaders of many smaller communities have already calculated the possible advantages offered by the EU. For example, Xabier Arzallus, leader of the Basque Nationalists, keeps in the corner of his office an EU flag with thirteen yellow stars instead of the usual twelve. The flag is a symbol of the Basque National Party's proposal for a distinctive and equal place for the Basque people within the European Union. The way forward, Arzallus argues, is through winning maximum autonomy now "so that we can find our way to Europe not through Spain, but as Basques."[88] To this end, the Basques have recently established an informal mission in Brussels alongside those of Catalonia, the German *Länder*, Scotland, Wales, and other regions. Such missions

---

[87] Zinkin, "Minorities," p. 269.
[88] "Spain: A Survey," *The Economist*, April 25, 1992, p. 23.

facilitate the growth of direct links between the Commission and regional authorities. The Basques have joined other communities in coordinating their lobbying efforts, in particular on the issue of extending their rights to express their communities' interests within EU institutions.[89]

Furthermore, the speeches of nationalist leaders within the former Soviet Union reveal that an appreciation of such international trends played a role in their demands for independence. In one representative example, when the Ukrainian historian Mykhailo Braichevs'kyi addressed the inaugural congress of the Ukrainian nationalist movement, Rukh, in September 1989, he pointedly questioned the relevance of the economic and security benefits of a large state:

> Today, it is probably clear to everyone that the union of republics, in the form it has assumed during the final quarter of this century, is very far from the ideal and requires a fundamental restructuring ... We are faced with the question of the viability, expedience and *necessity* of such a colossal federation comprising one sixth of the earth's surface. Once, great pride was taken in this colossus and it was regarded as an enormous achievement of mankind. Now quite a different tonality rules. Historical experience shows that it is the small nations which demonstrate the best standards of living: Belgium, the Netherlands, Sweden, Norway, Denmark, Iceland, Greece, etc. And the experience of our Baltic republics during their period of independent statehood also looks very instructive.
>
> The colonial system has collapsed; once subjugated people – large and small – have achieved independence ... If nowadays not only traditional teenies like Luxembourg, Andorra or San Marino, but also such tots as Mauritius or Barbados exist safely, and no one threatens them or intends to conquer them – then why cannot the 50-million-strong Ukraine, or small Estonia, exist as fully independent states? In what way is the Ukraine with her inexhaustible resources worse than 50-million-strong Britain, and 4-million-strong Azerbaijan worse that 4-million-strong Norway?[90]

Ukraine's secession from the Soviet Union in 1991 was certainly facilitated by an "opportune moment": the erosion of authority of the previously unifying, though now discredited, Communist Party, and the near collapse of the central government. Nevertheless, what is important to stress here is that for Braichevs'kyi, the leaders of Rukh,

[89] John Palmer, "Scotland and Wales Construct Power Bases in Europe," *The Guardian*, February 27, 1992, p. 8; "Spain: A Survey," p. 23.
[90] Bohdan Nahaylo and Victor Swoboda, *Soviet Disunion: A History of the Nationalities Problem in the U.S.S.R.* (New York: Macmillan, 1989), pp. 357–358. Emphasis added.

and many other Ukrainians, the success of other smaller states to provide defense and prosperity for their citizens within the contemporary international system enhanced the credibility of secessionist demands. Although their judgments with regard to economic constraints may prove mistaken, this type of analogy inspired many leaders of National Fronts throughout the former Soviet Union to press for independence.

These international political and economic developments have certainly not extinguished all benefits for smaller distinct communities embedded in Western liberal democracies. For some very small distinct communities such as the Romansch in Switzerland and the Frisians in the Netherlands, the state provides extensive financial subsidies for cultural, educational, and social programs. Part of the reason that the Swiss and Dutch governments do not have to contend with persistent separatist agitation from their Romansch or Frisian citizens is the recognition that their integration represents a means of obtaining greater financial resources to maintain their unique culture than they would be able to muster on their own even within the EU.[91]

Returning to the two original cases, recent instances of Catalan and Quebecois separatism become more comprehensible when set in the context of these international influences on the decision to secede. This context clarifies why, when both communities have secured extensive powers within their respective federations, separatist leaders find a constituency which believes that their proposals are worth sustained effort.

The growing public support for separation since the 1960s in Catalonia and Quebec – and in the Basque lands, Scotland, Wales, and other regions in Western societies – should therefore not be viewed as an atavistic phenomenon. It should not be seen as a revolt against governments perpetuating culturally repressive measures. Nor as a weakening of central government powers which provides an opportunity for withdrawal. Rather, it is the reaction to a gradual shift in the cost/benefit balance away from membership in existing states. Integration within established states is no longer judged as essential for

[91] Bud B. Khlief, "Issue of Theory and Methodology in the Study of Ethnolinguistic Movements: The Case of Frisian Nationalism in the Netherlands," in Edward A. Tiryakian and Ronald Rogowski. *New Nationalisms of the Developed West* (Boston: Allen & Unwin, 1985), pp. 176–196; and Kenneth McRae, *Conflict and Compromise in Multilingual Societies: The Case of Switzerland* (Waterloo: Wilfred Laurier University Press, 1983); William Keech, "Linguistic Diversity and Political Conflict: Some Observations Based on Four Swiss Cantons," *Comparative Politics*, 4, 3 (April, 1972), 384–404.

the protection and promotion of a distinct community's security and economic interests. This is especially the case if the community currently belongs either to a "small" state, or to a security alliance and a larger, effective economic association which protect some of the community's interests. The failure of these two relatively "small" states – Spain and Canada – to prevent the growth of secession movements becomes less obscure when understood in such terms. If these secession movements had been the consequence of specific grievances with the central government – as the Norwegian movement was – then one could expect that specific policy concessions could halt or reverse their growth. Certainly not all of the benefits associated with integration in larger, developed countries, have been eroded. Yet as the changing nature of the international system diminishes some of the original benefits of membership, the perception of such changes can and does influence the secession dynamic.

In closing, some may protest that as a consequence of changes in the very conception of sovereignty and the state outlined here, the potential decision by these Western communities to withdraw would no longer be one of secession. The concept of the state and the nature of its sovereignty are gradually but clearly being modified. Nevertheless, such changes do not negate the fact that the Catalans and Quebecois would still be withdrawing from existing, internationally recognized states in an attempt to create their own new independent states. Such an act does constitute secession. Only time will reveal whether this reduction in the benefits of membership, reinforced by the conviction that a community should be governed by its own members, will make persistent secession movements in Western liberal democracies grow into secession crises.

10   A rise in the benefits of secession

Evaluating the influence of a perceived rise in the benefits of secession on the decision to secede is difficult. Its effect frequently depends on the distinct community's expectations of its own future prospects rather than resting on historical experience. Chapter 6 introduced the two categories of benefits of secession: the greater financial opportunities for ethnic elites associated with sovereign statehood and the security and social advantages for the entire community of implementing the principle of national self-determination. This chapter first revisits these benefits to show that their allure continues to exert pressure in favor of a secession attempt. The main purpose of the chapter, then, is to argue that the gradual but discernible shift in the normative structure of relations between developed and developing countries can also have an impact on the secession dynamic. Wealthier states have assumed greater responsibility in ensuring the viability of their fledgeling counterparts. These newly established states have, to a certain extent, been exempted from the rigours of "normal" power politics. Some have also received considerable financial assistance from industrialised countries to alleviate their economic plight. This new political and economic infrastructure now underpins the numerous weaker states created mainly through the process of decolonization. These shifts become an incentive for secession.

Investigation of such a shift in the fundamental values underpinning international relations returns the focus to the difficult moral issues surrounding the decision to secede. The way the contemporary international system has undertaken the responsibility to promote the economic development, political stability and survival of the many weak states created through the process of decolonization only awkwardly fits into the analytical framework as a potential increase in the benefits of secession. Nevertheless, it deserves investigation since it can become a motivating force for future secessions.

The difficulties in relating the influence of these broader trends in the international system to the decision to secede are three-fold, and we will address each one in turn. First, some may question whether there has been such a shift in the international normative and legal structure; specifically, whether the developed world considers the needs of the developing world beyond what expediency, self-interest, and power politics would dictate. Many post-colonial governments accuse wealthy industrialised countries of disregarding their pleas for help.[1] Second, some may question whether such shifts can be extrapolated as a trend into the future. Without their intense ideological rivalry, the former superpowers and their allies are no longer pressured to provide development aid to unstable, poor countries in order to extend their influence. Third, the relatively recent nature of these changes makes it difficult to assess their implications on secession decisions. On the one hand, in the absence of mass violence, religious persecution, or forcible cultural assimilation, the desperate plight of many people in developing countries and the not inconsiderable economic benefits of membership within the existing state may, on the margin, weigh against secession. Withdrawal would thus be associated with the prospect of greater poverty, unemployment, and other economic ills. On the other hand, the possibility of receiving international financial assistance as one of the privileges of sovereign statehood acts as an incentive to secession. Certainly the maintenance of pre-secession levels of foreign assistance is an important issue for any newly independent state. A Bengali economist and former minister, Nusul Islam, recounts the way in which his high-level colleagues in the new government of Bangladesh protested that their country did not secede from Pakistan only to forfeit its foreign aid.[2]

Although as yet no secession can be linked directly to the gradual enhancement of such benefits, this factor is without doubt a relevant influence. Its discussion is primarily theoretical, and hence, remains tentative. It is included here in order to be as exhaustive as possible of all potential motives for secession. It may prove useful in analyzing tomorrow's secession crises.

[1] Robert Jackson, *Quasi-States: Sovereignty, International Relations, and the Third World* (Cambridge: Cambridge University Press, 1990), p. 115.
[2] Nusul Islam, *Development Planning in Bangladesh: A Study in Political Economy* (London: C. Hurst, 1977).

Elite interests revisited

Given the adverse conditions plaguing many developing countries, elites continue to gain opportunities and other advantages by dominating the mechanism of government. Frequently, the elites of a distinct community contemplate secession to further their own interests. Without a vibrant private sector to generate sufficient opportunities for the talented and ambitious, success in politics remains the sole guarantor of enrichment and social status. Fierce political competition, as witnessed in the Nigerian case, naturally follows. Nigeria's problems in the 1960s – before Biafra's secession – are representative of the domestic circumstances in many post-colonial societies. In this example, the convergence of four conditions – ethnic division, cultural hierarchy with a dominant ruling class, economic underdevelopment, and nominally democratic governing institutions – generated fierce political rivalry. Although at times it took on a mass character through political mobilization along communal lines, this rivalry primarily involved Hausa, Ibo, and Yoruba elites. They openly discussed secession as a means to promote and protect their vested interests. One could reasonably argue that improved economic growth would generate more opportunities for social mobility, and thus mitigate ethnic rivalry. The difficulty so far, however, has been that population growth in many developing countries has far outstripped economic expansion, thereby further aggravating existing political competition for scarce resources.

Furthermore, the example of Quebec indicates that economic development does not necessarily alter the basic patterns of ethnic rivalry, although perhaps the resulting competition is less fierce. Historian Rudy Fenwick argues that the incentives motivating the new urban Francophone middle classes closely resemble those motivating Nigeria's elites. A product of the Quiet Revolution's reforms, this upward mobility depended on the creation of new job opportunities for French speakers. Speaking French was historically considered a liability – fluency in English was an asset. For many members of this rising class, therefore, Quebec's potential secession from Canada presents several benefits. First, an independent Quebec would most likely be a unilingual state, and thus, the ability to speak French would become a competitive advantage in obtaining employment. Second, Quebec would no longer have to share its tax revenues with Ottawa. Some reasonably question whether Quebec would benefit financially from severing formal ties with Canada since it would forfeit its federal subsidies as well.[3] Others argue that independence would result in more tax monies being available for the Quebecois *projet de societé:* its educational reforms, social programs, and corporatist economic strategy. Further, the prospective expansion of Quebec's bureaucracy required to administer additional social services would also provide more opportunities for the new educated Francophone class. "The result is that the Francophone elite even outside the Parti Quebecois views increased Quebec autonomy favorably as a means of attaining greater financial resources."[4] The continuing power of elite self-interest in both developing and developed societies acts as an incentive toward a secession attempt.

The principle of national self-determination revisited

If the power of elite self-interest has not been diminished by time and economic development, neither has the influence of the principle of national self-determination. It continues to inspire the political goals of stateless peoples, frequently providing the justification for their ensuing secessionist struggles. Tamil representatives have consistently maintained that a meaningful resolution to Sri Lanka's conflict must include official recognition of their right to self-determination.[5] The Karen National Union has stipulated in its proposed Draft Constitution for Burma that every one of the twelve ethnic groups within Burmese territory possesses the right to self-determination.[6] The Tigre

---

[3] For example, leading Quebecois businessmen affiliated with the Conseil du Patronat du Quebec have made forceful public statements against movement toward an independent Quebec. Their arguments rely on an assessment of the economic costs which secession would entail. See Bertrand Marotte, "Unity Debate Biting into Business, CEOs Say: Independence would be Worse," *The Nation of Toronto*, March 6, 1992, p. B1; Clyde Farnsworth, "Separatist Fervour Fades in Quebec: The Cost of Seceding Is Seen As Too High," *The New York Times*, September 16, 1991, p. C1.

[4] Rudy Fenwick, "Social Change and Ethnic Nationalism: An Historical Analysis of the Separatist Movement in Quebec," *Comparative Study of Society and History*, 23 (1981), 215.

[5] At negotiations in Thimpu, Bhutan, among the governments of India, Sri Lanka, and representatives of Tamil organizations, this demand was included in the joint Tamil presentation. See *At Thimpu* (Cambridge: Tamil International Working Group, 1985), p. 6.

[6] Karen National Union, *Draft Constitution of the Federal Union of the Democratic National States of Burma*, Summer 1990, and declarations and statements made by the Karen National Union or the National Democratic Front have been provided to the author by the Karen National Union Secretary, Dr. Em Marta.

People's Liberation Front in Ethiopia consistently justified their protests by using the language of self-determination.[7] James Mayall assesses the continuing impact of the principle in the following manner:

> Domestication of the concept has allowed it to support the sovereignty of existing states rather than subvert it. However, it still has *enormous subversive appeal* to all those actual and potential secessionists who remain convinced that their fundamental rights have been denied ... The subversive appeal of national self-determination is not confined to Third World secessionists.[8]

Elite interests and self-determination continue to exert pressure in favor of secession. We now turn our attention to the influence on the secession dynamic of the recent gradual transformation of relations between wealthier and poorer countries.

"Quasi-statehood"

The fact that international economic and political support for weak newly independent countries has become expected and unquestioned represents arguably one of the most significant changes in the underlying values of the international system in the post-World War II era. State opposition and reluctance by the international community to extend diplomatic recognition still persist as barriers to secession. Even so, if a community were to establish an independent state through secession, then it could expect to receive the rewards of independence: the political support and economic aid which the international community provides to such newly emerging recognized states. The political support rests on progressive changes in diplomacy, such as the mutual recognition of sovereign equality, the elevation of territorial integrity to nearly an absolute level, and the restriction of the legitimate use of force to self-defense. Such conventions of statecraft originally facilitated the birth of many post-war states and have since then reinforced their political survival. Further, the growth of international aid bolsters the economic viability of many resource-limited states.

Discussion of such trends is not new. As early as 1960, B. V. A.

---

[7] Bereket Habte Selassie, *Conflict and Intervention in the Horn of Africa* (New York: Monthly Review Press, 1980), p. 89.

[8] James Mayall, *Nationalism and International Society* (Cambridge: Cambridge University Press, 1990), p. 150. Emphasis added.

Roling called attention to a gradual movement from the established "international law of liberty" to an emerging "international law of welfare."[9] This law of welfare presupposes active cooperation among developed and developing countries to address their pressing needs.[10] More recently, Robert Jackson traces "a normative shift from classical ideas of commutative justice based on reciprocity towards distributive justice necessitated by the gross material inequalities of states."[11] What is new is the study of the connection between these significant trends and secession.

Political infrastructure

The legacy of rapid decolonization was the arrival of numerous politically unstable states on to the international scene. After World War II, the prominence of the right of colonial people to self-determination rapidly eroded the legitimacy of imperial rule. Enduring much criticism in international fora, the European colonial powers quickly withdrew from their overseas empires, thereby creating many new states which Robert Jackson and Carl Rosberg have defined as "weak."[12] Without the requisite resources or institutions, these new regimes could not meet the challenges posed by the rapid acquisition of sovereignty. The emergence of a political infrastructure reinforcing the stability of these weak states, therefore, was the response of industrialised countries to that legacy.

In the political sphere, the large number of internal wars and coups in recently decolonised states indicates the weakness of their governing institutions. Three factors hinder such governments' control over their territory: insufficient domestic authority, a lack of a clear

---

[9] B. V. A. Roling, *International Law in an Expanded World* (Amsterdam, 1960), p. 83.

[10] Roling concludes, "The world community is bound to become a welfare community, just as the nation-state became a welfare state," Roling, *International Law*, p. 83. The 1980 Report of the Independent Commission on International Development Issues chaired by the former chancellor of West Germany, Willy Brandt, argues that from the basis of rights to sovereign equality derive rights to an equitable distribution of the world's resources. The Report asserts, "The international debate on development, at the threshhold of the 1980s, deals not just with 'assistance' and 'aid' but with new structures ... Such a process of restructuring and renewal has to be guided by the principle of equal rights and opportunities," *North–South: A Programme for Survival, The Report of the Independent Commission on International Development Issues* (London: Pan Books, 1980), p. 10.

[11] Jackson, *Quasi-States*, p. 117.

[12] Robert Jackson and Carl Rosberg, "Why Africa's Weak States Persist: The Empirical and the Juridical in Statehood," *World Politics*, 35, 1 (October 1982–July 1983), 1–24.

apparatus of power, and insufficient economic resources.[13] Rarely were colonial peoples, to whom the right of self-determination was supposedly ascribed, empowered with participation in their government – the fundamental tenet behind popular sovereignty. No systems of checks and balances constrained the excesses of power. Moreover, governing institutions rarely outlasted their original, forceful indigenous leaders. In their characterization of these new states, Bull and Watson point out that "still less do they reflect respect for constitutions or acceptance of the rule of law."[14] Plagued by disorganization and instability, few governments protect human rights, let alone provide for civil liberties or a decent standard of living. In the economic sphere, problems revolve around inadequate food production, high birth rates, weak industrial base, burgeoning and unproductive state sectors, insufficient capital for investment in new development projects, and high unemployment. Jackson refers to such post-colonial regimes as "quasi-states" since they do not "possess the institutional features of sovereign states as ... defined by classical international law."[15]

A survey of European history would reveal that there is nothing inherently novel about "weak" countries like those created through decolonization. States lacking strong internal cohesion, political institutions, or natural resources have been virtually a perpetual feature since the seventeenth-century evolution of the European states system. In the age of imperial conquest, weaker powers were routinely subjugated or relegated to protectorate status. Their domestic affairs were rarely free of external interference, manipulation, and sometimes even invasion.

The significant change between the eighteenth and nineteenth-century international system and the post-World War II era is the emergence of a political infrastructure which underpins these weaker states and supports their long-term viability. Because decolonization involved the legal transfer of formal sovereignty from colonial powers to their ex-colonies, it reinforced the juridical conception of sovereignty over the empirical one. As a result, ex-colonial states acquired the same external privileges – the same status in international law – as all other established states. They engage in international relations on

---

[13] Jackson and Rosberg, "Africa's Weak States," p. 1, 7.
[14] Hedley Bull and Adam Watson, *The Expansion of the International Society* (Oxford: Oxford University Press, 1984), p. 430.
[15] Jackson, *Quasi-states*, p. 21.

the basis of formal equality: each country has one vote in the United National General Assembly. The international community's respect for weaker states' formal sovereignty and equality has provided the ex-colonies with new opportunities to protect their interests.

Furthermore, the widespread acceptance of non-intervention and territorial inviolability as organizing principles of relations among states has lessened external military threats. In general, despite enormous inequalities in state power, the use of military force to intervene in others' domestic affairs requires compelling reasons. This is not to argue that intervention does not occur, but only to point out that it does not occur as frequently as it might. When states do intervene, they carefully justify their actions in terms of international law which may allow interventions in abnormal circumstances.

More importantly, those countries most disrupted by domestic strife continue to enjoy diplomatic recognition by the international community. Jackson's keen observations on this matter deserve to be quoted in full:

> What is different, therefore, is the existence of an international society that has presided over the birth of numerous marginal entities, guarantees their survival, and seeks at least to compensate them for under-development if not to develop them into substantial independent countries. Before the present century there was no special international regime that catered for small or weak states. All sovereign states today including some which are far more chaotic that the Austro-Hungarian or Ottoman Empires ever were – such as Chad or Lebanon – enjoy an unqualified right to exist and high prospects for survival despite their domestic disorganization and illegitimacy.[16]

The management of such diversity of sovereign states in terms of size, resources, economic progress, and cultural attributes therefore rests on the keystone of post-war international society: the mutual recognition of equal sovereignty. Despite the fact that many elements of a "mature anarchy" are more readily accepted in principle than incorporated in practice, this evolution in norms has nevertheless impaired the classical functioning of power politics. It has served to exempt weaker states from power contests in which they could not compete effectively.

---

[16] Ibid., p. 24.

Economic infrastructure

Moving beyond mutual respect for equal sovereignty, the contemporary international system also promotes the economic development and stability of newly independent states.[17] This unprecedented level of financial aid reveals the first impressions of a new benefit of secession. Distinct communities seeking secession, once they have achieved sovereign statehood, can and do expect to receive financial support. The Third World's claims to a "fair" share of the world's resources represent a morality which the West can deny or ignore only with increasing difficulty. Industrialised countries have gradually, although reluctantly, recognized the need for active cooperation to address the pressing needs of economic development. More specifically, Western countries, the United Nations, and international agencies now provide emerging states with economic aid, technological assistance, loans at concessional rates of interest, debt relief, food programs, and other humanitarian assistance.

In the 1960s, profound disillusionment with the gap between the aspirations engendered by independence and the associated harsh economic realities motivated the Third World's efforts to reform the international economic order. Most developing states endured economic stagnation having won independence. Inadequate domestic savings and foreign direct investment crippled attempts to industrialise production. Unstable raw material export prices meant widely fluctuating national incomes. The income differential between developing and industrialised countries continued to widen.[18] Thus, Third World leaders understood that their recently acquired political sovereignty would be a shallow victory if their countries could not confront the associated problems of economic dependence.

The elevation of weak powers to formal equality in international organizations provides them with both a voice and a forum to address these escalating economic concerns. Leaders of the Third World shrewdly utilized these privileges to place these concerns on the international agenda. As Martin Wight describes this achievement: "The existence of the United Nations has exaggerated the international importance of the have-not powers, enabling them to orga-

---

[17] Ibid.
[18] The Third World did produce a few exceptional cases of economic success during this time period including the rapid industrial development of South Korea, Taiwan, Singapore, Hong Kong and a few other countries.

nize themselves into a pressure group with much greater diplomatic and propaganda weight than they would otherwise have had."[19] The proliferation of new programs in trade, finance, and development specifically designed to address such issues reveals the growing legitimacy of these demands.

The Third World's challenge found its most stark expression in the New International Economic Order (NIEO) in 1974. It encompassed unprecedented claims for economic entitlements in compensation for its members' current disadvantaged status.[20] The UNGA's Charter of the Economic Rights and Duties of States,[21] which launched the NIEO, was an effort to rewrite the very norms governing global economic relations. Although the Charter's thirty-four articles were phrased in abstract terms as an idealized code of conduct, the message was quite clear. In drafting the resolution, the ex-colonies presented a revolutionary program to restructure international relations on the basis of redistributive justice:

> Article 14[22]
> Every State has the duty to cooperate in promoting a steady and increasing expansion and liberalization of world trade and an improvement in the welfare and living standards of all peoples, in particular those of developing countries.

Beyond this general "duty," the Charter outlined the actions demanded by the developing world.

> Article 22[23]
> All States should respond to the generally recognized or mutually agreed development needs and objectives of developing countries by promoting increased net flows of real resources to the developing countries ... in order to reinforce their effort to accelerate their economic and social development ... [All states] should endeavor to increase the net amount of financial flows from official sources to developing countries and to improve the terms and conditions thereof.

[19] Martin Wight, *Power Politics*, 2nd edn (Harmondsworth, 1986), p. 238.
[20] Antecedents of the NIEO can be discerned as early as the Bandung Conference's final communique in April, 1955, and the creation of the UN Conference on Trade and Development (UNCTAD) in 1964.
[21] The Charter of the Economic Rights and Duties of States is reprinted in Phillipe Braillard and Mohammad-Reza Djalili, *The Third World and International Relations* (London: Pinter, 1986), pp. 226–236.
[22] Braillard and Djalili, *Third World*, pp. 231–232.
[23] Ibid., p. 233.

In an important statement of intent, Article 18 called upon the
"developed countries" to extend the already established "system of
generalised non-reciprocal and non-discriminatory tariff preferences
to the developing countries." These modifications were later incorporated into GATT rules. Thus, one of GATT's founding precepts was
relinquished: that of reducing trade restrictions based on reciprocity.
In the assessment of two development legal scholars, GATT rules now
acknowledge that not all members "are economically equal and that
among unequal parties, the principle of reciprocity does not obtain."[24]

Many critics question the practical significance of these resolutions.
Wealthy states frequently take little notice of UN stipulations. With
the exception of an appeal to human morality, the Third World
possesses no mechanism by which to compel industrialised states to
provide greater financial assistance. Although a UN resolution formalized the principle that all developed states should contribute 0.7
percent of GNP to the developing world, very few countries outside
of Scandinavia have ever met these modest targets.[25] A striking gap
remains between the demands for structural reform of the economic
relations between industrialised and developing countries and the
effective results obtained so far. Many of the more strident demands
of the Charter and the NIEO were thus largely ignored by the
developed world.[26]

Nevertheless, one should not underestimate the significance of the
moral issues at stake in the Third World appeal. The mere presence in
world politics of claims for economic entitlements signifies a shift
away from the classical functioning of power politics. In more
concrete terms, aid and development programs have proliferated.

[24] Francis G. Snyder and Peter Slinn (eds.), *International Law of Development: Comparative
Perspectives* (Abingdon: Professional Books, 1987), p. 194.
[25] Jackson, *Quasi-states*, p. 115.
[26] It is important to stress that when the Charter was put to a vote in the United
Nations, its eventual approval was far from unanimous. Although many industrialised
countries were willing to engage in the relatively vague and idealistic rhetoric of
cooperation, they were unwilling to sacrifice their own perceived vital interests for the
achievement of these ideals. In the final vote, six industrialised governments voted
against the Charter, while a further ten abstained. The absence of a true consensus on
the main thrust of the proposed resolution led to an impasse in reaching an agreement
not only on the implementation of its provisions but even on a procedure for the
establishment of global negotiations. (The six countries which opposed the resolution
were Belgium, Britain, Denmark, the United States, Luxembourg, and West Germany.
The ten countries which abstained from the vote were Austria, Canada, Spain, France,
Ireland, Israel, Italy, Japan, Norway, and the Netherlands. See Braillard and Djalili, *Third
World*, p. 171.)

Wealthy countries have taken some collective steps toward providing economic assistance to weak states. Nearly all UN organizations now participate in aid disbursement. Within their own designated fields, the WHO, UNICEF, FAO, and UNHCR[27] provide material assistance, information, and technology to many struggling governments to address the urgent problems concerning health, children's education and welfare, agriculture, and refugees. The Commonwealth, *La Francophonie*, the European Union, individual governments and private agencies now organize initiatives encompassing famine relief, agricultural extension projects, development loans, technology transfers, and other forms of humanitarian assistance. In fact, during the late 1980s, over half of the UN members became net recipients of some form of economic aid.[28]

To illustrate this unprecedented change, the International Monetary Fund and the World Bank in conjunction with the Asian, African, Caribbean, and Inter-American Development Banks have increasingly become intimately involved not only in infrastructure project planning but also in formulating domestic monetary and fiscal policies as well. Due to economic mismanagement, political instability, and civil strife, many former colonies and especially those in Sub-Saharan Africa, cannot attract private capital. Such countries provide few attractive investment opportunities as the risks of investment are so high. Under these circumstances, if it were not for IMF and World Bank loans, many countries could not embark on infrastructure or industrial projects. In general, although expectations of aid have certainly outpaced its supply, this in itself does not detract from the movement toward what Jackson refers to as "international affirmative action."[29]

Perhaps the most remarkable evidence of this shift is the end of *pacta sunt servanda* as the basic criteria for loans to the developing world. Despite having defaulted or having had their loans written off, Third World finance ministers still receive a sympathetic reception in banking capitals. When such ministers arrive requesting preferential treatment and justifying their requests in terms of the developed world's moral obligations, they are not shown the door, but are instead invited to negotiate loans at concessional rates of interest. The

---

[27] The acronyms signify the World Health Organization, the United Nations International Children's Education Fund, the Food and Agricultural Organization, and the United Nations High Commission for Refugees.
[28] *World Development Report 1988* (New York, 1988), Table 17.
[29] Jackson, *Quasi-states*, p. 131.

waiving of normal considerations of sound banking practice, and, in particular, calculations of whether potential returns exceed the cost of invested capital, indicates the extent of the shift already experienced. Historically, international law simply recognized the right of sovereign states to provide for their citizens' welfare free from external intervention; now some level of external assistance has come to be expected.

To summarise, the emergence of this new international political and economic infrastructure impacts the secession dynamic as both a restraint and an incentive for secession. The legal entrenchment of such principles as non-intervention and the sanctity of borders serves to bolster the survival of existing post-colonial regimes, however arbitrarily created or precariously balanced, and therefore poses a significant obstacle to secession. Consequently, the distinct community seeking secession has no reason to expect special treatment from the international community during its struggle, although it may still enlist the support of specific external allies.

However, if it is successful in establishing governing institutions and having them legitimated by diplomatic recognition, then the community is likely to benefit from this substantial infrastructure supporting quasi-states. For example, much international assistance in the form of loans, food, and humanitarian aid was forthcoming to Bangladesh after it received diplomatic recognition. In another more recent example, once Eritrea seceded from Ethiopia and its popular Eritrean People's Liberation Front government was both confirmed in democratic elections in 1993 and recognized by foreign governments, multilateral and bilateral aid donors quickly stepped in to assist both in the reconstruction after the civil war and in economic development. By some estimates, by the early 1990s Eritrea had already received millions of dollars in economic aid.[30]

Moreover, these changes act as a further incentive toward secession by raising the stakes for discontented communities. Whereas assistance programs are intended to alleviate the destitute conditions of the very poor in former colonies, these interactions are initiated, negotiated, and settled mainly at the government level. Economic assistance is limited specifically to internationally recognized states. Multilateral aid packages do not normally benefit sub-state communities

---

[30] "Ethiopia: The Healing Touch," *The Economist*, December 14, 1991, p. 80; "Morning in Ethiopia," *The Economist*, September 14, 1991, p. 79; "Eritrea: An Unborn Nation," *The Economist*, October 20, 1990, p. 104.

directly. The possibility remains that material aid will not reach those most desperately in need of it; ruling elites may channel it toward political patronage and other personal uses. To benefit from the new economic infrastructure and aid, discontented communities must control their own sovereign states.

Given the recent nature of these changes, it is difficult to judge the extent to which the possibility of financial aid encourages those communities currently contemplating secession. Further investigation into the emerging infrastructure to support "quasi-states" may provide insights into future secession crises, as well as into unresolved ones of the present. Nevertheless, the multiple access to large, if overall inadequate, amounts of finance disbursed through many different channels combined with the diminished threat of external intervention surely acts as another incentive for aspiring elites and their communities to form new states through secession.

11 Conclusion

The two central claims of this book can be briefly stated: that *the distinct community's decision to secede can usefully be thought of as a function of its appraisal of its circumstances – in other words, the costs and benefits of both membership and secession*, and that *this appraisal is continuous.* The implications of these claims are significant. First, *independence for the distinct community has a relative, not absolute, value.* Second, *the decision to secede can be affected by changes in the circumstances in which the distinct community finds itself.* The purpose of this concluding chapter is fourfold: to summarize the main arguments as to the reasons why groups secede, to draw out the implications of these arguments for the concept of sovereignty, to indicate some of the policies which may be effective in the prevention and resolution of secession crises, and finally, to speculate on the main factors which may affect future trends in secession.

Speculation as to future trends is a hazardous enterprise which scholars embark upon only at their peril. Nevertheless, such contemplation on the future of secession movements may be valuable, if only to crystalize the lessons from the preceeding analysis. As the Ibo, Bengali, Southern Sudanese, Norwegian, and other secession crises arising as "last resorts" or at "opportune moments" revealed, some secession attempts are a direct reaction to changes in official policies. Accordingly, the conclusion comments both on the changing nature of sovereignty and on the way government policies can affect the decision to secede in certain cases, indirectly reflecting on some of the possible ways to prevent or resolve secession crises. Alternately, trends in political and economic relations among states and other factors beyond the direct control of states limit the influence that

216

government policies can have on secession. The chapter ends with a few thoughts on the factors upon which future secession crises will most likely hinge.

Main conclusions

To support the two central claims of this book, it is important to return to the original question raised by the Introduction: why do groups secede? The general answer proposed here is that the timing of the decision to secede can be understood as a function of four primary variables: the costs and benefits associated with both membership and secession. Secessions require four elements: a distinct community, territory, leaders, and discontent. Furthermore, critical to any secession is its moral justification. The dynamic of secession, however, cannot be provoked by static conditions. Secessions arise only when the distinct community determines there has been a shift in, and therefore an imbalance among, the four costs and benefits.

Intimately connected to these four costs and benefits are the four causal patterns of secession. This is where the detailed answers to the question of why groups secede lie. First, the rapid and painful rise in the costs of membership – in the form of escalating threats to lives, livelihoods, or cultural autonomy – can provoke a secession attempt. Confronted with such dire circumstances, the Ibos, Bengalis, and Southern Sudanese decided to fight secessionist wars as a "last resort" to protect their lives and cultural inheritance from threats by their respective ruling regimes. Second, a sudden reduction in the potential costs of secession, either through the weakening of central government authority or external support for the seceding community, can generate secession attempts. The collapse of tsarist rule, and the Indian and Turkish military interventions in Bangladesh and Cyprus, respectively, provided "opportune moments" for secessions by the peripheral communities of imperial Russia and by the Bengalis and Turkish-Cypriots. Third, changes in state policies or the international system which reduce the security and economic benefits of membership precipitate secessions or at least reinforce separatist policies. Sweden's neglect in providing adequate consular services prompted Norway's secession because Norwegians perceived that Sweden no longer provided the important benefits that they required. Further, evolution in the international system, and more specifically, the acceptance of mutual recognition, adoption of collective security measures, and growth in economic integration, has enhanced the viability of independence for many small distinct communities like the Catalans and Quebecois, and thus, bolstered the credibility of separatist movements. Fourth, a rise in the benefits of secession, and in particular the gradual transformation of the international normative structure which promotes the economic development and political stability of weaker states, may precipitate a secession crisis. If a seceding community were to succeed in overcoming state opposition and gain international recognition, like Eritrea, then it could expect to receive political support and financial assistance as well. Although as of yet no secession can be directly attributed to the recent rise in the benefits of secession, it remains a relevant influence on the secession dynamic.

The approach in determining the causes of secession has been the detailed scrutiny of numerous case studies. Since secession is the dramatic eruption into the international arena of a crisis for some distinct community, then the starting point of analysis of this phenomenon must be the needs, perceptions, and aspirations of the community. As a means to render the numerous case studies comparable, the study formulated the idiosyncratic motivations of each specific secession decision in more general terms, and thus, identified the causal patterns.

In presenting this analysis, I have attempted to make explicit assumptions regarding the distinct community, the state, the international community, and the nature of such an investigation. The analysis of secession crises involved reflections on the institutions of international law, the foreign policies of some states, and the domestic policies of others. In seeking to avoid moral judgments, I have not questioned the ability of communities formed over time by blood, kinship, shared religious or cultural values and suffering class, interest or factional divisions to rule themselves, despite the fact that many examples exist where just such a question could legitimately be posed. The proposed framework simply recognizes that such an assumption underlies any secession attempt.

Implications for the concept of sovereignty

Sovereignty is central to secession, as it is the essential characteristic of statehood to which secessionist communities aspire. Through the perspective afforded by the study of secession, we can discern the seeds of two general changes in the conception of sovereignty. First, it would appear that the juridical concept of sovereignty has begun to prevail over the empirical conception. In other words, sovereignty is gradually coming to signify more of an international legal status conferred on a state through recognition by other states rather than the focal point of power within a specified territory. Second, in circumstances where sovereignty is still conceived of as supreme authority over a population residing in a certain territory, evolution of the international system is gradually eroding some aspects of states' sovereignty in certain parts of the world. The first change raises the already substantial costs of secession by reinforcing the international community's hostility to the creation of new states through secession, while the second gradually decreases the benefits of membership, and thus, reduces the implicit restraints on secession.

James Crawford asserts that the historical and more empirical definition of sovereignty is that: "Sovereignty, in its origin merely the location of supreme power within a particular territorial unit, necessarily came from within and therefore did not require the recognition of other States or princes."[1] The numerous cases cited in this book reveal examples where the state clearly is not the "supreme power" within a given territory. A secessionist movement, by its very nature, questions the legitimacy of a government's authority over some people and territory. Several secessionist communities have not only challenged this authority, but have defeated it on the battlefield. The Karen National Union in the 1970s and 1980s, the Liberation Tigers of Tamil Eelam in the 1980s, the Eritrean People's Liberation Front in the late 1980s, and the Kurds in Iraq in the 1990s are but a few examples of secessionist communities who successfully challenged the central government and established civilian administrations in their territories to maintain order and to provide basic social services to their people. Despite the fact that these communities are likely to have satisfied the more traditional empirical requirements for sovereign statehood – namely, independence from external control and effective authority over population and territory – the international community did not recognize these instances of self-rule as states.[2] The double

---

[1] James Crawford, "The Criteria for Statehood in International Law," *British Yearbook of International Law* (London, 1976–1977), p. 96.
[2] In the early 1990s the international community was in the process of extending diplomatic recognition to Eritrea.

standard is striking given comparisons of the performances of these *de facto* administrations and many weak states. Many post-colonial states have lost control of their territory and are unable to maintain social order within their societies. Yet, since these governments were the beneficiaries of the formal process of decolonization, their sovereignty is not questioned.

It would appear, then, that in the post-war era, the meaning of sovereignty has subtly changed. In the essays of Jean Jacques Rousseau, popular sovereignty was most frequently identified with the inalienable right of the whole community to do as it wills. Some confusion arose over whether sovereignty was located with the people or with the supreme authority within a territory, if these were not the same. Nevertheless, it arose from domestic circumstances. Now sovereignty resembles more of an international legal status. Because the process of decolonization required the legal transfer of sovereignty from the imperial powers to the indigenous institutions of their former colonies regardless of whether those institutions were in fact prepared to exercise authority in their circumscribed territory, it reinforced the view of sovereignty as a status in international law rather than as the supreme authority in a territory.

Established states possess the power to recognize new states, and thereby bestow the legal status of sovereignty. Those which the international community does not recognize are relegated to diplomatic isolation, like the Turkish Republic of North Cyprus. The international system has even exhibited outright hostility to some secessionist entities – note the explicit condemnation of the Katanga crisis in the Congo and the Biafra withdrawal from Nigeria. Christopher Brewin discloses the trend toward conceiving sovereignty as a set of rights and duties toward other states and suggests that: "instead of being perceived as a relationship between the state and a particular territory, sovereignty is rather perceived as a social relationship between states where each recognizes the rights of others."[3] The previously cited examples of *de facto* administrations of secessionist communities without *de jure* international recognition indicate that existing states exercise this power of recognition with discretion.

Consequently, the entrenchment of the juridical conception of sovereignty reinforces the present level of international hostility

---

[3] Christopher Brewin, "Sovereignty," in James Mayall (ed.), *The Community of States: A Study in International Political Theory* (London: George Allen & Unwin, 1982), p. 43.

toward secession attempts. Even the eruption of secessionist activity in the former Yugoslavia, Soviet Union, Ethiopia, and Czechoslovakia has not reversed this trend. The early 1990s were characterized by the massive assault upon the *status quo* by a multitude of new states demanding recognition.[4] Western governments and international organizations, like the United Nations and the Red Cross, needed to establish diplomatic ties quickly in order to organize aid distribution and disarmament, and to assist with the cessation of hostilities. This assault, however, did not force a long-term reconsideration of sovereignty and international recognition. In fact, communism's collapse in Eastern Europe created a situation parallel to European decolonization in the 1950s and 1960s. Once again a certain class of states was deemed acceptable to join the international community, namely the constituent republics of the former Soviet Union and Yugoslavia. Nevertheless, entry into the international community would not be extended to other secessionist communities within these new countries. For example, such opposition can be discerned in the fact that Chechen rebels have received no diplomatic recognition, in Croatia's intransigence toward Serb irredentism, in Georgia's opposition to Ossetian demands for reunification with their kinsmen in North Ossetia within the Russian Federation, and in the Armenian – Azerbaijani conflict over the future of the predominantly Armenian enclave of Ngorno-Karabakh within Azerbaijan. In fact, new states such as Croatia, Georgia and Azerbaijan use their position as equal members of international fora to condemn secessionist movements within their own borders.

It is certainly in the vested interests of states to deny territorial challenges to their authority. Most states recognize that the international order would be severely threatened if territorial disputes were to be settled in a manner that would encourage similar demands elsewhere. As Immanuel Wallerstein has so succinctly put it, "every African nation ... has its Katanga. Once the logic of secession is admitted, there is no end except in anarchy."[5] As a result, the current division of global territory – with the exception of radical changes in

---

[4] The list of new states includes Lithuania, Latvia, Estonia, Slovakia, Slovenia, Croatia, Bosnia-Hercegovina, Macedonia, Byelorussia, Ukraine, Moldova, Georgia, Armenia, Azerbaijan, Turkmenia, Tadjikistan, Uzbekistan, Kazahkstan, Kirghizia, Eritrea, and the rump states of Russia, Yugoslavia, Ethiopia, and the Czech Republic.
[5] Quoted in Lee Buchheit, *Secession: The Legitimacy of Self-Determination* (New Haven: Yale University Press, 1978), p. 14.

the form of decolonization and communism's collapse – is deemed worthy of preservation. The international community promotes stability over other considerations such as justice or reform. With respect to the state and the international community there is a: "... determination to retain the existing political map and to reject virtually out of hand any belated demands for self-determination however worthy or just the cause may be. The conservatism of international society on this question is profound."[6] The recent onslaught on principles of diplomatic recognition by these newly independent republics has not changed the existing states' perception of the illegitimacy of secession, and ultimately may reinforce the international community's conservatism toward territorial change. This "profound conservatism" renders the costs of secession for distinct communities very high.

By looking through the prism of secession, the changing nature of its dynamic reveals a second change in the nature of sovereignty. The progressive transformation of international relations – along both security and economic dimensions – has altered the challenges faced by states in the West and reduced their ability to deal independently with those challenges. More specifically, the destructiveness of war and nuclear weapons has limited a state's independent ability to defend itself. In response, international security arrangements like NATO have become the focus of efforts to reduce vulnerabilities and improve self-defense. Vastly increased international trade and financial flows have limited a state's ability to control its own economy. Consequently, supra-national organizations like the European Union have become the focus of initiatives to regulate the economy and stimulate growth and prosperity. In fact, the original twelve European Community governments relinquished their sovereignty over specific fields of traditional state activity, like industry and consumer product standards, and educational requirements, in the Single European Act of 1987 to enable the European Commission to pursue the common goal of a single market in goods, services, labor, and capital. EU governments relinquished their sovereignty over some aspects of law and order to improve the effectiveness of cross-border police coordination and crime prevention initiatives. In arguably one of the most significant examples of the voluntary surrender of sovereignty, a majority of the EU countries renounced the formal control of

---

[6] Robert Jackson, *Quasi-States: Sovereignty, International Relations, and the Third World* (Cambridge: Cambridge University Press, 1990), p. 190.

monetary policy with the adoption of a single currency through the Economic and Monetary Union (EMU) on January 1, 1999. No longer can central governments in Western Europe and North America be considered "sovereign" in security and economic matters in the traditional sense. An understanding of these subtle changes, and their consequent enhancement of the viability of the independence option, has strengthened the secession dynamic in Catalonia, Quebec, and many other distinct communities.

The prevention and resolution of secession crises

By emphasising the distinct community's appraisal of the general costs and benefits associated with political alternatives, the analytical framework systematically isolates the economic, political, and social factors which influence the decision to secede. Understanding these factors suggests some of the policies useful in the prevention and resolution of secession crises and the circumstances which may limit their effectiveness. Discussion of a distinct community's general priorities establishes the context in which to analyze the main elements of state policies which could influence the secession decision.

The secession decision depends first and foremost on the distinct community's perceptions of its physical safety. Perhaps more interestingly, directly behind the understandable concern for the preservation of life lie concerns for the community's cultural identity, and the necessary power within the existing state or in an independent state to assure its security. Members of distinct communities whose cultures are under threat seem to value highly the prospect of their descendants participating in their cultural inheritance, and thus struggle to protect their shared identity. The basis of any community – culture, tradition, language, religion – is constantly changing, yet communities strive to pass on this changing identity to future generations. Economic and political issues, and not simply social ones, underlie the pursuit of this objective. Communities strive for the freedom to promote their culture. They also struggle for the financial means to do so, which translates into desires for the opportunity to earn a livelihood and to achieve social advancement whilst speaking one's own language and following one's own traditions. Therefore, of fundamental value to a community is also the security of the cultural bonds which maintain its coherence.

The community's judgment of how best to accomplish these two

223

priorities is necessarily a function of historical and existing circumstances, which leads to two implications deserving repetition. First, for the distinct community, independence in and of itself possesses a relative, not an absolute, value. Independence is but one means to the end – the protection of the distinct community's physical safety and cultural inheritance. In this sense, secession is like federalism, autonomy, or power-sharing at the center: each political configuration could be a satisfactory means to the end. The value to the distinct community of a particular form of rule, a particular political institution, or a particular policy, depends upon the circumstances. To argue that independence is a worthwhile goal in itself is to surrender secession to the realm of dogma. It is unfortunate that much of the debate about secession in general, and various secessionist struggles in particular, has frequently degenerated into two opposing sides advocating uncritical support for self-determination and the equally dogmatic defense of territorial integrity, leaving little common ground for discourse, negotiation, and compromise. In contrast, this book consistently argues that secession is best understood when such ideological confrontations are discarded. The secession dynamic can be understood in the context of an implicit weighing by the community of the advantages of all its political alternatives. In the end it may very well be the case that secession is the best means currently available to protect its safety and its identity, but the community would not draw such a conclusion before an appraisal of the costs and benefits associated with its alternatives.

Secondly, and more optimistically, under certain conditions the state can at least partially affect the decision to secede by altering its policies. These insights could be utilized to design a state's approach to its discontented minority communities. The findings presented in Parts II and III provide the building blocks for an analysis of the general ingredients critical to state initiatives designed to influence the secession decision. Some factors which impact on the secession dynamic, however, like the evolution in the international system, are clearly beyond the influence of individual states and consequently limit the effectiveness of state policies. Specifying those aspects of the secession dynamic which the state can influence facilitates the subsequent speculation on potential future trends in secession crises.

The design of state policies is predicated on an understanding of two categories of influences: the restraints on secession and the impetus for secession attempts. Many distinct communities have been

224

reluctant to withdraw from the existing political authority because they judged that they could ill afford to sacrifice the security, economic, and social benefits of membership. This has proved to be a powerful restraint on secession. Czech demands for the restitution of the Bohemian Kingdom within the Austro-Hungarian Empire at the turn of the century, the very rapid creation of Yugoslavia as the amalgamation of the Slovene, Croat, and Serb communities at the close of World War I, and the recent efforts exerted by the former Soviet Central Asian republics for an economic refederation of parts of the former Soviet Union all reveal the influence of such benefits. The renunciation of the Karen, Kachin, Mon, and other secessionist groups of their ultimate goal of independence in 1984 in part revealed their expectation of obtaining greater educational, financial, and social opportunities within the larger and wealthier Burmese state once the process of reconciliation had begun. Conversely, the rising costs of membership in terms of either threats to life or threats to cultural inheritance provide a powerful impetus for secession crises – witness the Ibo, Bengali, and Southern Sudanese secessions.

The crucial point here is that appraisal of both the benefits and costs of membership can, to a large extent, be influenced by state initiatives. Therefore, policies which enhance the benefits and lower the costs of membership would constitute one possible means for a heterogeneous state to earn the political loyalty of the different communities residing within its jurisdiction. In such a manner, the state could decrease the likelihood that it would suffer a painful and costly secession crisis.

The meaningful redistribution of political and economic power away from the central government and toward the institutions of the distinct community is a recurring element in successful government strategies. Policies of devolution empower the community to ensure its own preservation and promote its culture. The specific design of particular government proposals depends on addressing the community's unique needs and acknowledging the central government's abilities and constraints. Successful policies naturally differ as they address such varied community concerns as cultural assimilation, the control of their land, religious persecution, economic exploitation, political domination, and educational discrimination.

Heterogeneous states composed of deeply divided societies do continue to exist in peace. Their governments have found innovative ways of empowering communities and alleviating their grievances. In such ways, many Western liberal democracies have been successful in capturing aspects of the secession process within the realm of daily politics, instead of suffering its manifestation in the form of secessionist conflict and crisis. A mixture of meaningful devolution, accommodation of special ethnic needs, and acceptance of diversity has assisted in the prevention of crises, since it has served to decrease the perceived social costs of membership for many communities. Examples of innovative compromises include the cultural councils in Belgium constituted in 1970 by members of parliament and the constitution-mandated autonomy for the four "historic" regions of Spain. Countries outside the developed West have also employed devolution to resolve secession crises; the institution of special regional status and autonomy for the South in Sudan in 1972, and the creation of Nagaland in India in 1963 are but two examples. Policies which provide specific additional advantages associated with integration into the existing state include the Dutch central government's assistance to its small Frisian community and the Swiss federal government's policy of subsidising cultural, educational, and social programs for its small Romansch community.

Future trends in secession

With this analytical grounding, it is now possible to consider future trends in secession. We begin such contemplation first by restricting its scope to those situations where considerable economic and social benefits of membership still exist for members of particular communities. This restriction is relaxed later, since it is important to investigate secessions under circumstances where developments in the international system have begun to erode the "balance of advantages" associated with remaining a part of the established states of the developed West. None the less, this temporary restriction is justified since it depicts relatively accurately the experience of numerous groups, especially those residing in developing countries and small groups such as the Frisians and Romansch in the developed world. Communities such as the Nagas in India, the Southern Sudanese, and the Karen in Burma either obtain significant advantages from political integration into a larger and wealthier state or seek to obtain such potential benefits once a process of accommodation has began.

Speculation on the future prospects of secessionist struggles, nearly a perpetual challenge in many developing countries, generally sketches a rather bleak outlook, with only a few mitigating circumstances. Adverse conditions continue to plague many developing countries. Disparate communities compete fiercely for limited economic resources to facilitate their social advancement. This competition perpetuates commensurate political rivalry for power to allocate and appropriate these scarce resources. This is likely to lead to continued exploitation, discrimination, or domination of some communities by ethnic elites who control the government. Due to the already high and potentially escalating costs of membership under these conditions and with no other recourse besides assimilation or second-class status, many communities will probably choose to continue to fight for secession.

This pessimism is perhaps rendered more frustrating by the fact that the pattern of domestic relations in many developing countries affords the possibility of resolving secessionist wars short of granting full independence. These conflicts have become endemic not because of the structure of relations, but because of the specific choices made by both government and distinct community elites. In fact, the structure of such conflicts implies that elements for their resolution exists. The preceeding discussion demonstrated that in these circumstances of high costs combined with large benefits of membership, secession decisions are mainly reactions to government policies. Consequently, if ruling elites were to alter their policies, many of these crises would have the potential of being resolved. The book has consistently pointed out historical cases in developing countries where compromise resolved secessionist confrontations. Devolution and empowerment of discontented communities have been the foundation of solutions; examples include the Sixteen Point Agreement in 1960 between the Naga Political Convention and the Indian government which inaugurated the state of Nagaland three years later, and the Addis Ababa Agreement in 1972 which provided the foundation for a decade of peaceful reintegration of the Southern Sudanese community within Sudan on the basis of a special regional status.

However, even if the structure of the secession crisis may be conducive to a potential resolution of the confrontation, it still depends upon the will and commitment of the leaders on both sides. Even though the Introduction acknowledged their role, the importance of elites must be re-emphasized. Sometimes it is simply not in their personal interest to negotiate a resolution to their secession crisis. The state and the distinct community can only be used as the proper units of analysis as long as their leaders implement decisions which are of benefit to their constituency as a whole. When their decisions differ from those more closely associated with the perceived good of the entire country or community, the appropriate unit of analysis may become the individuals who wield power. One of the most important parts of a compromise remains elite commitment. Even with devolutionary ingredients at its foundation, an agreement cannot be imposed by external force.

Indeed, ruling elites may not adopt proposals which could resolve a secession crisis, such as the redistribution of power domestically, because it could be anathema to their own personal interests. The combination of the vested interests of the military establishment and Karachi businessmen and the ambitions of Pakistani politicians prevented these influential men from accepting a constitution based on the Bengali proposals encapsulated in the Awami League's Six Point Program. They were unwilling to relinquish their own personal power to pursue a policy that may have prevented their country's dismemberment. In the 1980s and early 1990s, the Burmese military elites did not negotiate with the Karen National Union or the other insurgents, for two reasons. The civil war against ethnic minorities provided an excuse for martial law and perpetuated the army's power within Burmese society. Furthermore, with the direct command of territory and soldiers, many military leaders profited handsomely from the sale of contracts to foreign companies, exploiting Burma's vast natural resources. In pursuit of such interests, the military regime presided over the economic stagnation of this potentially wealthy country, condemning the Burmese people to life in ever-worsening poverty.

Secessionist leaders may also perpetuate a struggle for their own interests – for personal gain and power. Having tasted power, many leaders have difficulty relinquishing it. The Naga military leadership continued its war of attrition against the Indian Army long after it became clear to other Nagas that violence was not the most effective means to achieve their primary goal of protecting Naga culture. The Nagaland Federal Government and its military wing, the Nagaland Home Guard, eventually lost their leadership role as Nagas began to consider statehood within the Indian Union as an acceptable proposal upon which to negotiate an end to the war. New Naga leaders emerged to negotiate the agreement with India. By contrast, in the early 1990s, the Tamil Tigers controlled the Jaffna Peninsula and provided a basic civilian administration for the area. Their leaders were unwilling to negotiate an end to the civil war in Sri Lanka, partly because such a resolution would imply the diminution of their own power. Moreover, the extent of their support among the Tamil population was difficult to gauge. Tiger commanders gained a reputation for murdering members of their own community who opposed their decisions.

Several factors could mitigate this pessimistic outlook: first, the growth of international humanitarianism, and second, the spread of democratic principles of government. Even though the international community continues to tolerate states which do not adequately protect the rights of their citizens, awareness and action concerning human rights abuses has been growing. In their concern for human rights, some international agencies, many under the auspices of the United Nations, and non-governmental organizations such as Amnesty International, Helsinki Watch, and Asia Watch have intruded more into the domestic affairs of states.

None the less, the practical effectiveness of international humanitarianism is limited by three considerations. First, the international community's respect for the principle of non-intervention is not about to be discarded. Second, the influence of Western humanitarian interventionist policies depends upon other countries' economic dependence on the West, as economic sanctions are one of the most frequently employed forms of external pressure. Countries like Burma, whose autarkic policies have left it with little or no economic relations with the rest of the world, remain immune from most external pressure for human rights. Third, the selectivity of the international community as to whose interests it deems require protection necessarily limits the effectiveness of such policies. After Iraq's defeat in 1991, the American, British, and French forces initially intervened only on behalf of the Kurds in the north, not the Shias in the south. Only more time will reveal how these international systematic shifts will affect the domestic policies of developing states. Nevertheless, if humanitarian concern by the international community does succeed in mitigating discriminatory, exploitative, and violent policies pursued by the many authoritarian regimes, then secessionist activity might gradually decrease as a result.

Furthermore, the prominence in many parts of the world of liberal democratic principles such as individual freedom and consent of the governed may ultimately mitigate some governments' resistance to secession. If the decision to secede were to be presented in a liberal democracy as the clear wish of a majority of the distinct community, as evinced through referenda or elections, then the government's possible reactions would be limited. If the state opposed the secession, it would perhaps cause irreparable damage to its domestic political institutions. It is difficult to imagine how Canada, without negating the very principles upon which Canada's federal institutions were founded, could prohibit the secession of Quebec, if demands for independence were endorsed by a Quebecois majority. An independent Quebec might also face a similar challenge, if the Indians living in the northern part of its territory were to present their own potential secession as the clear desire of their community.

Nevertheless, a word of caution is required here. It is already very difficult to speculate on the future trends of secessionist activity, but it is nearly impossible to predict the manner in which a particular government would react to a potential secession crisis. No doubt the Canadian government would employ numerous compromises to retain Quebec within its federation, as it has done on several occasions. Moreover, democratic forms of government are not a guarantee for official accommodation of distinct community concerns. As witnessed by the recent Estonian language laws directed against their Russian minority, even new democracies can disregard the needs of portions of their population, discriminating against minority communities. Perhaps it is sufficient to comment that over time and with the greater acceptance of liberal democratic values, many states' calculations of their economic, security, and prestige interests in a secession crisis may experience a gradual shift. This shift would decrease the likelihood that the political community would be maintained by force. More importantly, for the many distinct communities who reside in states which do not even pretend to embrace liberal political philosophy, the costs of secession remain high. These governments would not have the same scruples in avoiding the use of force to maintain their territorial integrity.

It is conceivable that even if states pursued flexible policies intended both to decrease the costs of membership, by promoting diversity and granting extended autonomy, and to increase the benefits of membership, perhaps by providing financial assistance to distinct communities for cultural programs, they could still be insufficient to prevent or resolve a secession crisis. This is because influences outside the parameters of a specific secession confrontation impact on the decision to secede and necessarily limit the effectiveness of central government initiatives.

Catalan and Quebecois separatism persists despite the efforts to alleviate community concerns on the part of the Spanish and Canadian governments. As one of the four "historic" regions of Spain, Catalonia has been accorded extensive political and fiscal jurisdiction in self-government. The Generalitat has subsequently employed these rights in decisions of symbolic and substantive importance, including those concerning the language, education, flag, local civil law, public works, commerce, energy, industry, property, and local urban planning. Despite these changes, as revealed by the public quarrels surrounding Catalan demands for the right to speak their native tongue in federal government institutions, Catalan separatism continues to threaten and anger the Spanish government. Similarly, the Quebec provincial government is arguably one of the most powerful of any sub-state units of administration. It possesses wide powers to regulate its economy, administer educational policy and social welfare programs, and promote vigorously the French language. Through its efforts to create a bilingual society, Canada has recognized Quebec's unique position in North America as a French-speaking enclave. Yet the Parti Quebecois, on an avowedly secessionist agenda, continues to receive support among significant portions of the Quebecois community. Although the referendum on independence in 1995 was defeated by the narrowest of margins, it is quite possible that the secessionist agenda will return to the fore in the next decade.

Since Spanish and Canadian governments are presently dealing with their distinct communities in an accommodating fashion, the implications are two-fold. First, Catalan and Quebecois self-rule has been judged to be a success, and, thus, has strengthened and legitimized the separatists' claims. This experiment in political autonomy has reduced the perceived costs of secession. Second, and with perhaps more serious ramifications for the future integrity of many heterogeneous societies, domestic politics are insufficient to explain the persistence of some secessionist movements. The combination of developments on the international systemic level which have served to diminish the benefits of membership and the successful experience of self-rule improve the viability of an independent Catalonia or Quebec. As a consequence, these trends limit the effectiveness of even the most accommodating government policies.

Preoccupation with the conflict surrounding a particular secessionist struggle obscures the fact that the main protagonist in this drama, the distinct community, is in large part motivated by reasonable calculations. Within the parameters of the values and priorities it holds dear, it assesses its various political options. The fact that the modern study of revolution has successfully led to its removal from the realm of dogma and polemic indicates that rational discourse is possible even on the most difficult of subjects. It is possible to subject the conflicting moralities associated with secession crises to objective and detached analysis. This book has attempted to lay out a structured framework for just such an analysis of the decision to secede. It neither denies nor minimizes the moral questions which impinge on the decision to secede. Having identified the elements necessary for a secession crisis – a distinct community, territory, leaders, and discontent, it describes the secession dynamic as a function of the multiple political, economic and social factors which constitute the costs and benefits associated with the community's political alternatives – continued integration in the larger existing state and secession. It argues that changes in the balance of these costs and benefits can and do provoke secession crises. I hope that it has made a small contribution toward a better understanding of secession. This has been my agenda.

Bibliography

THEORY

Acton, H. B. *John Stuart Mill: Utilitarianism, On Liberty, and Considerations on Representative Government*. London, 1972.

Alcock, Antony, Brian K. Taylor, and John M. Welton (eds.). *The Future of Cultural Minorities*. London: Macmillan, 1979.

Anderson, Benedict. *Imagined Communities: Reflections on the Origin and Spread of Nationalism*, 2nd edn. London: Verso, 1991.

Aristotle. *The Politics* (trans. T. A. Sinclair), Harmondsworth: Penguin, 1981.

Bailey, Sydney D. *How Wars End: The United Nations and the Termination of Armed Conflict, 1946–1964*. Oxford: Clarendon Press, 1982.

Balibar, Etienne and Immanuel Wallerstein. *Race, Nation, and Class: Ambiguous Identities*. London: Verso, 1991.

Barry, Brian. "The Consociational Model and its Dangers." *European Journal of Political Research*, 3 (December, 1975), 393–412.

Beitz, Charles (ed.). *International Ethics*. Princeton: Princeton University Press, 1985.

Political Theory and International Relations. Princeton: Princeton University Press, 1979.

Beran, Harry. *The Consent Theory of Political Obligation*. London: Croom Helm, 1987.

"A Liberal Theory of Secession." *Political Studies*, 33 (1984), 21–31.

Birch, Anthony H. "Minority Nationalist Movements and Theories of Political Integration." *World Politics*, 30, 2 (April 1978), 325–344.

Braillard, Phillipe, and Mohammad-Resa Djalili. *The Third World and International Relations*. London: Printer, 1986.

Brass, Paul R. "Ethnicity and Nationality Formation." *Ethnicity*, 3 (1976), 225–241.

Buchanan, Allen. *Secession: The Morality of Political Divorce from Fort Sumter to Lithuania and Quebec*. San Francisco: Westview Press, 1991.

Buchheit, Lee C. *Secession: The Legitimacy of Self-Determination*. New Haven: Yale University Press, 1978.

233

Bull, Hedley. *The Anarchical Society: A Study of Order in World Politics*. London: Macmallan, 1987.

Bull, Hedley, and Adam Watson. *The Expansion of the International Society*. Oxford: Oxford University Press, 1984.

Bull, Hedley, Benedict Kingsbury, and Adam Roberts. *Hugo Grotius and International Relations*. Oxford: The Clarendon Press, 1990.

Buzan, Barry. *People, States, and Fear: An Agenda for International Security Studies in the Post-Cold War Era*. 2nd edn. London: Wheatsheaf, 1991.

    People, States, and Fear: The National Security Problem in International Relations. London: Wheatsheaf, 1983.

Cable, James. "Nationalism: A Durable Cause?" *International Relations*, 10, 3 (1991), 227–236.

Calvert, Peter. "On Attaining Sovereignty, " in Anthony D. Smith (ed.), *Nationalist Movements*. London: Macmillan, 1976.

Carnoy, Martin. *The State and Political Theory*. Princeton: Princeton University Press, 1984.

Carter, Gwendolen M. (ed.). *National Unity and Regionalism in Eight African States*. Ithaca: Cornell University Press, 1966.

Chazan, Niaomi. *Irridentism and International Politics*. London: Adamantine, 1991.

Cobban, Alfred. *National Self-Determination*. London: Oxford University Press, 1944.

    The Nation State and National Self-Determination. London: Collins, 1969.

Cohen, Roland. "Ethnicity: Problem and Focus in Anthropology," *Annual Review of Anthropology*, 7 (1978), 379–403.

Connor, Walker. "Nation-Building or Nation-Destroying." *World Politics* (April, 1972), 24, 3, 319–355.

    "The Politics of Ethnonationalism," *Journal of International Affairs*, 24, 3 (1973–1974), 1–21.

Cooper, Richard N. *Economic Policy in an Interdependent World: Essays in World Economics*. Cambridge, MA: Massachusetts Institute of Technology Press, 1986.

Dahl, Robert A. (ed.). *Political Oppositions in Western Democracies*. New Haven: Yale University Press, 1966.

Deutsch, Karl, W. *Nationalism and Social Communications*. Cambridge, MA: Harvard University Press, 1966.

Deutsch, Karl, W. *et al. Political Community and the North Atlantic Area: International Organization in the Light of Historical Experience*. Princeton: Princeton University Press, 1957.

Dudley, B. J. *Instability and Political Order*. Ibadan: Ibadan University Press, 1973.

Dunn, Otto and John Dinwiddy (eds.). *Nationalism in the Age of the French Revolution*. London: Hambledon, 1988.

Eagleton, Clyde. "The Excesses of Self-Determination." *Foreign Affairs*, 31, 4 (July 1953), 592–604.

Enloe, Cynthia H. *Ethnic Conflict and Political Development*. Boston: Little, Brown, 1973.

Ergang, R. *Gustav Herder and the Foundations of German Nationalism*. New York: Columbia University Press, 1931.

Esman, Milton (ed.). *Ethnic Conflict in the Western World*. Ithaca: Cornell University Press, 1977.

Febvre, Lucien and Martin, Henri-Jean. *The Coming of the Book: The Impact of Printing, 1450–1800*. London: New Left Books, 1976.

Finer, Samuel Edward. *Comparative Government*. London: Allen & Unwin, 1970.

Furnivall, J. S. *Race, Ethnicity, and Social Change*. London, 1972.

"Colonial Policy and Practice," in J. Stone (ed.). *Race, Ethnicity, and Social Change*. London, 1972.

Gellner, Ernest. *Nations and Nationalism*. Oxford: Basil Blackwell, 1983.

George, Alexander L. "Case Studies and Theory Development: The Method of Structured, Focused Comparison," in Paul Gordon Lauren (ed.), *Diplomacy: New Approaches in History, Theory, and Policy*. New York: Macmillan, 1979.

George, David Lloyd. *The Truth about the Peace Treaties*. London, 1938.

Gerth, H. H. and C. W. Mills (eds.). *From Marx to Weber*. New York: Oxford University Press, 1972.

Gordon, Charles. "Instability and the State: Sudan," in Caroline Thomas and Paikiasotby Saravananuttu (eds.), *The State and Instability in the South*. London: Macmillan, 1989.

Gourevitch, Peter Alexis. "The Reemergence of 'Peripheral Nationalisms': Some Comparative Speculations on the Spatial Distribution of Political Leadership and Economic Growth." *Comparative Studies in History and Society*, 23 (1981), 303–322.

Gurr, Ted Robert. *Why Men Rebel*. Princeton: Princeton University Press, 1970.

Haas, Ernst. *The Uniting of Europe*. Stanford: Stanford University Press, 1968.

Hah, Chong-Do and Jeffrey Martin. "Toward a Synthesis of Conflict and Integration Theories of Nationalism," *World Politics*, 27, 3 (April 1975), 361–386.

Hannum, Hurst. *Autonomy, Sovereignty, and Self-Determination: The Accommodation of Conflicting Rights*. Philadelphia: University of Pennsylvania Press, 1990.

Hazelwood, Arthur (ed.). *African Integration and Disintegration*. London: Oxford University Press, 1967.

Hechter, Michael. *Internal Colonialism: The Celtic Fringe in British National Development, 1537–1966*. Berkeley: University of California Press, 1973.

"On Separatism and Ethnicity: A Response to Sloan's 'Ethnicity or Imperialism?'" *Comparative Studies in History and Society*, 21 (1979), 126–129.

Heraclides, Alexis. "Secessionist Minorities and External Involvement." *International Organization*, 44, 3 (Summer 1990), 341–378.

The Self-Determination of Minorities in International Politics. London: Cass, 1990.

Hobbes, Thomas. *Leviathan*, (ed. Crawford Brouger MacPherson). Harmondsworth: Penguin Books, 1985.

Hobsbawm, E. J. *Nations and Nationalism Since 1780: Programme, Myth, and Reality.* Cambridge: Cambridge University Press, 1990.

Hofstadter, R. *The American Political Tradition.* New York: Vintage, 1973.

Horowitz, Donald. *Community Conflict: Policy and Possibilities.* Coleraine: University of Ulster Press, 1990.

"Patterns of Ethnic Separatism." *Comparative Studies of History and Society,* 23 (1981), 165–195.

"Three Dimensions of Ethnic Politics." *World Politics* 23, 3(January 1971), 232–244.

Jackson, Robert. *Quasi-States: Sovereignty, International Relations, and the Third World.* Cambridge: Cambridge University Press, 1990.

Jackson, Robert and Carl Rosberg. "Why Africa's Weak States Persist: The Empirical and the Juridical in Statehood." *World Politics,* 31, 5 (October 1982–July 1983), 1–24.

Jennings, Ivor. *The Approach to Self-Government.* Boston: Beacon Press, 1963.

Joy, J. Richard. *Languages in Conflict.* Toronto: McClelland & Stewart, 1968.

Kahn, Robert L. and Mayer N. Zald. *Organizations and Nation-States: New Perspectives on Conflict and Cooperation.* San Francisco: Josey-Bass, 1990.

Kamanu, Onyeonoro S. "Secession and the Right of Self-Determination: an O.A.U. Dilemma," *Journal of Modern African Studies,* 12, 3 (1974), 355–376.

Kasfir, Nelson. "Explaining Ethnic Political Participation." *World Politics,* 32 (1979), 365–388.

"Peacemaking and Social Cleavage in Sudan," in V. Montville (ed.), *Conflict and Peace-Making in Multi-Ethnic Societies.* New York: Lexington Books, 1990.

Kavanagh, Dennis and Gillian Peele. *Comparative Government and Politics: Essays in Honor of S. E. Finer.* London: Heinemann, 1989.

Kedourie, Elie. *Nationalism.* London: Hutchinson University Library, 1960.

Keohane Robert O. and Joseph S. Nye. *Power and Interdependence.* Boston: Little Brown, 1977.

King, Roger. *The State in Modern Society: New Directions in Political Sociology.* London: Macmillan, 1986.

Kohn, Hans. *The Age of Nationalism.* New York: Harper, 1962.

Kuper, Leo. *Genocide.* New Haven: Yale University Press, 1981.

International Action Against Genocide. London: Minority Rights Group, 1982.

The Prevention of Genocide. New Haven: Yale University Press, 1985.

Kymlicka, Will. *Liberalism, Community, and Culture.* Oxford: Oxford University Press, 1989.

Lansing, Robert. *The Peace Negotiations, A Personal Narrative.* New York, 1921.

Lauren, Paul Gordon (ed.). *Diplomacy: New Approaches in History, Theory, and Policy.* New York: Macmillan, 1979.

Lijphart, Arend. "The Comparable-Case Strategy in Comparative Research." *Comparative Political Studies*, 8 (July, 1975), 158–177.

 Democracy in Plural Societies: A Comparative Exploration. New Haven, CT: Yale University Press, 1977.

 Ethnic Conflict in the Western World. Ithaca: Cornell University Press, 1977.

 Democracies: Patterns of Majoritarian and Consensus Government in Twenty-One Countries. New Haven, CT: Yale University Press, 1984.

Lorwin, Val R. "Segmented Pluralism: Ideological Cleavages and Political Cohesion in the Smaller European Democracies." *Comparative Politics*, 3, 2 (January 1971), 141–174.

Macartney, C. A. *National States and National Minorities.* Oxford: Oxford University Press, 1934.

McLennan, Gregor, David Held, and Stuart Hall (eds.). *The Idea of the Modern State.* London: Open University Press, 1984.

McRae, Kenneth (ed.). *Consociational Democracy: Political Accommodation in Segmented Societies.* Toronto: McLelland and Stewart, 1974.

Mayall, James (ed.). *The Community of States: A Study of International Political Theory.* London: George Allen & Unwin, 1982.

 Nationalism and the International Society. Cambridge: Cambridge University Press, 1990.

Mayall, James and Mark Simpson. "Ethnicity is Not Enough: Reflections on Protracted Secessionism in the Third World" (unpublished), 1990. Text provided by authors to Dr. Benedict Kingsbury who then provided it to the author.

Mill, John Stuart. *Collected Works*, vol. XIX. London, 1963.

 Considerations on Representative Government. Indianapolis: Library of Liberal Arts Press, 1958.

 Three Essays. London: Oxford University Press, 1975.

 Utilitarianism, Liberty, and Representative Government. London: J. M. Dent & Sons, 1972.

Miller, David and Larry Siedentrop. *The Nature of Political Theory.* Oxford: Clarendon Press, 1983.

Milliband, Ralph. *The State in Capitalist Society: The Analysis of the Western System of Power.* London: Quartet Books, 1973.

Mitra, Subra Kumar. *The Post-Colonial State in Asia.* London: Harvester Wheatsheaf, 1990.

Newman, Saul. "Does Modernization Breed Ethnic Conflict?" *World Politics*, 43 (April 1991), 451–478.

North-South: A Programme for Survival, The Report of the Independent Commission on International Development Issues. London: Pan Books, 1980.

Olson, Mancur. *The Logic of Collective Action: Public Goods and the Theory of Groups.* Cambridge, MA: Harvard University Press, 1965.

Osterud, Oyvind (ed.). *Studies of War and Peace*. Oslo: Norwegian University Press, 1986.

Polanyi, Karl. *The Great Transformation*. New York: Rinehart, 1944. Reprint, Boston: Beacon Press, 1985.

Porter, A. N. and A. J. Stockwell. *British Imperial Policy and Decolonization: 1938–1964*, vol. I. Cambridge: Cambridge University Press.

Premdas, Ralph, S. W. R. de A. Samarasinghe, and Alan B. Anderson (eds.). *Secessionist Movements in Comparative Perspective*. London: Pinter, 1990.

Presthus, Robert. *Elites in the Policy Process*. Cambridge: Cambridge University Press, 1974.

Ra'anan, Uri, Maria Mesner, Keith Armes, and Kate Martin (eds.). *The State and the Nation in Multi-Ethnic Societies: The Breakup of Multinational States*. Manchester: Manchester University Press, 1991.

Raz, Joseph. *The Morality of Freedom*. Oxford: Clarendon Press, 1986.

Rousseau, J. J. *The Social Contract*. Harmondsworth: Penguin, 1976.

Ryan, Stephen. "Explaining Ethnic Conflict: The Neglected International Dimension." *Review of International Studies*, 14, 3 (July 1988), 161–177.

Seton-Watson, Hugh. *Nationalism: Old and New*. Sydney: Sydney University Press, 1964.

   Nations and States: An Inquiry into the Origins of Nations and the Politics of Nationalism. London: Methuen, 1977.

Sidgwick, Henry. *The Elements of Politics*. London: 1891.

Sklar, Richard L. "Political Science and National Integration – A Radical Approach" *Journal of Modern African Studies*, 5, 1 (1967), 1–11.

   "The Nature of Class Domination in Africa." *Journal of Modern African Studies*, 17, 4 (1979), 531–552.

   "The State of the Nation-State." *The Economist*, December 22, 1990, pp. 73–78.

Sloan, William. "Ethnicity or Imperialism?" *Comparative Studies of Society and History*, 2 (1979), 113–125.

Smith, Anthony D. *Theories of Nationalism*. London: Duckworth, 1971.

Smith, Anthony D. (ed.) *Nationalist Movements*. New York: Macmillan, 1976.

Sugar, Peter F. and Ivo J. Lederer (eds.). *Nationalism in Eastern Europe*. Seattle: University of Washington Press, 1969.

Tajfel, Henri. *The Social Psychology of Minorities*. London: Minority Rights Group, 1978.

Tiryakian, Edward A. and Ronald Rogowski. *New Nationalisms of the Developed West*. Boston: Allen & Unwin, 1985.

Van Dyke, Vernon. "The Individual, the State, and Ethnic Communities in Political Theory." *World Politics*, 29, 3 (April 1977).

Verba, Sidney. "Some Dilemmas in Comparative Research." *World Politics*, 20 (October 1976).

Walter, Andrew. *World Power and World Money: The Role of Hegemony and International Monetary Order*. London: Harvester Wheatsheaf, 1991.

Waltz, Kenneth. *Man, The State, and War*. New York: Columbia University Press, 1959.

Walzer, Michael. *Just and Unjust Wars: A Moral Argument with Historical Illustrations*. New York: Basic Books, 1977.
"The Reform of the International System," in Oyvind Osterud (ed.), *Studies of War and Peace*. Oslo: Norwegian University Press, 1986.
Wambaugh, S. *Plebecites Since the World War*. Washington, DC: Carnegie Endowment for International Peace, 1933.
Weber, Max. "Politics as Vocation," in H. H. Gerth and C. W. Mills (eds.), *From Marx to Weber*. New York: Oxford University Press, 1972.
Wight, Martin. *Power Politics*, 2nd edn. Harmondsworth: Penguin, 1986.
Williams, Colin H. (ed.) *National Separatism*. Cardiff: University of Wales Press, 1982.
Wood, John. "Secession: A Comparative Analytical Framework." *Canadian Journal of Political Science*, 14 (1981), 107–134.
World Development Report 1988. New York, 1988.
Young, Crawford. *The Politics of Cultural Pluralism*. Madison: University of Wisconsin Press, 1976.
Zinkin, Maurice. "Minorities, Immigrants and Refugees: The Problems of Integration." *International Relations*, 10, 3 (May 1991), 267–276.

LAW

Brownlie, Ian. *Basic Documents on African Affairs*. Oxford: Clarendon Press, 1971.
Basic Documents on Human Rights. Oxford: Clarendon Press, 1981.
International Law and the Use of Force by States. Oxford: Clarendon Press, 1963.
Principles of Public International Law. Oxford: Oxford University Press, 1979; 4th edn., Oxford: Clarendon Press, 1990.
Crawford, James. *The Creation of States in International Law*. Oxford: Clarendon Press, 1979.
"The Criteria for Statehood in International Law" *British Yearbook of International Law*. London, 1976–77.
The Rights of Peoples. Oxford: Oxford University Press, 1988.
Cristescu, Aureliu. *The Right to Self-Determination: Historical and Current Development on the Basis of United Nations Instruments*. New York: United Nations, 1981.
The Events in East Pakistan, 1971. Geneva: Secretariat of the International Commission of Jurists, 1972.
Gros Espiell, Hector. *The Right to Self-Determination: Implementation of United Nations Resolutions*. New York: United Nations, 1980.
Higgins, Rosalyn. *The Development of International Law Through the Political Organs of the United Nations*. Oxford: Oxford University Press, 1963.
Okeke, Chris N. *Controversial Subjects of Contemporary International Law*. Rotterdam, 1979.

Bibliography

Palley, Claire. *Constitutional Law and Minorities.* London: Minority Rights Group, 1978.
Roling, B. V. A. *International Law in an Expanded World.* Amsterdam, 1960.
Snyder G. Francis. and Peter Slinn (eds.). *International Law of Development: Comparative Perspectives.* Abington: Professional Books, 1987.
Thornberry, Patrick. *Minorities and Human Rights Law.* London: Minority Rights Group, 1986.

CASES

Belgium – Flanders/Walloonia

"Devolve and Rule." *The Economist*, October 12, 1991, pp. 64–69.
Dunn, James. "'Consociational Democracy' and the Language Conflict: A Comparison of the Belgian and Swiss Experiences." *Comparative Political Studies*, 5, 1 (1972), 3–40.
"The Revision of the Constitution in Belgium: A Study in the Institutionalization of Ethnic Conflict." *Western Political Quarterly*, 27, 1 (1974), 143–163.
Heisler, Martin. "Institutionalizing Societal Cleavages in a Cooptive Polity: The Growing Importance of the Output Side in Belgium," in Martin Heisler (ed.), *Politics in Europe.* New York, 1974.
Kossman, E. H. *The Low Countries: 1780–1940.* Oxford: Clarendon Press, 1978.
Lorwin, Val. "Belgium: Religion, Class, and Language in National Politics," in Robert A. Dahl (ed.), *Political Oppositions in Western Democracies.* New Haven, CT: Yale University Press, 1966.
"Linguistic Pluralism and Political Tension in Modern Belgium." *Canadian Journal of History*, 5–6 (1970–1971), 1–23.
Miller, Jonathan. "Poll Farce Pushes Belgium Nearer Break-up." *The Sunday Times*, December 1, 1991, p. 25.
"Putting the Carthorse in Front." *The Economist*, March 14, 1992, p. 66.

Bengalis – Pakistan

Ahmed, Akbar S. "Identity and Ideology in Pakistan: An Interview." *Third World Quarterly*, 11 (October 1989), 54–69.
Ali, Tariq. *Can Pakistan Survive? The Death of a State.* New York: Penguin, 1983.
Ayub Khan, Mohammad. *Friends Not Masters – A Political Biography.* London, 1967.
Bangla Desh Documents, vols. I and II. Madras: B. N. K. Press, 1972.
Bangladesh Liberation Struggle, 1971: The Role of the United States, China, the Soviet Union, and India. London: Radical Asia Publications, 1990.
Bhutto, Zulfiqar Ali. *The Great Tragedy.* Karachi: Vision Publications, 1971.
Budhray, Vijay S. "Moscow and the Birth of Bangladesh" *Asian Survey*, 13 (May 1973), 482–495.
Chakravarty, S. R. (ed.). *Bangladesh: History and Culture* (vol. I) and *Domestic Politics* (vol. II). New Delhi: South Asia Publishers, 1986.

Choudhury, G. W. *The Last Days of United Pakistan*. London: C. Hurst & Co., 1974.

Government of Pakistan. *Reports of the Advisory Panel for the Fourth Five Year Plan, 1970–1975*. Karachi: Planning Commission, Government of Pakistan, 1970.

Islam, Nurul. *Development Planning in Bangladesh: A Study in Political Economy.* London: C. Hurst, 1977.

Keesing's Contemporary Archives, London, 1969–1975.

Khanal, Y. N. "Bangladesh in 1972: Nation-Building in a New State." *Asian Survey*, 13 (February 1973), 199–210.

LaPorte, Robert, Jr. "Pakistan in 1971: The Disintegration of a Nation." *Asian Survey*, 12 (February 1972), 97–108.

"Pakistan in 1972: Picking up the Pieces" *Asian Survey*, 13 (February 1973), 187–198.

Mishra, Gulab. *Indo-Pakistan Relations*. New Delhi: Ashish Publishing House, 1987.

Mohmood, Safdar. *Pakistan Divided*. New Delhi: Alpha Bravo, 1988.

Oldenberg, Nicholas and Philip Oldenberg. *Bangladesh – The Birth of a Nation*. Madras, 1972.

Rahman, Sheikh Mujibur. *Bangladesh, My Bengladesh*. Dhaka, 1972.

Rashiduzzaman, M. "The Awami League in the Political Development of Pakistan," *Asian Survey*, 10 (July 1970), 574–588.

"Leadership, Organization, Strategies, and Tactics of the Bangla Desh Movement" *Asian Survey*, 12 (March 1972),185–200.

Singh, Jagdev. *Dismemberment of Pakistan: The 1971 Indo Pak War*. New Delhi: Lancer International, 1988.

Sisson, Richard and Leo Rose. *War and Secession: Pakistan, India, and the Creation of Bangladesh*. Berkeley: University of California Press, 1990.

Biafra – Nigeria

Achebe, Chinua. *The Trouble with Nigeria*. London: Heinemann, 1983.

Anber, Paul. "Modernization and Political Disintegration: Nigeria and the Ibos." *Journal of Modern African Studies*, 5 (1967), 165–6.

Bello, Ahmadu. *My Life*. Cambridge: Cambridge University Press, 1962.

Choudhury, S. *The Genesis of Bangladesh: A Study in International Legal Norms and Permissive Conscience*. Dhaka, 1972.

Diamond, Larry. "Class, Ethnicity, and the Democratic State: Nigeria, 1950–1966." *Comparative Studies in Society and History*, 25 (1983), 457–489.

Dudley, B. J. *Instability and Political Order*. Ibadan: Ibadan University Press, 1973.

Parties and Politics in Northern Nigeria. London: Frank Cass, 1968.

The Events in East Pakistan, 1971. Geneva: Secretariate of the International Commission of Jurists, 1972.

"Floating Towards Democracy." *The Economist*, March 14, 1992, pp. 86–90.

"Form of Association for Nigeria. Paper by the Northern Nigeria Delegation," in *The Ad Hoc Conference on the Nigerian Constitution*. Eastern Nigeria, 1966.

Forsyth, Frederick. *The Biafra Story*. Baltimore: Penguin, 1969.

The Making of an African Legend: The Biafra Story. London: Severn House, 1983.

Hazelwood, Arthur (ed.). *African Integration and Disintegration*. London: Oxford University Press, 1967.

Introducing the Republic of Biafra. Enugu, Biafra: Government Printer, 1967.

Kirk-Green, A. H. M. *Crisis and Conflict in Nigeria: A Documentary Source Book, 1966–1970*. 2 vol. Oxford: Oxford University Press, 1971.

Genesis of the Nigerian Civil War. Uppsala: Scandinavian Institute of African Affairs Report No. 27, 1975.

Mackintosh, John P. *Nigerian Government and Politics*. Evanston, IL: Northwestern University Press.

Melson, Robert. and Howard Wolpe (eds.). *Nigeria: Modernization and the Politics of Communalism*. East Lansing: Michigan State University Press, 1976.

"Memorandum by the Western Region and Lagos Delegations to the Ad Hoc Committee on Constitutional Arrangements for Nigeria, 1966, in *The Ad Hoc Conference on the Nigerian Constitution*. Eastern Nigeria, 1966.

"New Breed, Old Ways." *The Economist*, August 17, 1991, pp. 37–38.

Nigeria and Biafra: The Parting of Ways. Enugu, Biafra: Government Printer, 1967.

Nixon, Charles, R. "Self-Determination: The Nigeria/Biafra Case." *World Politics*, 24, 4 (1972), 473–497.

O'Connell, James. "Political Integration: The Nigerian Case," in Arthur Hazelwood (ed.). *African Integration and Disintegration*. London: Oxford University Press, 1967.

Ostheimer, John M. *Nigerian Politics*. New York: Harper & Row, 1973.

Post, K. W. J. "The Crisis in Nigeria," *The World Today*, February 1966, pp. 43–47.

Nigerian Federal Election of 1959. London: Oxford University Press, 1963.

Proclamation of the Republic of Biafra. Enugu: Government of Biafra Press, 1967.

"Seething." *The Economist*, May 23, 1992, p. 72.

Sklar, Richard L. "The Nature of Class Domination in Africa." *Journal of Modern African Studies*, 17, 4 (1979), 531–552.

Nigerian Political Parties. Princeton: Princeton University Press, 1963.

"Political Science and National Integration – A Radical Approach." *Journal of Modern African Studies*, 5, 1 (1967), 1–11.

Sklar, Richard L. and C. S. Whitaker, "The Federal Republic of Nigeria," in Gwendolen M. Carter (ed.), *National Unity and Regionalism in Eight African States*. Ithaca: Cornell University Press, 1966.

Sobhan, Rehman. "Negotiating for Bangla Desh: A Participants View." *South Asian Review*, July 1971.

Stremlau, John J. *The International Politics of the Nigerian Civil War (1966–1970)*. Princeton: Princeton University Press, 1977.

Tamuno, Tekena N. "Separatist Agitation in Nigeria Since 1914." *Journal of Modern African Studies*, 8, 4 (1970), 563–584.

Young, Crawford. *The Politics of Cultural Pluralism*. Madison: University of Wisconsin Press, 1976.

Cyprus

Adams, T. W. "The First Republic of Cyprus: A Review of an Unworkable Constitution." *Western Political Quarterly*, 19, 3 (1966), 475–490.

Attalides, Michael. *Cyprus, Nationalism, and International Politics*. London: Q. Press, 1979.

Ertekun, Necati Munir. *The Cyprus Dispute and the Birth of the Turkish Republic of Northern Cyprus*. Nicosia, 1981.

Kyle, Keith. *Cyprus*. London: Minority Rights Group, 1984.

Kyriakides, Stanley. *Cyprus: Constitutionalism and Crisis Government*. Philadelphia: University of Pennsylvania Press, 1968.

Lijphart, Arend. "Constitutional Failure in Cyprus, 1960–1963," in *Democracy in Plural Societies: A Comparative Exploration*. New Haven, CT: Yale University Press, 1977.

Polyviou, Polivios. *Cyprus: Conflict and Negotiations, 1960–1980*. London: Duckworth, 1980.

Souter, David. "The Cyprus Conundrum: The Challenge of Intercommunal Talks." *Third World Quarterly*, 11 (1989), 78.

Czechoslovakia

Barber, Tony. "Slovaks near to split with Czechs." *The Independent* (London), June 20, 1991, p. 10.

Benĕš, Eduard. *Memoirs*. Paris, 1919.

Bradley, J. F. N. *Czechoslovakia: A Short History*. Edinburgh: Edinburgh University Press, 1971.

"A Central European Divorce." *The Independent* (London), June 19, 1991, p. 18.

Crawshaw, Steve. "Czechoslovak federation set to split today." *The Independent* (London), June 19, 1991, p. 1.

"The Danger of Delinquency." *The Economist*, March 16, 1991, pp. 44–45.

Dobbs, Michael. "Trauma of the New Order: Czechs and Slovaks Drift Toward Schism." *International Herald Tribune*, October 2, 1991, p. 2.

Genillard, Arianne and Anthony Robinson. "Bratislava Break-up Negotiations." *The Financial Times*, June 20, 1992, p. 3.

Greenberg, Susan. "Czechoslovaks Set for Quickie Divorce." *The Guardian* (London), June 20, 1992, p. 21.

Krcmar, Jan. "Slovaks fear the prospects of a future of their own." *The Independent* (London), June 19, 1991, p. 10.

Mamatey, Victor S. and Radomir Luza (eds.). *A History of the Czechoslovak Republic: 1918– 1948*. Princeton: Princeton University Press, 1973.

Meixner, Bernard. "Bratislava talks make progress." *The Times* (London), June 20, 1992, p. 12.

"One Country, Two Elections." *The Economist*, May 30, 1992, pp. 42–43.

Schmidt, William E. "Splitting Czecho/Slovakia." *The International Herald Tribune*, June 8, 1992, pp. 1–4.

Stern, Evzen. *Opinions of T. G.Masaryk*. Prague, 1918.

"Velvet Divorce?" *The Economist*, June 13, 1992, pp. 47–50.

Webb, W. L. "Czechs and Slovaks Find Fellow Feeling." *The Guardian* (London), December 18, 1991, p. 20.

Zacek, Joseph F. "Nationalism in Czechoslovakia," in Peter F. Sugar and Ivo J. Lederer (eds.), *Nationalism in Eastern Europe*. Seattle: University of Washington Press, 1969.

Zaninovich, M. George and Douglas A. Brown. "Political Integration in Czechoslovakia: The Implications of the Prague Spring and Soviet Intervention." *Journal of International Affairs*, 27, 1 (1973), 66–79.

Eritrea – Ethiopia

Cliff, Lionel. "Forging a Nation: the Eritrean Experience." *Third World Quarterly*, October 1989, 131–147.

Crowder, Michael (ed.). *The Cambridge History of Africa, Vol 8: 1940–1975*. Cambridge: Cambridge University Press, 1984.

"Eritrea: An Unborn Nation." *The Economist*, October 20, 1991, p. 104.

Fage, J. D. and Roland Oliver (eds.). *The Cambridge History of Africa, Vol. 7: 1905– 1940*. Cambridge: Cambridge University Press, 1986.

"Flying Food." *The Economist*, August 31, 1991, pp. 33–34.

"The Healing Touch." *The Economist*, December 14, 1991, p. 80.

Legum, Colin. *Eritrea and Tigray*. London: Minority Rights Group, 1983.

Markakis, John. "Nationalities and the State in Ethiopia." *Third World Quarterly*, October, 1989, pp. 118–130.

"Morning in Ethiopia." *The Economist*, September 14, 1991, p. 79.

Selassie, Habte, Bereket. *Conflict and Intervention in the Horn of Africa*. New York: Monthly Review Press, 1980.

India

"Ballots and Bullets." *The Economist*, April 27, 1991, pp. 63–64.

Brass, Paul. "Class, Ethnic Group, and Party in Indian Politics." *World Politics*, 33, 3 (1981), 449–467.

   The Politics of India Since Independence. Cambridge: Cambridge University Press, 1990.

"The Case against War." *The Economist*, September 7, 1991, pp. 34–35.

"A chance for Punjab." *The Economist*, January 25, 1992, pp. 60–63.

Embree, Ainslie T. "Pluralism and National Integration: The Indian Experience." *Journal of International Affairs*, 27, 1 (1973), 1–21.

"Flight of Fancy." *The Economist*, February 1, 1992, pp. 64–64.

Shackle, Christopher. *The Sikhs*. London: Minority Rights Group, 1985.

"Throwing Punches in Punjab." *The Economist*, January 5, 1991, p. 50.

"With the Punjabi commandos." *The Economist,* September 28, 1991, pp. 83–84.

Nagas

Dutt-Luithui, Ela. "Violence in India: The Case of the Naga National Movement." *South Asia Bulletin,* 5, 2 (1985), 39–42.

Endless War: Disturbed Areas in the North-East. New Delhi: Peoples Union for Democratic Rights, 1983.

Luithui, Luingam and Nandita Haksar. *Nagaland File: A Question of Human Rights.* New Delhi, 1984.

Maxwell, Neville. *India, the Nagas, and the Northeast.* London: Minority Rights Group, 1980.

The Naga Nation and Its Struggle Against Genocide. Copenhagen: The International Work Group on Indigenous Affairs (Document No. 56), 1986.

Nuh, V. K. *The Nagaland Church and Politics.* Kohima, Nagaland, India: Vision Press, 1986.

Pimomo, Paul (ed.). *Nagaland Yearbook.* Shillong, India: Neelam Press, 1984.

Short, Martin and Anthony McDermott. *The Kurds.* London: Minority Rights Group, 1975.

Yonou, Asoso. *The Rising Nagas: A Historical and Political Study.* New Delhi: Vivek Publishing House, 1974.

Karen – Burma

Amnesty International. *Burma – Extrajudicial Execution and Torture of Members of Ethnic Minorities.* London: Amnesty International, 1988.

Prisoners of Conscience in Myanmar: A Chronicle of Developments Since September 1988. New York: Amnesty International, 1989.

Asia Watch. *Human Rights in Burma (Myanmar).* New York: Asia Watch, 1990.

Killing Its Own People: Asia Watch Condemns Burma's Death March of Prisoners and Crackdown Against Opposition. New York: Asia Watch, 1989.

Burma In Brief. Washington, DC: The International Center for Development Policy, 1989.

Burma Situation Report. Bloomington, IN: Kachinland Foundation, 1990.

"Cry of Desperation." *Far Eastern Economic Review,* January 3, 1991, pp. 10–11.

"An Interview With Saw Maung." *International Affairs.* February 3, 1989.

Karen National Union. "Draft Constitution of the Federal Union of the Democratic National States of Burma" (unpublished), Summer, 1990. Text provided by the Karen National Union foreign secretary, Dr. Em Marta.

Lintner, Bertil. "Burma Profile." *Far Eastern Economic Review,* 8-part series. September 8–October 27, 1988.

"Class Distinctions." *Far Eastern Economic Review,* December 6, 1990, p. 28.

"An Inside Job: Communists' Disappearing Act All Their Own Work." *Far Eastern Economic Review,* June 1, 1989, p. 28.

Land of Jade. Bangkok: White Lotus Press, 1988.

Bibliography

"Left in Disarray: Ethnic Rank-n-File Ousts Communist Party Leaders." *Far Eastern Economic Review*, June 1, 1989, pp. 26–27.

"Oiling The Iron Fist." *Far Eastern Economic Review*, December 6, 1990, pp. 28–30.

Outrage: Burma's Struggle for Democracy. Bangkok: White Lotus Press, 1990.

McDonald, Hamish. "The Generals Buy Time." *Far Eastern Economic Review*, February 22, 1990, pp. 16–18.

"Partners in Plunder." *Far Eastern Economic Review*, February 22, 1990, p. 16.

Mirante, Edith T. "Burma – Frontier Minorities in Arms." *Cultural Survival Quarterly*, 11, 4 (1987).

"Burma Update: Urban Uprising and Frontier Rebellion." *Cultural Survival Quarterly*, 13, 1 (1989).

Moynihan, Daniel Patrick. "Testimony to the Subcommittee on East Asian and Pacific Affairs and to the Subcommittee on Human Rights and International Organizations, United States House of Representatives" (unpublished), September 13, 1989. Text provided by the Senator's Legislative Assistant, Tomasz Malinowski.

National Democratic Front. "The Panglong Agreement" (unpublished), February 12, 1947. Text provided by the Karen National Union foreign secretary, Dr. Em Marta.

"Statement Issued by the Third Plenary Central Presidium Meeting" (unpublished), October 30, 1984. Text provided by the Karen National Union foreign secretary, Dr. Em Marta.

"Statement Issued by the Second Congress of the National Democratic Front" (unpublished), July 8, 1987. Text provided by the Karen National Union foreign secretary, Dr. Em Marta.

Scigliano, Eric. "Burma: The Long Road Back." *Seattle Weekly*, May 24, 1989.

Silverstein, Josef. "In Burma, A Civil War Has Gone On For 41 Years." *New York Times*, September 12, 1989.

Burmese Politics: The Dilemma of National Unity. New Brunswick, NJ: Rutger's University Press, 1980.

Smith, Martin. "Dark Days in Burma." *Anti-Slavery Society Reporter*, December 1989, pp. 70–79.

Overholt, William H. "Dateline – Drug Wars Burma: The Wrong Enemy." *Foreign Policy* (Fall 1989), 172–191.

United States Committee on Refugees. *The War Is Growing Worse: Refugees and Displaced Persons on the Thai-Burmese Border.* Washington: United States Committee on Refugees, 1990.

United States Department of State. *Report on Human Rights.* Washington, DC: United States Government Printing Office, 1989, 1990.

United States General Accounting Office. *Drug Control: Enforcement Efforts in Burma Are Not Effective.* Washington, DC: United States General Accounting Office, 1989.

Katanga – Congo

Hoskyns, Catherine (ed.). *Case Studies in African Diplomacy; The Organization of African Unity and the Congo Crisis, 1964–1965*. Oxford: Oxford University Press, 1969.

The Congo Since Independence, January, 1960–December, 1961. Oxford: Oxford University Press, 1965.

Lemarchand, Rene. "The Limits of Self-Determination: The Case of the Katanga Secession." *The American Political Science Review*, 52 (1962), 404–416.

O'Brien, Cruise Conor. *To Katanga and Back: A UN Case History*. London, 1962.

Kurds – Turkey/Iraq/Iran

"Calvalry to the rescue." *The Economist*, April 20, 1991, pp. 69–70.

Chaliand, Gerard (ed.). *People Without a Country: The Kurds and Kurdistan*. London: Zed Press, 1980.

Destroying Ethnic Identity: The Kurds of Turkey. New York: US Helsinki Watch Committee, 1988.

"Elderly scraps of paper." *The Economist*, April 27, 1991, p. 74.

Entessar, Nader. "The Kurdish Mosaic of Discord." *Third World Quarterly*, 21, 4 (October 1989), 83–99.

"The Hammer of the Kurds." *The Economist*, April 6, 1991, pp. 9–10.

"Hope against Hope for Iraq's Kurds." *The Economist*, May 4, 1991, pp. 69–70.

"Independence by Stealth." *The Economist*, May 9, 1992, pp. 65–66.

Kinnane, Derk. *The Kurds and Kurdistan*. London: Oxford University Press, 1964.

"The Kurds' Bid for Freedom." *The Economist*, March 30, 1991, p. 37.

McDowall, David. *The Kurds*. London: Minority Rights Group, 1985.

Moreau, Ron. "Saddam's Slaughter." *Newsweek*, April 15, 1991, pp. 10–17.

Safire, William. "The Kurds' Dilemma." *New York Times*, September 12, 1991, p. A15.

"Sanctuary for the Kurds." *The Economist*, April 20, 1991, p.14.

"The Slippery Slope." *The Economist*, April 13, 1991, pp. 67–68.

"Trekking Home." *The Economist*, May 4, 1991, pp. 70–73.

"Wages of Defeat." *The Economist*, August 17, 1991, pp. 36–37.

"When Saddam Smiles, Make Sure You Count his Teeth." *The Economist*, April 27, 1991, pp. 73–74.

Norway – Sweden

Andersson, Ingvar. (trans. from Swedish, Carolyn Hannay), *A History of Sweden*. London: Weidenfeld and Nicolson, 1957.

Derry, T. K. *A History of Modern Norway: 1814–1972*. Oxford: Clarendon Press, 1973.

History of Scandinavia: Norway, Sweden, Denmark, Finland, and Iceland. London: George Allen & Unwin, 1979.

Bibliography

Heckscher, Eli. F. *An Economic History of Sweden*. (trans. Goran Ohlin), Cambridge: Harvard University Press, 1954.

Larsen, Karen. *A History of Norway*. Princeton: Princeton University Press, 1950.

"The Secession of Norway from Sweden," in Jane Jacobs, *The Question of Separatism: Quebec and the Struggle over Sovereignty*. New York: Random House, 1980.

Quebec – Canada

Ajzenstat, Janet. "Liberalism and Nationalism." *Canadian Journal of Political Science*, 4 (1981), 587–609.

Balk, Alfred. "Canada's Winter of Discontent." *World Press Review*, December 1991, pp. 24–25.

"Brian Mulroney's light brigade." *The Economist*, September 21, 1991, pp. 83–84.

Bumsted, J. M. (ed.). *Interpreting Canada's Past*, vols. I & II. Toronto: Oxford University Press, 1986, London: Edward Arnold, 1972.

Burroughs, Peter. *The Canadian Crisis and British Colonial Policy, 1828–1841*. London: Edward Arnold, 1972.

"Canada's Long, Hard Trail." *The Washington Post*, September 10, 1991.

Cook, Ramsay. *Canada, Quebec, and the Uses of Nationalism*. Toronto: McClelland & Stewart, 1986.

The Maple Leaf Forever. Toronto: Macmillan, 1967.

"Deadline Fever." *The Economist*, May 16, 1992, pp. 75–78.

"EEEk!" *The Economist*, June 13, 1992, pp. 66–68.

Farnsworth, Clyde. "Quebec Separatist Is Encouraged by Independence of Baltics." *The New York Times*, September 8, 1991, p. A8.

"Separatist Fervor Fades in Quebec: The Cost of Seceding Is Seen as Too High." *The New York Times*, September 16, 1991, p. C1.

Fenwick, Rudy. "Social Change and Ethnic Nationalism: An Historical Analysis of the Separatism Movement in Quebec." *Comparative Studies in History and Society*, 23 (1981), 196–216.

"For Want of Glue: A Survey of Canada." *The Economist*, June 29, 1991.

Guidon, Hubert. *Quebec Society: Tradition, Modernity, and Nationhood*. Toronto: University of Toronto Press, 1988.

Holmes, Jean. "A Note on Some Aspects of Contemporary Canadian and Australian Federalism." *Journal of Commonwealth and Comparative Politics*, 12–13 (1974–75), 313–322.

Jacobs, Jane. *The Question of Separatism: Quebec and the Struggle over Sovereignty*. New York: Random House, 1980.

Joy, J. Richard. *Languages in Conflict*. Toronto: McClelland & Stewart, 1968.

Legendre, Camille. *French Canada in Crisis: A New Society in the Making?* London: Minority Rights Group, 1980.

Lijphart, Arendt. "Semi-Consociational Democracy: Canada," in *Democracy in Plural Societies: A Comparative Exploration*. New Haven: Yale University Press, 1977.

Marotte, Bernard. "Unity Debate Biting into Business, CEOs Say: Independence would be Worse." *The Nation of Toronto*, March 6, 1992, p. B1.

McRae, D. Kenneth. "Consociationalism and the Canadian Political System." *Consociational Democracy: Political Accommodation in Segmented Societies.* Toronto: McClelland & Stewart, 1974.

McRoberts, Kenneth and Dale Postgate. *Quebec: Social Change and Political Crisis.* Toronto: University of Toronto Press, 1988.

Noel, S. J. R. "Consociational Democracy and Canadian Federalism." *Canadian Journal of Political Science*, 4 (1971), 15–18.

Ormsby, William. "The Providence of Canada: The Emergence of Consociational Politics," in Kenneth D. McRae (ed.), *Consociational Democracy: Political Accommodation in Segmented Societies.* Toronto: McClelland & Stewart, 1974.

Ornstein, Michael and H. Michael Stevenson. "Elite and Public Opinion Before the Quebec Referendum: A Commentary on the State in Canada." *Canadian Journal of Political Science*, 14 (1981), 745–774.

Pious, Richard. "Canada and the Crisis of Quebec." *Journal of International Affairs*, 27, 1 (1973), 53–63.

"Pulling together?" *The Economist*, March 7, 1992, pp. 76–78.

"Quebec Inc(omplete)." *The Economist*, March 7, 1992, p. 76.

Report of the Royal Commission on Bilingualism and Biculturalism, book III. Ottawa: Queen's Printer of Canada, 1969.

Sloan, Thomas. *Quebec: The Not So Quiet Revolution.* Toronto: Ryerson, 1965.

Smiley, V. Donald. *Canada in Question.* Toronto: McGraw-Hill, 1972.

"Something New in Canada's Frozen North." *The Economist*, January 4, 1992, pp. 47–48.

Spry, Graham. "Canada: Notes on Two Ideas of Nation in Confrontation." *Journal of Contemporary History*, 6 (1971), 147–158.

Verney, Douglas and Diana Verney. "A Canadian Political Community? The Case for Tripartite Confederalism." *Journal of Commonwealth and Comparative Politics*, 12–13 (1974–75), pp. 1–19.

Von Loon, Richard. and Michael Whittington, *The Canadian Political System: Environment, Structure, and Process.* Toronto: McGraw-Hill, 1976.

Zerker, Sally. "Another Imperfect Union." *The New York Times*, September 10, 1991, p. A19.

Soviet Union

"All the Fun of Yeltsinland." *The Economist*, January 4, 1992, pp. 13–14.

"Anatomy of a Botched Putsch." *The Economist*, August 24, 1991, pp. 17–18.

"The Bessarabians." *The Economist*, April 6, 1991, pp. 51–52.

"Bewildered." *The Economist*, January 25, 1992, pp. 52–54.

Clives, Francis X. "Last Rights." *The New York Times*, September 8, 1991, pp. 1–2.

"Proposal for Economic Union Offered." *The New York Times*, September 12, 1991, p. A7.

"Coming to Pieces?" *The Economist*, March 14, 1992, pp. 61–62.

Conquest, Robert. *The Nation Killers: The Soviet Deportation of Nationalities*. London: Macmillan, 1970.

   Soviet Nationalities Policy and Practice. London: Bodley Head, 1967.

"Countering the Counter-revolution." *The Economist*, August 24, 1991, pp. 18–19.

Ericson, Richard E. "The Classical Soviet-Type Economy: Nature of the System and Implications for Reform." *Journal of Economic Perspectives*, 5, 4 (1991), 11–27.

"Et tu, Minsk?" *The Economist*, April 20, 1991, pp. 47–48.

"Flight from the Kremlin." *The Economist*, August 31, 1991, pp. 13–14.

Fowler, Brenda. "Five Days After Proclamation, New Moldavia Feels Ignored." *The New York Times*, September 1, 1991, p. 9.

"Here's the RUB." *The Economist*, December 14, 1991, pp. 58–59.

Keenan, Edward L. "Rethinking the USSR, Now That It's Over." *The New York Times*, September 8, 1991, p. 3.

Keller, Bill. "Soviets Prepare to Design New System." *The New York Times*, September 1, 1991, pp. 1–6.

   "Tatars Seek Split with the Russians." *The New York Times*, September 8, 1991, pp. 1–11.

"Life After Gorbachev." *The Economist*, December 21, 1991, pp. 57–58.

McElvoy, Anne. "Republics Seek Reunion with Moscow." *The Times* (London), October 10, 1992.

"Meet Gagauzia and Transdniestria." *The Economist*, April 6, 1991, p. 52.

Nahaylo, Bohdan and Swoboda, Victor. *Soviet Disunion: A History of the Nationalities Problem in the U.S.S.R.* New York: Macmillan, 1989.

"The Next Bosnia?" *The Economist*, June 6, 1992, pp. 43–46.

Olcott, Martha Brill. "The Soviet (Dis)Union." *Foreign Policy*, 82, (Spring 1991), 118–136.

Rakowska-Harmstone, Teresa. "The Dialectics of Nationalism in the USSR." *Problems of Communism*, 23 (May–June 1974), 1–22.

Roeder, Philip G. "Soviet Federalism and Ethnic Mobilization." *World Politics*, 43 (January 1991), 196–232.

"The Russian Revolution." *The Economist*, August 21, 1991, pp. 37–39.

Schmemann, Serge. "Can the Soviets Avoid Chaos On the Way to a New Society." *The New York Times*, September 1, 1991, pp. 1, 3.

   "Soviet Congress Yields to Republics to Avoid Political and Economic Collapse." *The New York Times*, September 6, 1991, pp. 1, 6.

Szporluk, Roman. "Nationalities and the Russian Problem in the USSR: A Historical Outline." *Journal of International Affairs*, 27, 1 (1973), 41–52.

"Tatar Sauce." *The Economist*, September 7, 1991, p. 46.

"Their Coup, Really." *The Economist*, August 24, 1991, pp. 19–20.

Tishkov, Valeri. "Glasnost and the Nationalities within the Soviet Union." *Third World Quarterly*, October, 1989, pp. 191–207.

"Welcome to Slugonia." *The Economist*, December 21, 1991, p. 58.

The Baltic

"Backdown." *The Economist*, February 2, 1991, p. 50.

Encyclopedia Lituanica. Boston, 1972.

"Free, At Last." *The Economist*, August 31, 1991, pp. 40–41.

Gerutis, Alberas (ed.). *Lithuania: 700 Years*. Trans. from Lithuanian, Algirdas Budreckis. New York: Manyland Books, 1969.

Girnius, Kestutis K. *Partizanu Kovos Lietuvoje*. Chicago: Draugas, 1987.
    "Soviet Terror in Lithuania During Post-War Years." *Lituanus*, 32, 4 (1986).

Harmon, Danute S. "Lithuania: An Overview of a Struggle For National Survival." *Lituanus*, 36, 2 (1990).

Jakstas, Juozas. "Lithuania to World War I," in Albertas Gerutis (ed.) *Lithuania: 700 Years*. New York: Manyland Books, 1969.

Kaszeta, Daniel J. "Lithuanian Resistance to Foreign Occupation 1940–1952." *Lituanus*, 34, 3 (1988).

Lietuviu Enciklopedija, Boston, 1957.

Lieven, Anatol. "France Backs UN Quest as West Woos Republics," *The Times of London*, August 31, 1991, p. 8.

Lucas, Edward. "Hanging by a Thread." *The Independent on Sunday, London*, September 22, 1991, p. 6.

Pajaujis-Javis Joseph. *Soviet Genocide In Lithuania*. Chicago, 1980.

Pelekis, K. *Genocide: Lithuania's Threefold Tragedy*. Bonn, Germany, 1949.

"The Price of Freedom." *The Economist*, September 7, 1991, pp. 47–48.

Remeikis, Thomas. *Opposition to Soviet Rule in Lithuania – 1945–1980*. Chicago: Institute of Lithuanian Studies Press, 1980.

"The Two Sides of the Soviet Barricades." *The Economist*, January 26, 1991, pp. 47–48.

Vardys, Stanley V. *Lithuania Under the Soviets: Portrait of a Nation, 1940–1965*. New York: Frederick Praeger, 1965.

Welch, Irene. "Nationalism and Lithuanian Dissent." *Lituanus*, 29, 1 (1983).

Soviet Central Asia

"Auf Wiedersehen, Kazakhstan." *The Economist*, March 7, 1992, p. 60.

Imart, Guy G. "Kirgizia-Kazakhstan: Hinge or Faultline?" *The Problems of Communism*, 39 (1990), pp. 1–13.

"The Next Islamic Revolution." *The Economist*, September 21, 1991, pp. 58–60.

Ro'i, Yaacov. "The Islamic Influence on Nationalism in Soviet Central Asia." *The Problems of Communism*, 39 (1990), 49–64.

Schmemann, Serge. "Kazakh Chief, Seeking What Works, Backs Both Order and Free Economy." *The New York Times*, September 8, 1991, p.11.

"The Silk Revolution." *The Economist*, October 19, 1991, p. 71.

"Vegas of the East." *The Economist*, March 7, 1992, p. 60.

"A Way of Life Evaporates." *The Economist*, September 21, 1991, p. 59.

Transcaucasus

Allen, W. E. D. and Paul Muratoff, *Caucasian Battlefields*. Cambridge: Cambridge University Press, 1953.

"Armenia Lives." *The Economist*, May 23, 1992, p. 50.

Bryce, Viscount, James. *Transcaucusus and the Ararat*. London, 1896.

"Caspian Cauldron." *The Economist*, June 13, 1992, p. 51.

Dadrian, Vahakn N. "The Naim–Andonian Documents of the World War I Destruction of the Ottoman Armenians: The Anatomy of Genocide," *International Journal of Middle East Studies*, 18, 3 (August 1986), 311–360.

Dragadze, Tamara. "The Armenian-Azerbaijani Conflict: Structure and Sentiment." *Third World Quarterly*, 11 (January 1989), 55–71.

"Family at war." *The Economist*, January 11, 1992, pp. 46–47.

"First Things, Second." *The Economist*, September 21, 1991, pp. 65–66.

"Georgia Opponents Charge Republic Is Led by Dictator." *The New York Times*, September 6, 1991, p. A7.

Graves, Sir, Robert. *Storm Centers of the Near East: Personal Memories, 1879–1919*. London, 1933.

Lang, David Marshall and Christopher J. Walker. *The Armenians*. London: The Minority Rights Group, 1987.

"A Mess on a Map." *The Economist*, September 28, 1991, p. 64.

Nahaylo, Bohdan. and C. J. Peters. *The Ukrainians and the Georgians*. London: Minority Rights Group, 1980.

Nalbandian, Louis. *The Armenian Revolutionary Movement*. Los Angeles: University of California Press, 1963.

Rowley, Storer H. "Explosive Mix of Ethnic Groups Adds to Challenge in Georgia." *Chicago Tribune*, September 15, 1991, p. 5.

Saroyan, Mark. "The 'Karabakh Syndrome' and Azerbaijani Politics." *Problems of Communism*, 39 (September–October 1990), 14–29.

"Small War, Loud Bang." *The Economist*, March 7, 1992, pp. 51–52.

"A Time of Turmoil." *The Economist*, June 13, 1992, pp. 51–52.

Toynbee, A. J. B. "The Extermination of the Armenians," in *The Times History of the War*. vol. III. London 1916.

Wyszomirski, Margaret J. "Communal Violence: The Armenians and the Copts as Case Studies." *World Politics*, 27, 3 (April 1975), 430–455.

Ukraine

Barber, Tony. "Ukraine Secures Oil and Gas Supplies by Barter Deal with Iran." *The Independent of London*, January 31, 1992, p. 10.

"Coming Alive." *The Economist*, September 7, 1991, p. 47.

"Crimea Declares Independence." *The New York Times*, September 6, 1991, p. A8.

"The Crimean Question." *The Economist*, January 11, 1992, pp. 47–48.

Dejevsky, Mary. "Ukraine Saves Gorbachev Trade Treaty." *The Times of London*, November 7, 1991, p. 10.

"A Giant Starts to Stir." *The Economist*, October 6, 1990, pp. 63–64.

Mace, James E. "Famine and Nationalism in Soviet Ukraine." *Problems of Communism*, 33, 3 (1984), 37–51.

"Message to Kiev." *The Economist*, February 8, 1992, p. 17.

Nahaylo, Bohdan and C. J. Peters. *The Ukrainians and the Georgians*. London: Minority Rights Group, 1980.

"The New Cold War." *The Economist*, May 9, 1992, p. 50.

"A New Crimean war?" *The Economist*, February 1, 1992, pp. 52–53.

"Second to None." *The Economist*, September 28, 1991, pp. 64–65.

Seely, Robert. "Party Sent to Scrap Yard as Nationalists Take Control." *The Times* (London), August 31, 1991, p. 8.

"Ukraine as Nation." *The Economist*, October 5, 1991, p. 6.

Spain – Catalonia/the Basque lands

Berger, Suzanne. "Bretons, Basques, Scots, and Other European Nations." *Journal of Interdisciplinary History*, 3 (1972–1973), 167–175.

Gooch, Adela. "ETA and Madrid Engaged in a Battle of Nerves." *The Independent of London*, January 31, 1992, p. 10.

"Gibraltar Voters Shun Spain and Look to Europe." *The Independent* (London), January 16, 1992, p. 9.

Jones, N. L. "The Catalan Question Since the Civil War," in P. Preston (ed.), *Spain in Crisis*. London: Harvester Press, 1976.

Laitin, David. "Linguistic Revival: Politics and Culture in Catalonia." *Comparative Studies in History and Society*, 31 (1989), 297–317.

Medhurst, Kenneth. *The Basques and the Catalans*. London: Minority Rights Group, 1987.

Preston, P. (ed.). *Spain in Crisis*. London: Harvester Press, 1976.

"Spain: A Survey." *The Economist*, 25 April, 1992, p. 22.

Sudan

Beshir Hamid, Mohammad. "Confrontation and Reconciliation within an African Context: The Case of Sudan." *Third World Quarterly*, 5 (April 1983), pp. 320–329.

Beshir, M. O. *Southern Sudan: Background to Conflict*. London: C. Hurst and Co., 1966.

Gurdon, Charles. "Instability and the State: Sudan," in Caroline Thomas and Paikiasotby Saravananuttu (eds.), *The State and Instability in the South*. London: Macmillan, 1989.

Holt, P. M. and M. W. Daly. *The History of the Sudan*. London: Weidenfield and Nicholson, 1979.

"Islam's Star." *The Economist*, February 1, 1992, p. 73.

Johnson, Douglas H. *The Southern Sudan*. London: Minority Rights Group, 1988.

Kasfir, Nelson. "Peace-making and Social Cleavage in Sudan", in V. Montville (ed.), *Conflict and Peace-Making in Multi-Ethnic Societies*. New York: Lexington Books, 1990.

Lesch, Anne M. "Rebellion in the Southern Sudan." *University Field Staff Reports*, no. 8, 1985.

Malwal, Bona. *People and Power in Sudan – The Struggle for National Stability.* London: Ithaca Press, 1981.

Mayall, James and Mark Simpson. "Ethnicity is Not Enough: Reflections ȯn Protracted Secessionism in the Third World" (unpublished), 1990. Text provided by authors to Dr. Benedict Kingsbury who then provided it to the author.

O'Fahey, R. S. and J. L. Spauding. *Kingdoms of the Sudan.* London: Methuen, 1974.

Ottaway, Marina. "Post-Numeiri Sudan: One Year On." *Third World Quarterly,* 9 (1987).

The Return to Democracy in Sudan. Geneva: International Commission of Jurists, 1986.

"Sudan's Famine: Please Don't Help." *The Economist*, January 19, 1991, p. 70.

Sudan Yearbook. Khartoum: Ministry of Guidance and National Information, 1983.

"Swamped." *The Economist*, June 6, 1992, p. 72.

"Twilight." *The Economist*, September 14, 1991, pp. 79–80.

Wai, Dunstan. *The African–Arab Conflict in the Sudan.* London: Holmes and Meier, 1981.

Switzerland

Daalder, Hans. "On Building Consociational Nations: The Cases of the Netherlands and Switzerland." *International Social Science Journal*, 23, 3 (1971), 355–370.

Dunn, James. "Consociational Democracy and the Language Conflict: A Comparison of the Belgian and Swiss Experiences." *Comparative Political Studies*, 5, 1 (April 1972), 3–40.

Keech, William. "Linguistic Diversity and Political Conflict: Some Observations Based on Four Swiss Cantons." *Comparative Politics*, 4, 3 (April, 1972), 384–404.

McRae, Kenneth. *Conflict and Compromise in Multilingual Societies: The Case of Switzerland.* Waterloo: Wilfred Laurier University Press, 1983.

Mayer, Kurt. "The Jura Problem: Ethnic Conflict in Switzerland." *Social Research*, 35, 4 (Winter, 1968), 707–741.

"The Swiss Fortify Romansch," *The Economist*, March 30, 1996, p. 51.

Tamils – Sri Lanka

"Another Round." *The Economist*, January 19, 1991, p. 68.

"Back on the Gold-painted Throne." *The Economist*, October 12, 1991, pp. 88–89.

Burger, Angela S. "Policing a Communal Society: The Case of Sri Lanka." *Asian Survey*, 27, 7(July 1987), 822–833.

Desmond, Edward W. "Sri Lanka's Tamil Tigers." *Time*, September 16, 1991, p. 41.

"Elephantine mistake." *The Economist*, August 17, 1991, p. 30.

Hennayake, Shantha K. "The Peace Accord and the Tamils in Sri Lanka." *Asian Survey*, 29, 4 (April 1989), 401–415.

Horwitz, Donald L. "Incentives and Behaviour in the Ethnic Politics of Sri Lanka and Malaysia." *Third World Quarterly*, October, 1983, pp. 18–35.

Hubbell, L. Kenneth. "The Devolution of Power in Sri Lanka: A Solution to the Separatist Movement" *Asian Survey*, 27, 11 (November, 1987), 1176–1187.

The Indo-Sri Lanka Agreement: An Emerging Consensus. Madras: ProTEG Publications, 1988.

Kodikara, Shelton U. "The Continuing Crisis in Sri Lanka: The JVP, the Indian Troops, and Tamil Politics." *Asian Survey*, 29, 7(July 1989), 716–724.

Matthews, Bruce. "Sri Lanka in 1988: Seeds of the Accord." *Asian Survey*, 29, 2 (February 1989), 229–235.

"Sri Lanka in 1989: Peril and Good Luck." *Asian Survey*, 30, 2 (February 1990), 144–149.

"Our Allies, the Tigers." *The Economist*, September 28, 1991, pp. 82–83.

Pfaffenberger, Bryan. "Sri Lanka in 1986: A Nation at the Crossroads" *Asian Survey*, 27, 2 (February 1987), 55–162.

"Sri Lanka in 1987: Indian Intervention and the Resurgence of the JVP." *Asian Survey*, 28, 2 (February 1988), 137–147.

Premdas, Ralph, and S.W.R. de A. Samarasinghe. "Sri Lanka's Ethnic Conflict: The Indo-Lanka Peace Accord." *Asian Survey*, 28, 6 (June 1988), 676–690.

Rao, P. Venkateshwar. "Ethnic Conflict in Sri Lanka: India's Role and Perception" *Asian Survey*, 28, 4 (April 1988), 419–436.

Saravanamuttu, P. "Ethnic Conflict and Nation-building in Sri Lanka." *Third World Quarterly*, October, 1989, pp. 313–327.

Schwarz, Walter. *The Tamils of Sri Lanka.* London: Minority Rights Group, 1988.

Singer, Marshall R. "New Realities in Sri Lankan Politics." *Asian Survey*, 30, 4 (April 1990), 409–425.

"Taming the Tigers." *The Economist*, June 6, 1992, pp. 80–83.

At Thimpu. Cambridge: Tamil International Working Group, 1985.

"Under the Stones of Sri Lanka." *The Economist*, September 14, 1991, p. 74.

United Kingdom – Scotland/Wales

"The Battle is Joined." *The Economist*, February 1, 1992, p. 16.

Berger, Suzanne. "Bretons, Basques, Scots, and Other European Nations." *Journal of Interdisciplinary History*, 3 (1972–1973), 167–175.

"Oil Be Off Now." *The Economist*, February 8, 1992, p. 32.

Palmer, John. "Scots and Welsh Construct Power Bases in Europe." *The Guardian* (London), February 27, 1992, p. 8.

"The 39 Steps to Home Rule." *The Economist*, February 1, 1992, p. 36.

"Towards Edinburgh." *The Economist*, June 13, 1992, p. 42.

"Welsh spoken here." *The Economist*, May 16, 1992, p. 30.

Yugoslavia – Slovenia/Croatia

"Against the Grain." *The Economist*, December 15, 1990, p. 58.

Allcock, John B. "In Praise of Chauvinism: Rhetorics of Nationalism in Yugoslav Politics." *Third World Quarterly*, October 1989, pp. 208–222.

"And so to Bosnia." *The Economist*, January 4, 1992, pp. 39–41.

"Another Twist." *The Economist*, October 5, 1991, p. 58.

"Back from the Brink." *The Economist*, February 2, 1991, pp. 46–47.

Banac, Ivo. *The National Question in Yugoslavia: Origins, History and Politics.* Ithaca: Cornell University Press, 1984.

Bertsch, Gary K. "Currents in Yugoslavia: The Revival of Nationalism." *Problems of Communism*, 22, 6 (November-December 1973), 1–15.

"Blowing Up History." *The Economist*, October 12, 1991, p. 64.

"Body and Soul." *The Economist*, March 23, 1991, p. 62.

Burg, Steven. L. *Conflict and Cohesion in Socialist Yugoslavia: Political Decision Making Since 1966.* Princeton: Princeton University Press, 1983.

"Bust-up in the Balkans." *The Economist*, October 13, 1991, pp. 19–20.

"A Case of Serb-atomic particles." *The Economist*, March 16, 1991, p. 49.

Champion, Marc. "A Land in Fear of Predatory Neighbours." *The Independent* (London), January 16, 1992, p. 8.

Clissold, Stephen. (ed.). *A Short History of Yugoslavia: From Early Times to 1966.* Cambridge: Cambridge University Press, 1966.

"Countdown to Recognition." *The Economist*, December 21, 1991, p. 59.

Crawshaw, Steve. "Zagreb Promises Concessions to Serb Aspirations." *The Independent* (London), January 16, 1992, p. 8.

Engelberg, Stephen. "Carving Out a Greater Serbia." *The New York Times Magazine*, September 1, 1991, pp. 18–32.

"Et tu, Skopje?" *The Economist*, September 14, 1991, pp. 63–64.

"Democracy in Eastern Europe." *The Economist*, February 1, 1992, pp. 58–59.

Graff, James L. "Serbia's Land Grab in Yugoslavia. " *Time*, September 16, 1991, pp. 40–41.

"Hail, Croatia." *The Economist*, December 21, 1991, p. 12.

"History's Victims." *The Economist*, December 14, 1991, p. 66.

"Into the Dark." *The Economist*, September 21, 1991, p. 57.

Job, Cvijeto. "Yugoslavia: Stop Humpty Dumpty Before He Falls." *International Herald Tribune*, September 9, 1991, p. 6.

Judah, Tim. "Dubrovnik's Heart Survives the Onslaught." *The Times* (London), November 16, 1991, p. 11.

Lambert, Sarah. "Croatia and Slovenia Recognised." *The Independent* (London), January 16, 1992, p. 1.

Lederer, Ivo J. "Nationalism and the Yugoslavs," in Peter F. Sugar and Ivo J.

Lederer (eds.), *Nationalism in Eastern Europe*. Seattle: University of Washington Press, 1969.

Lendvai, Paul. "Yugoslavia without Yugoslavs: The Roots of the Crisis." *International Affairs*, 67, 2 (April 1991), 251–262.

"The Lilliputian is Still Wriggling." *The Economist*, June 6, 1992, pp. 42–43.

"Macedonia: Next on the List." *The Economist*, February 8, 1992, pp. 56–57.

"Men of Blood." *The Economist*, August 17, 1991, p. 43.

Montgomery, Paul L. "Europe Plans Yugoslav Peace Talks." *The New York Times*, September 4, 1991, p. A3.

"Yugoslavs Trade Accusations as Peace Meeting Opens in the Hague." *The New York Times*, September 8, 1991, pp. A6.

"Next, please." *The Economist*, March 7, 1992, pp. 52–57.

"Not 1914, But Not 1991 Either." *The Economist*, August 10, 1991, pp. 37–38.

"The Pattern of Evil." *The Economist*, May 16, 1992, pp. 44–45.

"Quiet, But No Peace." *The Economist*, September 28, 1991, pp. 63–64.

Rowley, Storer H. "Fighting Flares Despite Yugoslav Cease-fire. " *Chicago Tribune*, September 1, 1991, pp. 1–6.

"Terror Cuts Both Ways in Fight Between the Croatians and Serbs." *Chicago Tribune*, September 1, 1991, p. 3.

"Yugoslav Army, Croatian Police Class." *Chicago Tribune*, September 1, 1991, p. 3.

Rustinow, Dennison. "Yugoslavia: Balkan Breakup?" *Foreign Policy*, 83 (Summer 1991), 143–159.

Shoup, Paul. "The National Question in Yugoslavia." *Problems of Communism*, 21, 1 (January–February, 1972), 18–29.

Tagliabue, John. "Croatia Cuts Off Army's Supplies and Seizes Officer." *The New York Times*, September 15, 1991, p. 3.

"Croatia Shuts Off Oil Pipeline To Serbia. " *The New York Times*, September 12, 1991, p. A3.

"Croatia's Dying Dream." *The New York Times*, September 15, 1991, p. 2.

"Renewed Fighting Wounds Yugoslav Economy." *The New York Times*, September 5, 1991, p. A3.

"Serbia Says It Is Accepting European Peace Proposal." *The New York Times*, September 1, 1991, p. 3.

"Serbian Rebels Harden Control of Croatia Coast." *The New York Times*, September 14, 1991, p. 6.

"Serbs Cut Off Croatian Capital From South Coast." *The New York Times*, September 13, 1991, p. A7.

"Wartime Demeanor for Serbs in Croatian Cities: Quiet and Invisible." *The New York Times*, September 6, 1991, p. A4.

"Yugoslav Republic Votes To Secede, The Third To Do So: Big Macedonia Majority." *The New York Times*, September 12, 1991, pp. 1, 6.

Tanner, Marcus. "Yugoslavia Lives On, says Belgrade." *The Independent* (London), January 16, 1992, p. 8.

"The Truce Will Out." *The Economist*, October 12, 1991, p. 63.

257

"Turning Point in Yugoslavia." *The Economist*, January 11, 1992, pp. 45–46.
"Waiting for Slobo." *The Economist*, January 5, 1991, pp. 44–45.
"War?" *The Economist*, October 6, 1990, pp. 67–68.
"Yugo This Way, Yugo That Way." *The Economist*, May 11, 1991, pp. 13–14.
"Yugoslavia: Hitch for the UN." *The Economist*, February 1, 1992, p. 57.
"Yugoslavia: In Parts." *The Economist*, August 31, 1991, p. 44.
"Yugoslavia on the Brink." *The Economist*, May 11, 1991, pp. 51–52.

OTHER CASES
American South, Saharawis, Tibet

Crofts, Daniel W. *Reluctant Confederates: Upper South Unionists in the Secession Crisis*. Chapel Hill, NC: University of North Carolina Press, 1989.
Ford, Lacy K. Jr. *Origins of Southern Radicalism: The South Carolina Upcountry, 1800–1860*. Oxford: Oxford University Press, 1988.
Hodges, Tony. "The Origins of Saharawi Nationalism." *Third World Quarterly*, 5 (1983), 28–57.
"Horror Story That Falls on Deaf Ears." *The Independent*, March 6, 1991.
"In Search of a God." *The Economist*, October 12, 1991, p. 86.
Mullin, Chris and Phuntsog Wangyal. *The Tibetans: Two Perspectives on Tibetan-Chinese Relations*. London: Minority Rights Group, 1989.
"Prayers From the Top of the World." *The Economist*, October 27, 1990, p. 82.
Sandburg, Carl. *Abraham Lincoln: The War Years*. New York: Harcourt, Brace Publishers, 1939.
Shuyun, Sun. "Tibet: A Study of Anglo-Tibetan Relations." M. Phil. Thesis, Oxford University, 1990. Text provided by the author.
Van Walt Van Praag, Michael. *The Status of Tibet*. New York: Westview Press, 1987.
Wills, Garry. *Lincoln at Gettysburg: The Words that Remade America*. New York: Simon & Schuster, 1992.

Index

Index

CAMBRIDGE STUDIES IN INTERNATIONAL RELATIONS